Jesse Portman Chesney

Shakespeare as a Physician

Comprising every word which in any way relates to medicine, surgery or obstetrics,

found in the complete works of that writer, with criticisms and comparison of the

same with the medical thoughts of to-day

Jesse Portman Chesney

Shakespeare as a Physician
Comprising every word which in any way relates to medicine, surgery or obstetrics, found in the complete works of that writer, with criticisms and comparison of the same with the medical thoughts of to-day

ISBN/EAN: 9783337386047

Printed in Europe, USA, Canada, Australia, Japan

Cover: Foto ©Thomas Meinert / pixelio.de

More available books at **www.hansebooks.com**

SHAKESPEARE

AS A

PHYSICIAN.

COMPRISING EVERY WORD WHICH IN ANY WAY RELATES TO MEDICINE,
SURGERY OR OBSTETRICS, FOUND IN THE COMPLETE WORKS OF
THAT WRITER, WITH CRITICISMS AND COMPARISON
OF THE SAME WITH THE MEDICAL
THOUGHTS OF TO-DAY.

—BY—

J. PORTMAN CHESNEY, M. D.,

Ex-Secretary Medical Society of the State of Missouri; Corresponding Member of the
Gynæcological Society of Boston; Prof. of Gynæcology in the Northwestern
Medical College, St. Joseph, Mo., etc., etc.

"SIR:—I hear you are a schollar—I will be brief with you—and you
have been a man long known to me, though I had never so good means, as I
desire, to make myself acquainted with you. I shall discover a thing to
you wherein I must very much lay open mine own imperfection; but, good
sir, as you have an eye upon my follies, as you hear them unfolded, turn
another into the register of your own, that I may pass with a reproof the
easier, sith yourself know, how easy it is to be such an offender."

J. H. CHAMBERS & CO., Publishers,

CHICAGO, ILL.,   ST. LOUIS. MO.,   ATLANTA, GA.

1884.

CONTENTS.

CHAPTER I.

OBSTETRICS, - - - - - 17

Blue-eyed hag—Go to "Texas"—The "fly young man"—Dr. Rosenweig and Madam McCarthy—Poor Alice Bowlsby and Miss Jennie Cramer—The horsewhip and "navy"—The poor duke's constable—Longing for stew'd prunes—Shakespeare's sagacity—The "craving" appetite in females—The blood is the life—Anorexia and delirium—"Good cheer" for pregnant women—Pompey Bum and the "social evil"—"Quick" at the second month—Puck and his girdle—Exploring the moon—Normal ovariotomy—The nubile age—Mental emotions and abortion—Three classes of causation—The fruit withers—Neoplasms—Endometritis—Syphilis and the nobility—Juliet and lady Capulet—Lord Campbell—Forensic medicine—Childbed privilege—The "medicine man" and his fee—Twenty money-bags—King John and his erroneous decision—Premature deliveries and the law—Two cases from Taylor—Groaned for him—The heyday of existence and the evening of age—"Hal" and Herbert Spencer—Alcohol and venery—Fish diet and sex—Abortion; never in the prostitute—The doctor's coat—Maid of Orleans—Commission on pregnancy—Difficulties in diagnosing pregnancy—Jorisenne's method—Apprehensions in the pregnant state—The "play" as a means of education—Richard the Third at his birth—Shakespeare's intuition—Teeth generated in error—Teretology; its varieties—Hunchbacks and their wit—Richard's villainy—The "grunting"—The accouchement of Anne Boleyn—Graphic description—Tamora, queen of the Goths—"He is your brother by the surer side"—Early marriages and premature decay—Excuses in America—Weaning of Juliet—Stand on the floor and suck—Inanition and little gilded tombs—"Twin sisters"—Chlorosis—Scoundrels made from the mothers' milk—The mother who nurses her own offspring—Cæsarian section should not be "untimely"—How fresh she looks.

CHAPTER II.

PSYCHOLOGY,   -   -   -   -   70

Definition—Shakespeare's profound knowledge of the subject—Bucknill's eulogium—"It is *all the best*"—Shakespeare's special study of insanity an absurdity—His intuition—Scene before an Abbey—Jealousy versus sanity—A foul conspiracy—A psychological charlatan—Sleeplessness but a symptom—Shakespeare draws on his own domestic experience—*Now* not a joke, but a dark reality—Thrown into a "dankish" vault—The cell of Foscari—Public institutions need surveillance—Preliminary abuses—Probate courts and examinations in lunacy — Monkey and medical expert—A ten-dollar fee—Charles Reade—"Why hast thou put him in such a dream?"—No darkness but ignorance—Make the trial of it in any constant question—Erroneous assumption—Bucknill on memory—What at any time have you heard her say?—"Out damned spot"—Here's the smell of blood still—Will she go now to bed?—Cure her of that—"Make thick my blood stop up the access and passage to remorse"—Cases from De Boismont—"He had a large knife in his hand and went straight to my bed"—He returned as he came—"I had so strange a dream"—His services were thereafter dispensed with—Somnambulism and insanity—The pulse as indicative of insanity—Did you nothing hear?—Hallucinations—The ghost—The spectre cat—The doctor's fright—Look! Amazement on thy mother sits—Lesions of structure necessary to lesions of function—I'm a'gwine to die!—One finale awaits the man and all his attributes—Love and sleeplessness—Age—"No man bears sorrow better"—The final cataclysm—King Lear not insane—A dog's obeyed in office—The "Bedlam beggar"—"How does the king?"—"You are a spirit, I know"—Lord Shaftesbury's opinion—The EMOTIONS—Their close relationship to actual mental diseases—Jealousy—With "pin and web"—Othello, the Moor—"O! now farewell the tranquil mind"—Alas the day! I never gave him cause—The ills we do their ill instruct as to—Ninety children the utmost limit—The relative procreative capacity of the sexes—Monogamistic relations—Abortion and polygamy—Love—All lovers swear more performance than they are able—Love-marks—"Did you ever cure any so?"—The pale complexion of true love—"He took me by the wrist and held me hard"—Mine eyes were not at fault, for she was beautiful—Lust—Not from Shakespeare—One man in every five—Love powders—My daughter! O my daughter!—Lucretius, the poet—A veritable letter—Venereal excitement not love—Let not the creaking of shoes—The will and conception—"Could I find out the woman's part in me"—Painful copulation (Dyspareunia)—Anger—Envy.

CHAPTER III.

NEUROLOGY,   -   -   -   -   -   121

Epilepsy—Falling Sickness—"Rub him about the temples"—Playing "wolf"—The prototype of Othello—"What, did Cæsar swoon?"—The epileptic zone—The trade-mark and "plug" hat—Mistaken diagnosis—This apoplexy will certain be his end—Gad's Hill and Sir John—I talk not of his majesty—It is a kind of *deafness*—Croups—Drowning as a consequence of popular delusion—The mad-stone and its votaries—Not known by medical men—The treatment as good as any—"John Jones, of Albany"—Odontology—Set up the bloody flag against all patience—The nurse's head-ache—"Let me but bind it hard"—Varieties of the malady—Sciatica—Syphilis as a complication—Gout—Plays the rogue with my great toe—Anorexia—Paralysis—" My firm nerves shall never tremble."

CHAPTER IV.

PHARMACOLOGIA, - - - - 132

Sleepy Drinks—Foster nurse of Nature—A liberal offer—A doctor's knowledge appreciated—What?—The perfumed dandy—Unbearable nonsense—What's in't?—Mandragora—Drowsy syrups—Superstition—Toxicology—The trusty pistol—Fashions of suicide—Difficulty of purchase—Poisoned by a monk—This tyrant fever—Swinstead abbey—Strange fantasies—North winds —A compound—Monks as physicians—Cardinal Beaufort—Liebreich anticipated—Republished—Was it chloral?—Comparison of conditions—Care. fully noted—Meagre were his looks—What, ho!—Famine is in thy cheek—Death's pale flag—Thus with a kiss—A nest of Death—A slight discrepancy—Oxalic acid—Discovery repeats itself—The insane root—Drugging the posset—"Hashish"—The unction of a mountebank—Rabies canina—Curara—From what derived?—A failure apprehended—Trap with double triggers—Fencing match—An unlooked for termination—A jealous sister—Kills and pains not—Immortal longings—Easy ways to die—Zest to a tragedy—A specific—Alconcito—A royal student—Soliloquy—Most likely I did—Moreton preceded.

CHAPTER V.

ETIOLOGY, - - - - - 156

Prefatory—Wine for an ague—Objects of commiseration—A promise redeemed—Icy burning—A marshy residence—Magna charta—Allegorical—An idea of antiquity—"Would to bed"—"Falstaff, he is dead"—Congestive chill—Gad's-hill—Prince Henry and his "pals"—This man has become a god—Is Brutus sick?—Acerbity—The Appian Way—Foes to life—Malaria as a demoralizing agent—Cross gartering—The tourniquet as a remedy—Same as a cause of disease—Farewell to neuralgia—Brunonianism.

CHAPTER VI.

DERMATOLOGY, - - - - 164

The beginning—Serpigo—A voluminous curse—Was it small-pox?—The cursed hebenon—Acarus scabiei—The disease in Paris—Falstaff as a " wen"—Kibes—Probably vaccinated—A string of rhymes—Good fruit only

from a good tree—Transmissibility of defects—Gynæcological phenomena—
The "convulsive zone"—Spreading it on "thick"—Rouge and pearl powders—'Tis beauty truly blent—Commendable caution—Danger in the dark—
A fastidious scoundrel—Supposition strengthened—We catch of you, Doll—
Baths in syphilis—Ricord and Bumstead—A beautiful picture—Durability of
a tanner—A curious but not creditable truth—A needed reform—Venesection
in the right iliac fossa.

CHAPTER VII.

Organology,   -   -   -   -   -   174

The stomach—Power of mind over function—Voluntary inanition—Its
Pathology—What a physiologist!—Dietetic ideas of a hostess—An apt comparison—The irritability of hunger—A plain road—An error explained—The
woodman and his belt—Seat of the affections—Gin-drinker's liver—Cause
for effect—Smiling at grief—Lewdness and poverty—Illustrated—Sentiment
reversed—The badge of cowardice—The truth in popular ideas—Then live,
Macduff—Sleep in spite of thunder—Pulmonary gangrene—Benedick, the
married man—Thaw'd out—A pertinent conclusion—A blind philosopher—
How are you 'fraid!—Latent senses—The green flap—Some new infection—
An enquiry—An amusing incident—"Hal's" vocabulary—Renal functions—
Sympathetic fibrillæ—Carry his water to the wise woman—What says the
doctor to my water?—A sensible doctor, for a wonder—Changes in the kidney—Nose painting—A sure sign—Taste not—A cheap article—"When I was
about thy years, Hal"—The lean and hungry Cassius—He smiles in such a
sort—Drawing the fire out—A parody—An exploded barbarity—Mr. Stribling, the druggist—The blood is the life—Blasting a good resolve—Man improves with his condition—A plea for the lancet—Palpitation—Good air as
an agent—Much effuse of blood, etc.

CHAPTER VIII.

Chirurgery,   -   -   -   -   -   192

Grows stronger for the breaking—Mistaken principle—Patching the over-
coat—Bad practice—Syncope—Mistakes in prognosis—Spare the blood—
Shakespeare a poor surgeon—A scar covered veteran—The money changer—
The surgeon's fee—Professional failing—Doctors and the clergy—A man
with a soul—The surgeon's tools—Surgeon's fort—Honors to whom honor,
etc.—Trichina spiralis—Who is responsible?—Doctors and their doings—
Little change—Cowardly knave—Jester for an hospital—The least merit—
A precedent for doctor "she"—"Malignant fistulæ"—Potent remedy—
Popular ignorance—The reformed hod-carrier—Professional honor—Another
comparison—A lame impostor and his lame detection—Doctor's untimely
end—The English Nero—Dr. Butts, the scoundrel—A want of faith—Woful
mistake—Danger of expectancy—In Macbeth—An absurd credulity—God
Almighty as a visiting physician—How does your patient, doctor?—Needs a
divine—No mean psychologist—Indiscreet—A self-constituted doctor.

CHAPTER IX.

MISCELLANEOUS,   -   -   -   -   212

A vile caricature—The Hunchback—Now is the winter of my discontent—Listening to the whispers of Vanity—I'll be at charge for a looking-glass—Troublous dreams—Sleep that knits up the raveled sleeve—Our life is two-fold—Sleep hath its own world—From Byron—Neuralgia—No guaranty of truth—Riot—Position in sea-sickness — Old quarantine regulations — The plague—From the cradle to the grave—Characteristics of senility—Take a man of honor, Kate—He brings his physic after his patient's death—An awkward predicament—Tests for death—Life a failure—Ay! but to die? Grim Death!

LIST OF ILLUSTRATIONS.

PAGE.

King Henry VIII. and the Midwife, - - - 49

The Midwife to Anne Bullen, on receiving her fee. - - 50

Aaron, the Moor, and the Illegitimate Child, - - 52

An Illustration of the Benefits of Protracted Lactation, - 59

Enquiry in Lunacy—(Medical Experts to the right), - 76

Lady Macbeth murders the sleeping Duncan, - - 82

The Doctor looks for the skeleton behind him, - - 90

The Effects of gathering the May-apple root, - - 136

Romeo and the Apothecary of Mantua, - - - 143

Romeo and Juliet in the " tomb of the Capulets," - - 144

Prince "Hal" manifests his friendship for Sir John Falstaff, 176

The Woodman, and his arrangement for "cheap boarding," 179

The Clown enlivening the inmates of an Hospital, - - 198

A Female Practitioner presents herself before the King, - 200

The famous "Dr. Sunrise" condescends to visit the good people
   of St. Joseph, - - - - - 203

A Gentleman who practices under the protection of a License
   issued by the highest authority, - - - - 211

PREFACE.

The thoughts of Shakespeare enter more or less into the productions of almost every one who writes in the English language. His works abound in such a profuse diversity of thought and expression, that they are laid under contribution to supply the gems which sparkle among the lowering effusions of the lawyer, the doctor, and the divine; they contribute the ornamentation for the title-pages of the wit, the poet and the fictionist,—whilst in miscellaneous writings of every conceivable kind and sentiment their wisdom is pruned or distorted to suit the " mellowing of occasion."

The idea even of making an entire volume based upon some single line of thought found in Shakespeare's writings is not new,—as a work embracing "Shakespeare's Legal knowledge " was written by Lord Campbell, and published in England some years ago ; and it is said, that even now, there are as many as twenty books in some way connected with the great dramatist, issued yearly from the British press. If in the vastness of this literature there has not at some time in the past appeared a work embodying "Shakespeare's Medical knowledge," it is a little strange,—though of the existence of such a work the present writer has no knowledge.

The conception of presenting Shakespeare's medical knowledge in a complete and connected form is, therefore, probably original as connected with the present work. We are not unmindful, however, that his thoughts on medicine have from time to time appeared in a fragmentary form,—the latest of which is a paper a few years ago published in this country, embracing the immortal poet's ideas of *Insanity;* of the scope and merit of the paper we can, however, say nothing, as it has never fallen into our hands.

15

In presenting, as we have endeavored to do, truly and faithfully, every line and precept in Shakespeare's complete works which in the remotest sense bears upon the science and practice of medicine, we may say that easy as the task may seem to one who has not essayed it,—yet the satisfactory accomplishment of the work has been attended with no small amount of difficulty and labor; and in extenuation of any faults which may be found in its pages, we will say to the " critics " that if in them the " antique and well-noted face of plain old form is much disfigured—and, like a shifting wind into a sail, it makes the course of thought to fetch about.—startles consideration,—makes sound opinion sick, and truth suspected, for putting on so new a fashioned garb,"—why, then, we shall hail with delight a *better* work upon the same subject from any one of them.

THE AUTHOR.

St. Joseph, Mo.,
    March 1st, 1884.

NOTE.—Since placing the present work in the hands of the publishers, I have been favored by Dr. George C. Catlett, Superintendent of the Missouri State Lunatic Asylum, with a copy of an English work, entitled " The Mad Folk of Shakespeare," by Dr. Jno. Charles Bucknill, and from its pages I have liberally drawn in amending my chapter on Insanity.—J. P. C.

CHAPTER I.

OBSTETRICS.

Blue-eyed hag—Go to "Texas"—The "fly young man"—Dr. Rosenweig and Madam McCarthy—Poor Alice Bowlsby and Miss Jennie Cramer—The horsewhip and "navy"—The poor duke's constable—Longing for stew'd prunes—Shakespeare's sagacity—The "craving" appetite in females—The blood is the life—Anorexia and delirium—"Good cheer" for pregnant women—Pompey Bum and the "social evil"—"Quick" at the second month—Puck and his girdle—Exploring the moon—Normal ovariotomy—The nubile age—Mental emotions and abortion—Three classes of causation—The fruit withers—Neoplasms—Endometritis—Syphilis and the nobility—Juliet and lady Capulet—Lord Campbell—Forensic medicine—Child-bed privilege—The "medicine man" and his fee—Twenty money-bags—King John and his erroneous decision—Premature deliveries and the law—Two cases from Taylor—Groaned for him—The heyday of existence and the evening of age—"Hal" and Herbert Spencer—Alcohol and venery—Fish diet and sex—Abortion; never in the prostitute—The doctor's coat—Maid of Orleans—Commission on pregnancy—Difficulties in diagnosing pregnancy—Joriscune's method—Apprehensions in the pregnant state—The "play" as a means of education—Richard the Third at his birth—Shakespeare's intuition—Teeth generated in error—Teretology; its varieties—Hunchbacks and their wit—Richard's villainy—The "grunting"—The accouchement of Anne Boleyn—Graphic description—Tamora, queen of the Goths—"He is your brother by the surer side"—Early marriages and premature decay—Excuses in America—Weaning of Juliet—Stand on the floor and suck—Inanition and little gilded tombs—"Twin sisters"—Chlorosis—Scoundrels made from the mothers' milk—The mother who nurses her own offspring—Cæsarian section should not be "untimely"—How fresh she looks.

Under this caption will be considered every thing connected with parturition and the science of gynæcology. The material, though sufficiently voluminous to constitute a chapter of value, is yet so difficult of arrangement into readable order, that the task I take upon myself in essaying its accomplishment is of some solicitude.

"The Tempest," A. i., S. ii., furnishes us with the first idea in this direction.

"This blue-eyed hag was hither brought with child," has reference to the former mistress of Caliban, but is not of sufficient moment for comment.

"'Tis my familiar sin with maids to seem the lapwing, and to jest, tongue far from heart, play with all virgins so: your brother and his lover have embrac'd: as those that feed grow full; as blossoming time, that from the seeding the bare fallow brings to teeming foison, even so her plenteous womb expresseth his full tilth and husbandry.

Isabella.   Some one with child by him?—My cousin Juliet?

Lucio.   Is she your cousin?

Isabella.   Adoptedly; as schoolmaids change their names by vain though apt affection.

Lucio.   She it is.

Isabella.   O, let him marry her."

The above conversation might have been overheard between a young lady and young gentleman, parties to the interesting play of "Measure for Measure," A. i., S. v., had the ear been applied to the key-hole; and though somewhat pointed to be had between a young couple—or at least would be now so considered—it was no doubt admissible at the date in which it purports to have been used.

Isabella but echoes the sentiment of a woman's heart. She would have her brother marry the girl he had wronged, and thus save her from the odium incident to the results of their improper intimacy. Not so the sentiment of masculine humanity. *Think* of it as he may, the man's *acts* are commonly to *get away* from the scenes of his villainies. Go to "Texas," *get away, go any where*, but leave the place of perfidy, leave his victim to the burden of both her own sorrows and his crimes is the usual mode. Some there are however essay another means of egress from the net closing around them— a means apparently less hazardous to them, but doubly so to the victim. Instead of either "marrying her" or escaping to Australia, the "fly young man" consults Dr. Rosenweig or Madam McCarthy, with one or the other of whom he perfects arrangements for boarding his "cousin" for a week or two. "My cousin, you know, has 'taken cold,' you know, and has dropsy." The result of this stay of a few days with the eminent doctor, coupled with the "treatments" he gives her to "bring her round again," is but too forcibly pictured in the fate of poor Alice Bowlsby, whose body, packed in a trunk, and shipped about the country for several days, so horrified New England a few years ago. Or then the victim's fate is sealed, and she hides her deep despair in the murky waters of a neighboring pond, the swift current of the river, the quiet depths of a lake—or, like the more recent case of Jennie Cramer, expiates, voluntarily, the unendurable bitterness of her folly by hiding her body and shame together in the dark waters of the sea. Those antiquated notions of "let him marry her" may find an occasional response in the bosom of some of our country swains, actuated to the performance of the noble and self-sacrificing duty by the horsewhip of an indignant father, or the point of a "navy" in the hands of a big brother; but in the city, among the refined and intelligent, where Madam M. and Dr. R. may be found almost in every block—never.

In continuation of this same case, wherein the party accused of fornication was by the edict of the ruler of the country to suffer death, we have these further details:

Escalus. "Well, heaven forgive us all!
    Some rise by sin, and some by virtue fall.

Elbow. Come, bring them away. If these be good people in a common-weal, that do nothing but use their abuses in common houses, I know the law; bring them away.

Angelo. [*The duke's deputy, who is executing the law with the utmost rigor on others, although violating it himself with the most flagrant hand.*] How now, sir? what's your name? and what's the matter?

Elbow. If it please your honor, I am the poor duke's constable, and my name is Elbow: I do not lean upon Justice, sir; and do bring in here before your good honor two notorious benefactors.

Angelo. Benefactors! Well, what benefactors are they! are they not malefactors?

Elbow. If it please your honor, I know not well what they are; but precious villains they are, that I am sure of, and void of all profanation in the world that good Christians ought to have.

Escalus. This comes off well; here's a wise officer.

Angelo. Go to: what quality are they of? Elbow is your name: why dost thou not speak, Elbow?

Clown. He cannot, sir; he's out at elbows.

Angelo. What are you, sir?

Elbow. He, sir? a tapster, sir; a parcel-bawd; one that serves a bad woman, whose house, sir, was, as they say, hot-house, which I think, is a very ill house too.

Escalus. How know you that?

Elbow. My wife, sir, whom I detest, before heaven and your honor.

Escalus. How! thy wife?

Elbow. Ay, sir; who, I thank heaven, is an honest woman.

Escalus. Dost thou detest her therefor?

Elbow. I say, sir, I will detest myself also, as well as she, that this house, if it be not a bawd's house, it is pity of her life, for it is a naughty house.

Escalus. How dost thou know that, constable?

Elbow. Marry, sir, by my wife; who, if she had been a woman cardinally inclined, might have been accused in fornication, adultery, and all uncleanliness there.

Escalus. By the woman's means?

Elbow. Ay, sir, by Mrs. Overdone's means; but as she spit in his face, so she defied him.

Clown. Sir, if it please your honor, this is not so.

Elbow. Prove it before these varlets here, thou honorable man; prove it.

Escalus. [*To Angelo.*] Do you hear how he misplaces?

Clown. Sir, she came in great with child, and longing (saving your honor's reverence) for stew'd prunes: sir, we had but two in the house, which at that distant time stood, as it were, in a fruit dish, a dish of some three pence: your honor have seen such dishes: they are not china dishes, but very good dishes.

Escalus. Go to, go to; no matter for the dish, sir.

Clown. No, indeed, sir; not of a pin; you are therefore in the right; but to the point. As I say, this Mistress Elbow, being, as I said, with child, and being great belly'd, and, longing as I said, for prunes, and having but two in the dish, as I said, Master Froth here, this very man, having eaten the rest, as I said, and, as I say, paying for them very honestly;—for, as you know, Master Froth, I could not give you three pence again.

Froth. No, indeed.

Clown. Very well; you being then, if you be remember'd, cracking the stones of the foresaid prunes.

Froth. And so I did indeed.

Clown. Why, very well; I telling you then, if you be remember'd, that such a one, and such a one, were past cure of the thing you wot of, unless they kept very good diet, as I told you."

The court scene above represented is a pretty fair representation of what may be heard most any day in our inferior tribunals,—the medical matter being better however in the above instance than the legal. The idea conveyed in the last paragraph, as to the necessity of good diet in the treatment of the "diseases you wot of," was ignored by the medical world until a period so recent as to come within the memory of our junior practitioners; and that its propriety, nay, *necessity*, should have forced its self upon the notice of a non-medical man three centuries and a half ago, when no medical mind had grasped the idea, is only one among the thousands of evidences we have of Shakespeare's unequaled sagacity. The craving appetite of pregnant women is in my mind a real demand made by nature for material with which to repair some specific waste incident to conception; and the guardians of a female in that condition, who pass lightly by the demands of their charge, are certainly derelict in the discharge of a sacred duty. The whole period of gestation is one of severe strain upon the tissues of the mother; every change in her structures during the nine months of the fœtal existence is to her a period of retrograde metamorphosis, and this is shown by nothing better than the qualities of her blood—the changes in the composition of which, so characteristic of the pregnant state— being recognized as an indubitable evidence in this direction. "The blood is the life," and when this fails to perform its wonted functions, the whole economy follows its lead. The demands upon the system of the mother are of course to supply the materials of a new being; and though we have no data at hand upon which to predicate an assertion that the strange and unusual articles of diet sometimes so longingly sought by the mother do contain ingredients essential to the elaboration of some of its tissues—yet it *may* be so. For some women to become pregnant is to become a new being— her whole aspect is changed. This metamorphosis is no where in her economy more apparent than in the digestive apparatus—the stomach more particularly participating in these perturbations in a degree often sufficient to endanger the life of the woman. Then the mental change, so noticeable a feature in some pregnant females, is doubtless due partially, if not essentially, to the disturbance of the nutritive balance in the system, whereby the brain and nervous system are deprived of some ingredient which is essential to their

healthy functional activity. At a later period doubtless may be
added, as a factor in these manifestations, the septic influences
engendered by a retention of a *materies morbi* in the system of the
mother—the products of the waste of the growing ovum, as also
of her own tissues, retained in her blood.

We notice analogous symptoms connected with many wasting
diseases, as, for example, in typhoid fever, where the anorexia and
the delirium are only the language of the conditions before suggested.
Supply, then, the woman with the "stew'd prunes," or any thing
she requests—her system demands it. The champagne found to be
of so much service to pregnant females by Meigs was but an example of how much "good cheer" may do for them.

The appetite should not be called "morbid," and passed over
carelessly; but our "great belly'd" patients should be well fed,
the fear of "plethora" to the contrary notwithstanding. Plethora,
uræmic disorders, etc., are the evidences of improper elimination
and impoverished organic tissues, rather than of over feeding and
undue assimilation.

This same Clown, Pompey Bum, entertained an idea that may
yet command the notice of the physicians, clergy and law-makers
of this country—namely, that to prevent some from living by the
trade of bawds, it will be necessary to geld and spay all the youths
of the country; and thus would the social evil and its physical
counterpart, venereal maladies, vanish together.

In "Love's Labor Lost," A. v., S. ii., we find:

Costard. "The party is gone: fellow Hector, she is gone; she is
two months on her way.

Armado. What meanest thou?

Costard. Faith, unless thou play the honest Trojan, the poor
wench is cast away; she is quick; the child brags in her belly
already."

The idea of a woman being quick at the end of the second
month is not borne out by the facts; yet it is probably not due to
a lack of definite knowledge on that point by Shakespeare, but is
made so to place it in keeping with the general spirit of exaggeration which pervades the whole plot of the comedy.

In "A Midsummer Night's Dream" we find reference to parturient fatality in these words: "But she being mortal, of that boy
did die;" which applied to the labor of Titian's companion, but
there is nothing further of interest can be deduced from it.

In the same play, and though somewhat irrelevant to our subject, I may mention the now somewhat notorious boast of "Puck" in regard to "putting a girdle round about the earth in forty minutes." Little did Shakespeare dream that this very thing, to him no doubt only a thought placed there to illustrate the extremist impossibility, should be an accomplished fact while yet his own great name is fresh in the minds and hearts of a majority of the civilized people of the earth. Less did he imagine that "forty minutes" should in so short a time be considered an absolute waste of the precious moments, and that the *necessities* of the age made it imperative that it be only forty seconds!

The speculations of the maniac who should now declare that the time will be when we shall be able to reach and explore the hidden mysteries of the moon, would seem to us as plausible as the prediction of "Puck;" now, we mortals behold his seemingly idle vagaries an accomplished fact. We know not what a day may bring forth. Shakespeare, with all his insight into the possibilities which reside in the human composition, did not reach, even in his wildest dreams, the ideas of the telephone, phonograph, etc., both of which have been perfected—nay, *conceived*, since the above paragraph was written. Wonderful as they are, are they much more so than the ability and utility found in connection with what may be accomplished with the pen? The pen and printing press are *grandest* after all. But to return to our theme: In "The Merchant of Venice" we find a coarse conversation between Lorenzo and Lancelot in regard to the pregnancy of a certain Moor, which, however, has little point, and need not be mentioned.

"All's well that ends well," act last, scene last, contains the following: "But for this lord, who hath abus'd me, as he knows himself, though yet he never harm'd me, here I quit him.

> He knows himself my bed he hath defil'd,
> And at that time he got his wife with child:
> Dead though she be, she feels her young one kick;
> So there's my riddle, one that's dead is ' quick.' ''

The lady in this case was Doctor Helena, who worked wonders in the cure of the king's "fistula," to be spoken of in a subsequent chapter of this volume.

"The Winter's Tale" supplies us with this: "The queen, your mother, rounds apace: she is spread of late into a goodly bulk "

This was the queen's ladies'-in-waiting in converse with a small boy, the "prince." Leontes, the boy's father, being wofully jealous of his wife, thought to annoy her by depriving her of the society of the child, and gave orders to his servants—"away with him; and let her sport herself with that she's big with, for 'tis Polixenes has made her swell thus."

One of the king's officers, who knew that the queen was innocent of the charges that were laid at her door, avowed that if she was proven guilty that he would geld his three daughters—fourteen they should not see, to bring false generations. The more euphoneous and polite term *normal ovariotomy* (instead of geld) was not found in the medical vocabulary of the age in which Shakespeare lived.

This idea that the age of fourteen is the beginning of the nubile age in females, is made prominent in more than one place in Shakespeare's writings, and will therefore receive a share of attention as the chapter progresses. Farther on in the same "tale" is found an illustration of the wide-spread popular error that abortion is so often the result of emotional causes. "How fares our gracious lady? As well as one so great, and so forlorne, may hold together. On her frights and griefs (which never tender lady hath borne greater), she is somewhat before her time deliver'd."

It is somewhat interesting to notice that in the above quotation Shakespeare held almost identically to the ideas widely extant to-day as to the part played by mental disturbances in the production of abortion. Strange indeed it appears, that upon this point the average medical man of this advanced age should have gone so little beyond in exact scientific positivism the inherent knowledge of the non medical mind of two hundred and fifty years ago. Many medical minds of the present can see few causes of abortion other than those of mental emotions—and even here cause and effect are not usually very clearly associated in their minds. It is here as is too often the case in other medical cases with this class of loose thinkers, a declaration merely—*a vague generality* meant to subserve, for the present, a lack of real knowledge in relation to the subject.

It is not denied that great mental shock may sometimes be the proximate agency in the production of premature uterine action and expulsion of the uterine contents; but with the experience of many years as a guide the writer is lead to think it an unusual source of such trouble. In fact, the causes of women's being "somewhat before their time deliver'd" are so numerous that to follow the subject through all its sinuosities, and into its multitudinous labyrinths, would make a volume. These causes may, for convenience, be formulated so as to cover most of the ground in this manner:

1st. Causes which reside in the general system of the mother.

2d. Those which reside alone (and are therefore local) in the reproductive system of the mother—and

3d. Those which pertain or belong exclusively to the ovum itself.

In regard to the first of these divisions it may be said to be by far the less frequent source of expulsion of the uterine contents. This fact is well illustrated by the well known truth that in tuberculosis, one of the gravest of the constitutional maladies, pregnancy seems actually to exert, for the time, a retarding influence in regard to its progress—abortions, premature deliveries, etc., being almost unknown occurrences as traceable to it. But there are other constitutional conditions in which the reproductive organs may participate only in a general way, in which miscarriages are very common indeed, and most noticeable among these is, perhaps, constitutional syphilis.

But it is not to chronic constitutional maladies alone that we may confine our remarks, as it is well known that *acute* maladies of various kinds affecting the system at large are prone to be attended with this danger when happening in the pregnant woman. Of this class may be named typhoid fever and the exanthematous fevers,—small-pox, scarlatina, etc., in particular. Defective nutrition is the essential factor in the production of these accidents when occurring under such circumstances quite probably. The fruit withers and falls from its parent stem from lack of the food proper for its growth and nourishment.

Causes of the second variety or class are almost innumerable, and therefore preponderate largely over all others in causing abortions. It is not to conditions of the uterus singly that this fact applies; the womb is not alone at fault always. It may be some organ or tissue entirely independent of the uterus, which by its diseased condition or by its trespass upon the womb and the space which by right belongs to it, which causes all the trouble. A distended urinary bladder or a loaded rectum may do this; an enlarged ovary, a dropsy of the Fallopian tube, an abscess in the veseco-uterine connective tissue, an hæmatocele in the recto-uterine cul-de-sac, tumors of the uterine walls, urinary calculi when large, exostoses when springing from any of the bony surfaces of the pelvic walls, tight corsets, and if it was said a thousand other extrinsic agencies local in their operation and outside of the womb itself operate as causes in the production of abortion, it would be no exaggeration.

Besides these there are the mal-conditions belonging to the uterus proper which go to swell the list of causation. It may be set down as an axiomatic truth that an absolutely healthy womb does not expel its contents spontaneously prematurely,—that is, before the expiration of nine months after conception has occurred. It must be normal in form, in structure, in size, in position, and in its attachments to insure a normal gestation.

Malformations of this organ are usually congenital, and consist of a lack of development in some portion—commonly, of one horn or lateral portion of the organ, leaving it asymmetrical in outline and abridging the normal space which should constitute a proper uterine cavity,—thus rendering a progressive gestation impossible. Or the change in form may be the result of neoplasms, as in the growth of interstitial or other fibroid tumors, the effect of which upon the fertile function of the organ is mostly the same as in the foregoing congenital condition. It is not always so, however, as pregnancy may and often does progress to its proper termination, a uterine tumor present notwithstanding. It must be normal in structure. The uterus, when its walls are thickened up with hyperplastic depositions, or when left in a state of sub-involution after child-birth or miscarriage, is in no condition to carry the burden of a pregnancy to the end.

The muscular and mucous coats of the organ may at the same time be involved in this condition of turgescence and thickening, and whether one or both are involved the results are nearly the same. The vascular supply is not in healthy trim,—the distorted tissues have distorted vessels and nerves accompanying them,—the blood supply is here too small and there too great, the nerve force is unequally distributed, and neuralgia from plethora may involve one nerve filament, while irritability of another may ensue from anemia. The local hemorrhage at one spot and local anemia at another, incident to change in the vascular structure of the organ, are incompatible with the growth and maturity of the fruits of conception. Changes in the size and position of the womb, when not the result of the progress of the pregnancy itself, are prejudicial to the continuation of pregnancy from the same general facts as narrated in the preceding paragraph, though in a less degree perhaps than when accompanied by direct local lesions of the lining membrane of the organ. Endo-metritis is no doubt a fruitful source of the early discharge of the ovum. The change in the membrane being non-consonant with the nutrition and development of the conception,—if even conception occur under such a condition of the membrane. Endo-cervicitis is, however, the greater obstacle to the function of merely impreg-nation.

The uterus is essentially a mobile organ when it is in its healthy condition, and anything that tends to interfere with this freedom of movement,—any event or condition which unduly encroaches upon or hampers it in its normal movements, surely have a tendency to pro-duce the unhappy event which ushers in and gave origin to this article. In its normal state it almost floats unconstrainedly in the pelvic cavity ; while the organ remains so we see few or no abortions.

Let a cellulitis occur, and the organ become agglutinated by in-flammatory products and closely tied to some of the neighboring organs, even at a single point, and abortion then becomes the rule instead of the exception.

Then again as to the causes which reside in the ovum itself. These may reside alone in the sperm-cell. It may have in it vital elements sufficient to fecundate the ovule, thereby exhaust itself and then wither and die. It may go further, but to die in the near future from the effects of a morbific principle inherent in its own organization, as from the poison of syphilis for example ; and this condition may pertain to the *germ*-cell as well as the sperm-cell. Like other animal poisons, this also has under these circumstances the power of multiplication, as we see the terrible effects of it upon the person of the premature little being.

The cause may reside or be engendered in the membranes, the umbilical cord, or in the placenta itself—inflammatory processes be-ing a large factor in such change as connected with these. Mechan-ical causes, such as detachments of the after-birth, knotting or twist-ing, or ruptures, etc., of the cord and membranes, are also among the contingencies which may cause a woman to be " before her time delivered." Enough has doubtless been said to prove that Shake-speare *might* have been correct in placing the miscarriage spoken of to the credit of fatigue and mental worry ; but then the chances are as one in a thousand that he *might* also have been mistaken. Syphilitic infection and hereditary taints are so common, doubtless among those whose marriages of consanguinity keep up the family chain for ages, that miscarriage should be the rule in place of the exception among the nobility of the old countries.

As regards the age at which the menses appear, Shakespeare makes his lord commit an error in placing it absolutely at the age of fourteen years. It will be remembered that the parties of whom he is writing are located in Sicily, in latitude 36° 40′ and 38° 20′ North, which, owing to its insular climate, would have much the same temperature as the south of France, where statistics show that the largest number of girls menstruate for the first time at from the fifteenth to the sixteenth year; but the error most noticeable in this regard is in the case of Juliet, a native of Verona, which is situated in latitude 45° 30′ North, and in the gorges of the Tyrol, where a robust constitution would naturally retard the eruption for a year or two; in this high latitude a large majority of young females do not "see" until beyond the sixteenth, and a large proportion not until the seventeenth or even the eighteenth year.

We find that Juliet was fourteen at the time of her death, and the language of lady Capulet that, "younger than you, here in Verona, ladies of esteem, are made already mothers: by my count, I was your mother, much upon these years that you are now a maid"— which would certainly have placed the good lady's first period as early as her thirteenth year.

I know it may be claimed by those critically inclined that the aristocratic families to which these personages are supposed to have belonged would have brought them "out" much sooner than the commonalty; and that the excitement incident to gay life could have brought about a premature development of the sexual system, which would save the "bard of Avon" any just criticism from a common pen; but this may be met with the fact that the luxurious ease common to the great in our day and nation was not enjoyed even among the princes and nobles of the barbarous age of which the scene and incidents in Romeo and Juliet claim to be a part. The author, no doubt, obtained his data from the time the menses usually appear among the women of England, and approximates the time or age with perhaps as much accuracy as do the doctors, notwithstanding their special enquiries.

In the passage next to be quoted, there is a legal question to be discussed, and as Lord Campbell once wrote a work entitled "Shakespeare's Legal Acquirements," I certainly should, if I knew just how and where, procure a copy of his work to assist me in the matter. It is the case of the doubtful progeny of the wife of Leontes, the king of Sicily. The king had thrown his queen into prison upon a charge of adultery with his former friend, Polixenes, king of Bohemia. The queen was delivered in prison, and the good lady in attendance on her desired to carry the babe to the king to see if its presence might not soften the rigor of his "unsane lunes," but the jailor had some doubts as to his powers under the law to let the babe pass out of the prison doors without a warrant; he was not sure but that he might gravely infringe the law in letting it pass, and thus bring down the wrath of the authorities upon his own devoted head. The lady was equal to the emergency however—as women always are when placed in trying positions of such a character, and pleaded with the prison officer in these terms: "You need not fear it, sir; the child was prisoner to the womb, and is, by law and process of great nature, thence freed and enfranchis'd; not a party to the anger of the king, nor guilty of, if any be, the trespass of the queen." It does not, however, come further in the scope of this work to treat of the legal aspects of this case, as forensic medicine will find a very limited place in its pages; but it matters little what the *lex scripta* of the case may have been, justice said "let her pass."

This same woman, in her desire to save the queen from the foul charge of inconstancy to her marriage vow, presented the babe to the king, and endeavored to convince him of the legality of its paternity by the following exhibit:

"Behold, my lords, although the print be little, the whole matter and copy of the father: eyes, nose, lip; the trick of his frown, his forehead; nay, the valley, the pretty dimples of his chin and cheek; his smiles; the very mould and frame of hand, nail, finger.—And, thou, good goddess Nature, which hast made it so like him that got it, if thou hast the ordering of the mind too, 'mongst all colours, no yellow in't; lest she suspect, as he does, her children not her husband's."

To throw the odium of induction of premature birth on the hands of the king, see how closely and with what tact Shakespeare keeps to his points; he says, "although the print be *little*," etc., thus making it correspond in size and age.

The queen was brought before the husband for trial, and makes her own defence in these words: "To me can life be no commodity: the crown and comfort of my life, your favor, I do give lost, for I do feel it gone, but know not how it went. My second joy, and first-fruits of my body, from his presence I am barr'd, like one infectious. My third comfort, starr'd most unluckily, is from my breast,—the innocent milk in its most innocent mouth, hal'd out to murder: (*The child had been banished by order of the king*) myself on every post proclaim'd a strumpet: with immodest hatred, the child-bed privilege denied, which 'longs to women of all fashion: lastly, hurried here to this place i' the open air, before I have got strength of limb.'' (''*Limit*'' *in Shakespeare.*)

It seems that the law of nature has so indelibly impressed this matter of the ''child-bed privilege'' upon the human race, that even the untutored savage is tamely subordinated to its sway. The deference paid even by the American Indian to his squaw, while in the parturient condition, was aptly illustrated in a story narrated to the writer once by an English lady of intelligence, who had long resided among the aborigines on our western border. The narrative interested me much at the time, but as the particulars have escaped my memory, I can only present it in substance. The wife and her lord, husband, or ''buck,'' or whatever title is used by them to denote the head of the household, had been on inimical terms for a time, had had a domestic broil for a few days, and to rid himself of the unpleasant contiguity of a morose wife, perhaps, had gone off on a hunt. While thus absent, the squaw took it into her head to be confined. She had, on all former occasions, been attended by an old woman, whose fee, if anything at all, was but a nominal one. This time she employed the ''medicine man,'' who confronted the ''buck'' on his return with his bill, the which the luckless wight was glad to liquidate at the expense of his most valuable pony. It was an *obstetric* fee, and *his* honor was too exalted to quibble over it, be the sum small or great. Herein could many of his pale-faced brothers learn a wholesome lesson.

The babe who had been banished by her father to a strange coast, and who was thought by the king to have been murdered by those to whose charge she was given, was however trusted to the tender mercies of a wilderness—found and raised by a shepherd, and when grown courted and married the prince of the country. She then returned to the land of her nativity, where she learned her own history, and was taken to see her mother's statue—who, it was supposed, had died in prison. The old king, who was yet alive, says to his son-in-law: '' *Your* mother was most true to wedlock, prince, for she did print your royal father (Polixenes) off, conceiving you;" whilst the bride reached forth her hand to the statue of her mother, saying: "Lady, dear queen, that ended where I began, give me that hand to kiss." *('Twas her mother, and not a statue.)*

Autolicus, at the shepherd's feast, tells the gaping plebeians of a usurer's wife who was delivered of twenty money-bags at a birth, one of his fair hearers praying to be excused from marrying a usurer!

In King John, A. i., S. i., occurs another case involving an amount of scientific inquiry, both medically and legally, to invest it with special interest. It is a case where a charge of illegitimacy was made, based upon the fact that a viable child was born fourteen weeks before " term "—counting from the period of the return of the husband, who had been from home in a distant country, in a very protracted absence. To get more fairly at the points in the case, it will be necessary to give a somewhat lengthy extract:

King John. "What men are you?

Philip Faulconbridge (called the Bastard). Your faithful subject I, a gentleman born in Northamptonshire, and eldest son, as I suppose, to Robert Faulconbridge, a soldier, by the honor-giving hand of Cœur-de-Lion knighted in the field.

King John. What art thou? *(To another.)*

Robert. Son and heir to that same Faulconbridge.

King John. Is that the elder, and thou the heir? You came not of one mother then, it seems.

Bastard. Most certain of one mother, mighty king; that is well known, and, as I think, one father; but for the certain knowledge of that truth I put you o'er to heaven and my mother: of that I doubt, as all men's children may. (Here we have, what occurs very rarely in Shakespeare's writings, a contradiction in the same paragraph; he first thinks he *is*, and then he thinks he *is not*, his brother's father's son—that is, old Robert Faulconbridge's son.)

Elinor. Out on thee, rude man! thou dost shame thy mother, and wound her honor with this diffidence.

Bastard. I, madam? No, I have no reason for it; that is my brother's place, and none of mine; the which if he can prove, 'a pops me out from fair five hundred pounds a year. Heaven guard my mother's honor and my land!

King John. A good blunt fellow. Why, being younger born, dost he lay claim to thy inheritance?

Bastard. I know not why, except to get the land. But once he slander'd me with bastardy: but whe'r I be as true begot, or no, that still I lay upon my mother's head; but that I am as well begot, my liege (fair fall the bones that took the pains for me!), compare our faces, and be judge yourself, If old Sir Robert did beget us both, and were our father, and this son like him,

> O! old Sir Robert, father, on my knee   ?
> I give heaven thanks I was not like to thee.

King John. Why, what a madcap hath heaven sent us here.

Elinor. He hath a trick of Cœur-de-Lion's face; the accent of his tongue affecteth him. Do you not read some tokens of my son in the large composition of this man?

King John. Mine eye hath well examined his parts, and finds them perfect Richard.—Sirrah, speak: what doth move you to claim your brother's land?

Bastard. Because he hath a half-face, like my father, with that half-face would he have all my land: a half-fac'd groat, five hundred pounds a year!

Robert. My gracious liege, when that my father liv'd, your brother did employ my father much.

Bastard. Well, sir, by this you cannot get my land. Your tale must be how he employ'd my mother.

Robert. And once despatch'd him in an embassy to Germany, there, with the emperor, to treat of high affairs touching that time. The advantage of his absence took the king, and in the meantime sojourn'd at my father's; when how he did prevail, I shame to speak, but truth is truth: large lengths of seas and shores between my father and my mother lay, as I have heard my father speak himself, when this same lusty gentleman was got. Upon his death-bed he by will bequeath'd his lands to me; and took it, on his death, that this, my mother's son, was none of his; and if he were, he came into the world full fourteen weeks before the course of time."

It has been argued, that if a child born at the fifth or even the sixth month survive, this fact alone should be held as evidence of illegitimacy—that is, where concurrent circumstances point to the fact; but according to common English law it is held that it is not essential that a child be born capable of living to any specific age, or to the full of a certain number of hours, days or months, to entitle it to inherit; but it is sufficient if the child have been born *alive.*

This construction of the law certainly would vest the rights of inheritance in the Bastard, the point of legitimacy alone considered: for if it was a fact that he was born at the end of the twenty-second week of gestation, he could not only have lived, but could even have grown into the "lusty gentleman" which we now find him. Though of the legal aspect of the case, as regards rights to property, it is not our province to write, but the question as to whether a child born fourteen weeks prior to the end of the time when an ordinary gestation is completed—that is, at the end of the twenty-second week—can live and grow to adult age, is clearly one for the science of medicine to settle. Upon theoretical assumptions alone this question could not be adjusted; only *facts* gathered from actual observation of the witness, or those derived from records of undoubted authenticity, should be offered as testimony by a medical expert in a case of this kind. From the most reliable data which we are able to gather, it does not seem improbable that a case may occasionally happen where a child even at the early period of the *twentieth* week may not only be born *viable,* but may survive to puberty or to old age. I quote two cases from Taylor:

"Dr. Barker, of Dumfries, narrates a case in which a child was born at the one hundred and fifty-eighth day of pregnancy, or at the end of twenty-two weeks and four days after intercourse. The child weighed one pound and measured eleven inches. It did not suck properly till after the lapse of a month, and she didn't walk until she was nineteen months old; was sprightly, but at the age of three and a half years only weighed twenty-nine and a half pounds."

On a trial involving the legitimacy of the child of the wife of a minister, which was born on the one hundred and twenty-fourth day after marriage, one reputable medical witness testified that he had "attended a case where the child was certainly born at the end of the *nineteenth* week of pregnancy, and the child lived a year and a half."

Occurrences of this kind are so rare, however, that the judgment rendered by king John—given upon that plea alone—that is, had he based his decision upon the fact that viability is probable in a child born at the end of twenty-two pregnant weeks, would certainly have been giving too great a weight to a fact which can only be admitted as a *possibility;* and besides, the *moral* circumstances connected with the case would, if proven before an impartial jury, have certainly reversed the judgment of the king. Indeed, after the decision had been rendered in favor of Philip, lady Faulconbridge admitted his illegitimacy. I will give the language used by the king, and the reasoning which he brought to bear in guiding him in his decision:

John. [*To Robert Faulconbridge.*] "Sirrah, your brother is legitimate: your father's wife did after wedlock bear him; and if she did play false, the fault was hers, which fault lies on the hazards of all husbands that marry wives."

The king did not pretend to found the verdict on justice, but only adhered blindly to a rule which had clearly been shown to have in this case an exception, that wedlock is presumptive evidence of the legality of all the progeny produced within its pale. Were we called to testify in a case of the kind, we should give it as an opinion that in a case where the child had been born fourteen weeks prior to the end of the thirty-sixth week of the gestative condition, that grave doubts might be entertained of its legitimacy, if its development and other circumstances gave any room for suspicion that the wife had been " sluc'd " in the husband's absence, and his " pond fish'd by Sir Smile, his next neighbor." This proved to have been the case with the Faulconbridge family, the lady herself admitting the fact thus:

"King Richard was thy father. By long and vehement suit I was seduc'd to make room for him in my husband's bed.—Heaven! lay not my trangression to my charge; thou art [*to Philip*] the issue of my dear offence." This is sufficient to establish the error of John's decision, and ought to have established the validity of Robert's title. But enough.

Elinor, widow of king Henry the Second, and her daughter-in-law Constance, were on inimical terms, and bandied foul epithets without stint or measure. The daughter thus accuses her mother: " Thy sins are visited upon this poor child; the canon of the law is laid on him, being but the second generation removed from thy sin conceiving womb."

It is natural to infer from the foregoing paragraph that history would give some data upon which to found the intimation which is there clearly made touching a lack of chastity on the part of Elinor, the widow'd queen of the second Henry ; from the history of that period now at my command, it is not apparent that such charges were really ever preferred against her. This same Constance, who seems to have been the widow of the king's eldest son, and who had died before his father, somewhere about 1185 or 6, leaving one son, Arthur, who his mother, then a scheming widow, wished to place upon the English throne ; and failing in accomplishing her purpose, even after entering into an arrangement with the king of France, who ultimately "went back on her."—her son in the meantime being taken prisoner by his uncle John, who was then king, and who was accused of murdering the boy with his own hand—she thus pours forth a tirade of bitterness against mankind in general, ending in these words : " Let wives with child pray, that their burdens may not fall this day, lest their hopes prodigiously be cross'd." Next we have, " Have we more sons, or are we like to have? Is not my teeming date drunk up with time, and wilt thou pluck my fair son from mine age, and rob me of a happy mother's name?" This was the language of the wife of the Duke of York, in Richard the Second, when expostulating with her husband, who had determined to acquaint the king of a plot against his life,—his own son being one of the conspirators ; she then goes on : " Hadst thou groan'd for him as I have done, thou wouldst be more pitiful. But now I know thy mind ; thou dost suspect that I have been disloyal to thy bed, and that he is a bastard, not thy son."

York flies to the king, and whilst he is divulging the plot his wife also hastens thither, when the old duke accosts her thus :

> " Thou frantic woman, what dost thou make here?
> Shall thy old dugs once more a traitor rear?"

It would seem that each of them had a keen sense of the desolation attending the " sere and yellow leaf " of age, and were sad in the prospect of henceforth walking the down grade to the tomb, without even a pleasing retrospection to win them for a moment from the cheerless monotony of their journey. Asperity is not, in general, a concomitant of this period of human existence—a pensive realization of the fact that the spring-time of life has passed—the seed has been sown, the heyday of existence has been reached and the harvest gathered in, and the husbandman has nothing more to do but set thoughtfully by through the autumn and winter, with his

hands resting on the top of his staff, contemplating the shadows
as they silently fall around him.

Patriotism, or love of one's king, would hardly, in these days of
self-love, bear such fruits of loyalty as was apparent in this good
but mistaken old York.

Prince "Hal," the riotous companion of Falstaff, and afterwards
the wise and good king, Henry the Fifth, was renowned for his
sound and pertinent witticisms. Upon the question of population,
on one occasion, he made the remark: "The midwives say, the
children are not in fault, whereupon the world increases, and kin-
dreds are mightily strengthened;" which makes it apparent that
"Hal," had he lived in this age, would no doubt be a worthy member of the London Dialectical Society, and discuss "Social Science"
with as much logic as Herbert Spencer and the rest of them.

It is also apparent that "Sir John" himself had an idea or two in
the same direction, as he places his estimate of prince John before
the world in plain language; he made the acquaintance of the
prince after the close of the military campaign in which he, Sir
John, won such renown. and upon the occasion when he delivered
up to the prince the rebel prisoner Colevile; here is the colloquy:

Falstaff. "My lord, I beseech you, give me leave to go through
Glostershire; and when you come to court, stand my good lord,
pray, in your good report.

Prince John. Fare you well, Falstaff; I, in my condition, shall
better speak of you than you deserve.

Falstaff. (To himself.) I would, you had but the wit: 'twere
better than your dukedom.—Good faith, this same young, sober-
blooded boy doth not love me, nor a man cannot make him laugh;
but that's no marvel, he drinks no wine. There's never any of
these demure boys come to any proof, for their drink doth so over-
cool their blood, and making many fish meals, that they fall into a
kind of male green-sickness; and then, when they marry, they get
wenches."

In these days, when the action of all alcoholic liquors upon the
human economy occupies so unsettled a position in the minds of
therapeutists, it is difficult to say whether the idea entertained as to
its powers in influencing the sex of our offspring, as suggested in
the last quotation, is true or false. Certain it is, however, that wine
is a great provocative to venereal appetite, and from that fact it

might be inferred that it might on occasions spur one of those cold youths into a condition of amorous excitement, whereby he might beget a boy in place of a " wench." This could only have reason for a basis however, under very special restrictions, or when administered by the direction of a scientific mind, with a view to build up the weakened functions, as in the following case, treated by Dr. Wilks. an English physician, very lately :

" A little boy, aged five years and a half, was admitted to Guy's hospital in an extreme state of emaciation on Oct. 25th. No disease could be found in him, and it was thought his ailments might be due merely to starvation. In spite, however, of good living and a little wine, he did not improve, and therefore, after having been in till Dec. 15th, he was ordered one drachm of rectified spirits four times a day. In a few days he was better, was soon able to leave his bed, and has been growing fatter and stronger ever since."

The " sack," wine, etc., taken in excess, according to the plan of Falstaff, would not have any tendency to aid in the production of robust children, either of the one sex or the other, as it is a lamentable fact that a large majority of the pitiful humanity that people our public charities are the offspring of drunken parents ; this is not only so where poverty is the cause of the change, but is also the case where physical and particularly *mental* infirmity is the cause which demands the interference of charity—thus plainly telling us that though Falstaff's idea might reach consummation one time in a thousand, it will not do to build upon as a rule. Besides, sack nor any of its kindred compounds are likely to benefit " chlorosis " either in the male or female.

The eating of fish certainly finds a misapplication in this instance, as it is now supposed that the white meats, and most noticeably among them fish, serves as the best pabulum for brain workers, thus conducing to a mental and physical state the exact antipode to both " green sickness " and the desire to the abuse of the sexual function. At least this is claimed as regards the application to more elegant society, though criticism might find vantage ground by referring to the mental, moral and physical status of the inhabitants of fishing villages—those whose diet consists almost solely of fish. The same might, perhaps, be said however of any people who are not accustomed to a diversity of alimentary substances. I do not find any statistical data to show that in fishing communities female predominates over male births.

If drinking " sack " had been the handmaiden of procreation in the day whereof we write, we might have reposed some confidence in the claim of pregnancy put in by the notorious bawd Mrs. Doll Tearsheet : but even with this beverage as a " partus accelerator " we doubt whether she ever conceived or brought forth anything save a bundle of notorious falsehoods, as is the wont of all her class. At the time she makes the asseveration of pregnancy she is in the hands of the officers of the law, and perhaps only feigned pregnancy to shield herself from the consequences of crime, as it is not at all likely that one so far gone as she in the trade of licentiousness would become fruitful. Here is what she says in conversation with the officer :

1st Officer. "The constables have delivered her over to me, and she shall have whipping-cheer enough I warrant her. There hath been a man or two lately killed about her.

Doll. Nut-hook, nut-hook, you lie. Come on : I'll tell thee what, thou damned tripe-visaged rascal, an the child I now do go with do miscarry, thou hadst better thou hadst struck thy mother, thou paper-faced villain.

Hostess. O, the lord, that Sir John were come! he would make this a bloody day to some body. But I pray God the fruit of her womb do miscarry ! "

The gestation of " Mistress Doll " was evidently a hoax, because, as stated above, it is seldom indeed that a female so old in sexual license as " Mrs. Doll " preserves the power of reproduction. The oft-repeated and finally the continued engorgement of the pelvic organs incident to the frequent erotic excitement to which such women are constantly exposed, produces a change in the tissues of the reproductive organs incompatible with fruitful ovulation and germination. It is well known that these women, when some years advanced in their lamentable trade, do not become pregnant—the probable sin of abortion, added to their other excesses, thus being spared to them.

In King Henry the Sixth is used, illustratively, the term " a child's bearing cloth." Obstetric literature and practice now recognize no article of the lying-in chamber by that name specifically, but the presumption is that the writer has reference to the cloth on which the nurse receives the new-born babe from the hands of the accoucheur, immediately after its separation from the secundines—the good nurse usually, in the hurry and excitement of the moment, seizing the first article with which her hand comes in contact, whether it be a bed comforter or a lace pocket-handkerchief.

I had a ludicrous incident in this connexion to befall myself on one occasion. As is usual, I believe, among doctors of the present day, I had "pulled off my coat and rolled up my sleeves," the better to facilitate my accoucheural duties; and when the labor was finished, my hands washed, etc., and I ready to take my leave, behold I could not find my coat! After much search and diligent enquiry, however, it was found deeply hidden in the recesses of the cradle, with the new-comer snugly ensconced therein! I consoled myself with the remembrance of the old saw that "accidents will happen," etc.

In Henry the Sixth is also an account of the trial and condemnation of the "Maid of Orleans," wherein the Poet attaches a foul blemish to the character of that unfortunate female, unworthy of a great man—one which should have called down the stern condemnation not only of the mighty and chivalrous nation to which Joan of Arc belonged, but also of the generous and noble of every land; this is more particularly so, since history gives us no shadow of a ground for sustaining him in an assumption, which he only put forth, doubtless, to gratify a national antagonism that has from the earliest days existed between the Celts and Anglo-Saxons. He brings her forward in a pretext to procure a stay of execution of the sentence of death by setting up a plea of pregnancy, which stay was allowable at that period, provided a commission of midwives, who were usually appointed to investigate the matter, reported that she the condemned were found actually to be in that condition. She says to her enemies: "Will nothing turn your unrelenting hearts? Then, Joan, discover thine infirmity, that warranteth by law to be thy privilege.—I am with child, ye bloody homicides: murder not, then, the fruit within my womb, although ye hale me to a violent death." It was decided not to entertain this appeal, and the unhappy "visionary" was roasted at the stake.

Referring to the custom then common of appointing a commission of midwives to determine a question in science which involved the life or death of an individual may seem to us in the highest degree farcical, but in reality a board of examiners composed of such material would *know* just as much with regard to the *certainty* of the pregnant condition as would a commission of the most enlightened physicians. By this I mean to say that there are no means yet known to the medical world by which pregnancy can be *positively* known. Certainly there are many ways •by which the truth is approximated, and by which the intelligent physician may be able to satisfy his own mind as to a given case, but to say *yes* or *no* under oath would be quite another matter. We are furnished with much better and more specific data when we wish to say a woman is *not* pregnant. *The uterus that is not increased in size above the normal* (to that woman) *is not pregnant.* It may be increased in its dimensions and yet not be pregnant however, and this is often, very often, the case.

In forming our diagnosis as to whether pregnancy exists, it must first be ascertained whether or not there has been a chance for contact between the seminal elements of the female and male; this is a requirement indispensable to fecundation. This union or blending of the sexual elements must find a proper nidus in which to germinate. It is not essential, as would appear from the investigations of Sims, that there be actual contact between the persons of the parties who furnish the spermatozoa and the ovule. The evidence positive that the copulative act has happened can only assure us that we have a first stepping-stone, and nowhere, in any direction, is, perhaps, to be seen a positive footing. Doubt of the pregnancy may yet be as prominent as ever unless there be present other phenomena characteristic of the condition. Of these, probably, suspension of the menses, morning nausea, irascibility of temper, appetite for unusual articles of diet, salivation, evident growth of the uterus—are as unfailing signs as can be observed during the early months. The click of the fœtal heart, at a later period, is of some value.

Of course it is not the province of a work like this to enumerate all that might be said upon a subject so extended, but the object sought in the foregoing is merely to call the attention of the reader to a realization of the fact of the limited amount of *positive* knowledge possessed, even at this late day, by the profession upon this seemingly simple subject. It is thought by persons outside of medicine, very generally, that any medical man ought to be competent to solve *positively* a problem which to their seeming is very plain.

The doctrine lately put forth by Jorisenne, that pregnancy may be diagnosed as early as the conclusion of the first month by a uniformity in the frequency of the pulse in the erect, reclining or horizontal position of the body of the female, is perhaps of little worth as a positive means; it has, however, the merit of easily being put to the test of actual experimentation. If found to be true upon further investigation, it will prove all the more valuable from the fact of its simplicity.

King Edward in battle with the forces led by the famous Warwick was defeated, and himself taken prisoner. Queen Elizabeth thus laments the catastrophe:

Rivers. "The news, I must confess, are full of grief;
Yet, gracious madam, bear it as you may:
Warwick may lose, that now has won the day.
Elizabeth. Till then fair hope must hinder life's decay; and I the rather wean me from despair, for love of Edward's offspring in my womb: this is it that makes me bridle passion, and bear with mildness my misfortune's cross: Ay, ay, for this I draw in many a tear, and stop the rising of blood-sucking sighs,

Lest with my sighs or tears I blast or drown
King Edward's fruit, true heir to th' English crown."

Pregnancy exerts a very powerful influence upon the mental condition of many patients, elevating and enlivening the spirits of some, while it causes depression and despondency in others. It is common, I apprehend, for a large majority of women to pass through the gestative process 'mid more of apprehension and solicitude than is generally supposed. This is a necessary accompaniment of the pains and certain amount of danger which every female instinctively recognizes as inseparably connected with the parturient function; it is under such circumstances that *hope*—that sentiment or principle of the human soul without which all in this life would be black and comfortless despair, comes in to sustain and encourage them. If there is ever an hour in human existence when a person needs the kindly offices and sympathies of husband and friends, it is found in the life of woman during pregnancy. To carry to a successful termination a gestation which is the product of the man she loves, a woman will make the most unheard-of sacrifices; and more particularly is this so if the partner to her condition be dead or in trouble. The whole idea of Elizabeth could be summed up in the simple sentence—"something to love and live for."

It is a curious but cogent commentary upon the force and character of the writings of Shakespeare, that although his delineations are drawn always in a merely histrionic spirit, yet they are so faithful a portraiture of the times, places and people to whom they apply, that even at this day, and among the most scholarly people, they are accepted as veritable history. There is little doubt, however, but that the paucity of books at the day in which he wrote rendered the drama a means not only of amusement but also a source of knowledge to the play-goers; and hence the incentive for keeping to the real as much as possible in the cultivation of theatric art. In the present age the morning paper is our educator, and something only to please is brought upon the stage. Fiction of the purest type is now the fashion.

The good but imbecile king, Henry the Sixth, whose reign was practically ended at the battle of Tewkesbury, and who, after a rigorous confinement in the Tower at London was supposed by historians to have been murdered by the usurping Richard the "hunchback,"—the same monster in partial human form who is made to commit the deed, with his own hand, by the dramatist,— had the history of his own entrance into the world given to him, by the imprisoned monarch, at the time when he went into the prison-cell to murder him.

The good king knowing full well his bloody intent, and the utter hopelessness of asking mercy at his relentless hands, makes good use of his few remaining moments to paint the monster, to his own face, in all his hideousness. He says: "The owl shriek'd at thy birth, an evil sign: the night-crow cried, a boding luckless tune; dogs howled, and hideous tempests shook down trees: the raven rook'd her on the chimney's top, and chattering pies in dismal discord sung. Thy mother felt more than a mother's pain, and yet brought forth less than a mother's hope; to-wit,—an indigest, deformed lump, not like the fruit of such a goodly tree. Teeth hadst thou in thy head, when thou wast born, to signify thou com'st to bite the world: and if the rest be true which I have heard, thou com'st to—"

Here Richard stabs him; but after he has committed the bloody tragedy, he concludes the history himself:—"I have often heard my mother say, I came into the world with my legs forward. Had I not reason, think you, to make haste and seek their ruin that usurped our right? The midwife wonder'd; and the women cried, 'Jesus, bless us! he is born with teeth;' and so I was."

We note in the foregoing description of the parturient stage in woman the same wonderful accuracy of detail in which our author is usually so fertile. Did he learn all this from his own observation, or was this wonderful tact in looking into human character *inherent?* I have thought it must be that he *knew intuitively*—that a man in an ordinary lifetime, no difference how profoundly observant powers might be developed in him, nor how favorable his opportunities for observation, could never have *learned* so much of human nature as is evinced in his writings.

See how he names the leading facts connected with labor. First he makes it occur in the night—making it coincide in this particular with the common time of its occurring ; then he makes the night one of the *dismal* kind,—thus placing it in close relation perhaps to fact. Night seems actually to be the time in which most labors happen, and *bad* nights are the ones most likely to be chosen by—what? for the occurrence of the labor. I was going to say chosen by the mother, but then accuracy of expression forbade my doing so, because the poor mother *has no choice* in the matter. I was then going to say the babe chose the time at which to come into the outer world, but here again I am checked in reckless assertion, and made to acknowledge humbly that no one knows why nights—nights in which hideous tempests shake down trees—are the most seemly for such occasions, in the view of that *nameless cause* which man knows not of.

We can see the profound superstition of the age holding place even in the mind of Shakespeare himself, in his allusions to the hooting of the owl, the boding luckless tune of the night-crow, the howling of the sleepless dog, the croak of the raven and the chattering of the pies. Who among us, even now, are *entirely* free from a small degree of the same? Then again, the assertion that Richard came into the world with teeth would no doubt in that age have excited wonder and been grounds for forebodings of good or of evil for the possessor, just as the whim of the nurses might have dictated. This departure from the ordinary law of development is not often observed even among professional midwives and obstetricians of large practice, although it has been many times noticed. Why it does not happen oftener is a matter for wonder, as of all the histological elements which go to make up the human body teeth are found to be oftener generated in error than any other tissue, and this always during intra-uterine life. This curious fact is, however, oftener observed to happen in females,—the favorite situation for their development being the ovary. As many as three hundred fully developed teeth have been found in a single ovary. They are however also noticed in tumors of the male—more particularly, I believe, as connected with the testes.

Deviations from normal development occurring previous to the termination of fœtal existence are embraced under the scientific name (cyphosis) Teratology,—the signification of which is "monster:"—an "indigest deformed lump" is what our author well names it in the case of Richard. The causes of these lacks of proper development are susceptible of being viewed from two stand-points—the one pertaining to the parents, the other to the fœtus itself. In regard to the first, it is believed that the germ furnished by either or by both parents may be diseased or defective in form or composition, and thus by transmission we will have lack of a perfect offspring. Or, then, the impression may be made on the plastic tissues of a healthy fœtus while in utero by various causes operating on it, such causes being themselves contained in the womb also in some instances, and thus acting directly upon the offspring; while another class of causes may be found to be extra uterine, but yet having their seat in the pelvic cavity,—or yet again they may reside outside of the mother's body, but produce, when brought into activity, like results. Of the first of these we can know but little. They may pertain to an undue proximity of some point in the developing tissue of the child with some point —as of a uterine tumor, for example, or a pelvic exostosis—in the mother. A nodule in the placental tissue, or a knotted umbilical cord may lie so in contact with the soft tissues during fœtal development as by its pressure to cause a failure of organization at a given point. Of course these are but hypotheses,—because, as I said above, etiological factors belonging to this category are very obscure.

These causes may operate upon one or more points of the fœtus at the same time, thus producing one or more species of malformation in the same person. The law which seems to be always followed in Teratology may be formulated somewhat intelligibly in the following manner:

1st, Dissimilar parts of the body never become united,—as a union between an arm and a foot; nor is a hand ever found attached to a leg. It is only parts which are developed from the same isolated mass or "germinal spot," if we may so term it, which become thus united.

2d. Malformed parts are restricted to their proper place on or in the body.

3d. No malformed organ ever loses entirely its own character; that is, *some* of its form, structure or function will remain, no difference how great the deformity. Nor will a deformed animal lose its generic distinction. The dog in the process of development may appear with an abbreviated tail, yet he is a dog all the same.

4th. Double deformities are always of the same sex. No mention is made by any observer worthy of credence wherein the male and female have been found united in the same or a similar manner as were the Siamese Twins.

The second class of causes which produce malformations of the fœtus, or arrest of its complete development, are to be found in the numerous class of external agencies which may operate through, of course, the medium of the mother's tissues. These would include mainly agencies of a mechanical nature, and are, therefore, so numerous and so diversified in kind that it would be superfluous to enumerate them here.

It would appear to one who gives thought to the subject, and analyzes closely the mental traits given to Richard by Shakespeare, that they belong more to that class of hunchbacks the deformity in whom occurs at a post natal period,—those who are congenitally decrepit usually lacking in their mental make-up the witticisms which render the others so companionable, and the sarcasm which is in them such a prominent characteristic. In the latter, also, what they lack in physical powers to render pugnacity successful they find supplied to them in the sting at the point of the tongue.

We find two causes operating to render the labor of Richard's mother severe, and to cause the woman who brought him forth to feel "more than a mother's pains." These were the deformity and the presentation of the feet, either of which was sufficient doubtless to produce more pain than in a normal labor; while both, occurring at once, would complicate the case yet more. Of course, in a case of presentation of the feet the preparatory stage of the labor is much prolonged, from the lack of the steady, even pressure of the head; and the pain and suffering are augmented accordingly. Many women also suffer much from an impossibility to speedily deliver the head. The accuracy of the observation then, as applied to these two points, in our author's description, mainly defy the criticism of even the present era.

But the foregoing description of the mental and physical components of Richard the Third is not by any means given in full, and consequently all that may be written upon them cannot be deduced from a text so incomplete. The *full* description of his make-up, and the construction which he himself places upon the anomaly, will be found under the heading " Miscellaneous " in the last chapter of this volume. Apology may here also be mentioned for the apparent repetition therewith associated, but it is considered better to hazard the risk of criticism in that direction than that for ambiguity.

In the next quotation we find some seeming contradictions to declarations given above—a fault seldom observed in Shakespeare's writings.

Of a piece with the description of the birth-night of Richard is that of the fearful tumult on the night of the murder of Duncan, and that of the night before the assassination of Cæsar, as witnessed by Casca. This same distorted cut-throat, Richard, on another occasion, whilst imprecating Nature for not bestowing upon him fairer fashion, declares he came into this breathing world before his time and only half " made-up;" whilst Margaret, the widow of the murdered king, tells what she knew of the miserable wretch in these words:

" Thou elvish-marked, abortive, rooting hog! thou that wast seal'd in thy nativity the strain of nature, and the scorn of hell! thou slander of thy mother's womb! thou loathed issue of thy father's loins! "

It is not probable that his "half make-up" was because of his having " come before his time into this breathing world," because premature children have imperfectly developed appendages, as the nails, etc., and would therefore not be likely to possess teeth, as it is asserted that this boy had, at birth; nor is it likely that the term "abortive" used by Margaret had reference to untimely birth, but only to lack of physical development.

The same Richard in an effort to enlist the populace in his favor and against his own brother, thus impeaches his mother's virtue:

(To one of his adherents.) "Tell them that when my mother went with child of this insatiate Edward, Noble York, my princely father,

then had wars in France; and by true computation of the time, found that the issue was not his begot."

It could with some plausibility be argued that the physical deformity of Richard was an inheritance from his parentage in the manner first discussed—namely, in the form of abnormal germ-life as the gift of one or the other of his parents, or of both the father and the mother. It is seen in the quotation above that he openly declares the lack of virtue in his mother, and it may thus have happened that it was some constitutional or sexual malady in her that retarded or arrested the development of the "hunch-back" while in utero.

On another occasion, where he wished to marry his own niece to assist him in his designs upon the crown, he uses the following argument to the girl's mother:

"If I did take the kingdom from your son, to make amends, I'll give it to your daughter; If I have killed the issue of your womb, (he had killed his two young nephews) to quicken your increase, I will beget mine issue of your blood upon your daughter. A grandam's name is little less in love than is the doting title of a mother: They are as children, but one step below, even of your mettle, of your very blood; of all one pain save for a night of groans endured of her for whom you did like sorrow."

Shakespeare denominated it a "night of groans" from the mouth of "Dick the Third," while in the tongue of our Native America it is often designated by the laconic term a "grunting." This is one of the popular terms used for labor among the good old country women of Missouri, and is about as significant an appellation as any in use. This appellation is also applied to labor by Hamlet in his somewhat broad conversation with Ophelia as is noted in the last paragraph of this chapter.

To this individual, Richard the Third, we can well apply the truism, that men's evil manners live in brass, whilst their virtues are written in water.

Henry the Eighth furnishes us a few lines on the subject of procreation.

A gentleman of the court in speaking of the manner in which the people did reverence to Anne Boleyn (*Anne Bullen in the drama*), the second wife of Henry, at the time of her marriage thus illustrated the matter: (*To a friend.*) "Believe me, Sir. She is the

goodliest woman that ever lay by man ; which when the people had
the full view of, such a noise arose as the shrouds make at sea in
a stiff tempest, as loud, and to as many tunes : hats, cloaks,
(doublets, I think) flew up ; and had their faces been loose this day
they had been lost, such joy I never saw before.   Great-bellied
women that had not half a week to go, like rams in the old time of
war, would shake the press, and make them reel before them.''

After this marriage, in due time it is announced, ''The queen's in
labor ; they say, in great extremity, and feared she'll with the labor
end.''

This was a conversation between two courtiers, and was follow'd
at another place by a talk between the King and an attendant on the
same subject :

King. ''Now, Lovell, from the queen what is the news?

Lovell. I could not personally deliver to her what you commanded me, but by her women I sent your message ; who return'd
her thanks in the greatest humbleness, and desir'd your highness
most heartily to pray for her.

King. What say'st thou? ha ! to pray for her? what! is she crying out?

Lovell. So said her woman ; and that her sufferance made almost
each pang a death.

King. Alas, good lady !

Suffolk. God safely quit her of her burden, and with gentle
travail, to the gladding of your highness with an heir !

King. 'Tis midnight, Charles ; pr'y thee to bed ; and in thy
prayers remember my poor queen.   Leave me alone, for I must
think of that which company would not be friendly to.

Suffolk. I wish your highness a quiet night ; and my good mistress will remember in my prayers.''

The queen's labor progressed in the meantime, and an old lady
enters the king's apartment in haste.

Gentleman. *(To the old lady.)* ''Come back ; what mean you?

Old Lady. I'll not come back ; the tidings that I bring will make my
boldness manners.—Now, good angels, fly o'er the royal head, and
shade thy person under their blessed wings !

"Now, by thy looks, I guess thy message."

King. Now, by the looks, I guess thy message; is the queen deliver'd? Say, ay; and of a boy.

Old Lady. Ay, ay, my liege; and of a lovely boy: The God of heaven now and ever bless her. 'Tis a *girl*, promise boys hereafter. Sir, your queen desires your visitation, and to be acquainted with the stranger: 'Tis as like you as cherry is to cherry.

King. Give her an hundred marks. I'll to the queen. *(Exit King.)*

Old Lady. An hundred marks! By this light, I'll ha' more; an ordinary groom is for such payment: I will have more, or scold it out of him. Said I for this the girl was like to him? I will have more, or I will unsay 't; and now, while it is hot, I'll put it to the issue."

In that portion of the quotation relating to the queen's labor, the description is graphic, and as true to nature as had it been drawn with the pen of a master in the science of obstetrics. How Shakespeare could have become possessed of a knowledge so accurate in regard to scenes and incidents in the lying-in chamber, is a problem. His domestic experiences in that particular were hardly of an order voluminous enough to have given him so correct an idea. It was another of his *intuitions.* How true to the life also are his doings of the old midwife flattering the old king and then grumbling over the amount of her fee! How more than natural for the penurious old monarch to award her niggardly pay. Verily, humanity presents itself in the same garb among the high and the low, the rich and the poor,—among all nations and in all ages.

A " Mark " in English money equaled about thirteen shillings and six-pence, which multiplied by one hundred would be considered a pretty liberal fee among modern accoucheurs in ordinary practice, but perhaps if you my reader, or I, had a royal patron we might indulge the thought that an " hundred marks " for a case of obstetrics was nothing extra in the way of remuneration ; and the king's action in the matter of the fee was in strict keeping with the humanity which hovers along the pathway of the physician " from the college to the grave."

In Coriolanus we find the good Virgilia declining a pressing invitation of her mother-in-law Volumnia, who wished her to accompany her on a visit to a good lady that " lies in ; " and in " Titus Andronicus," we have a goodly display of procreative knowledge in the details of the relations which existed between Tamora, queen of the Goths, and Aaron, her black paramour, whose " soul was black as his face." Tamora had been prisoner to Saturninus of Rome, and through his gallantry he had married her and placed her in high estate. Aaron, her black lover, had been prisoner also, and it seems that their familiarity, which existed at the time of their durance, had continued after she became empress of Rome, thus laying the foundation for the black-a-moor child which figures in the quotation.

Demetrius. "Come, let us go and pray to all the Gods for our beloved mother in her pains.

Aaron. Pray to the devils ; the Gods have given us over.

Demetrius. Why do the emperor's trumpets flourish thus?

Chiron. Belike, for joy : the emperor hath a son.

Demetrius. Soft ! Who comes there? *(Enter a nurse, with a black child in her arms.)*

"Look how the black slave smiles upon his father."

Nurse. Good morrow, lords. O! tell me, did you see Aaron the Moor?

Aaron. Well, more, or less, or ne'er a whit at all, here Aaron is; and what with Aaron now?

Nurse. O, gentle Aaron, we are all undone! Now, help, or woe betide thee ever more!

Aaron. Why, what a caterwauling dost thou keep; what dost thou wrap and fumble in thy arms?

Nurse. O, that which I would hide from heaven's eye, our empress' shame. our stately Rome's disgrace. She is deliver'd, lords; she is deliver'd.

Aaron. To whom?

Nurse. I mean she's brought to bed.

Aaron. Well, God give her good rest! What hath he sent her?

Nurse. A devil.

Aaron. Why, then, she's the devil's dam; a joyful issue.

Nurse. A joyless, dismal, black and sorrowful issue. Here is the babe,—as loathsome as a toad amongst the fairest burdens of our clime. The empress sends it thee, thy stamp, thy seal, and bids thee christen it with thy dagger's point.

Aaron. Zounds! ye whore, is black so base a hue?—Sweet blowse *(to the babe)*, you are a beauteous blossom sure.

Demetrius. Villain, what hast thou done?

Aaron. That which thou canst not undo.

Chiron. Thou hast undone our mother.

Aaron. Villain, I have done thy mother.

Demetrius. And therein, hellish dog, thou hast undone.
    Woe to her chance, and damn'd her loathed choice!
    Accurs'd the offspring of so foul a fiend!

Chiron. It shall not live.

Aaron. It shall not die.

Nurse. Aaron, it must: the mother wills it so.

Aaron. What! must it, nurse? then let no man but I do execution on my flesh and blood.

Demetrius. I'll broach the tadpole on my rapier's point. Nurse, give it me; my sword shall soon dispatch it.

Aaron. Sooner this sword shall plow thy bowels up. *(Takes the child from the nurse.)* Stay, murderous villains! Will you kill your brother? Now, by the burning tapers of the sky, that shone so brightly when this boy was got, he dies upon my scimitar's point, that touches this my first-born son and heir. What, what, ye sanguine, shallow-hearted boys! Ye white-lim'd walls! ye alehouse painted signs! coal-black is better than another hue, for all the water in the ocean can never turn the swan's black legs to white, although she lave them hourly in the flood. Tell the empress from me, I am a man to keep my own; excuse it how she can.

Demetrius. Wilt thou betray thy noble mistress thus? By this our noble mother is forever shamed.

Aaron. *(Speaking of the babe.)* Look how the black slave smiles upon the father; he is your brother, lords.—of that self blood that first gave life to you, and from that womb where you imprisoned were, he is enfranchised and come to light: he is your brother by the surer side. Not far hence lives Muli, my countryman; his wife was but yesternight brought to bed. His child is like to her, fair as you are; go pack with him, and give the mother gold, and tell them both the circumstances of all; and how by this their child shall be advanced and be received for the emperor's heir, and substituted in the place of mine to call in this tempest whirling in the court, and let the emperor dandle him for his son.''

Cornelia, a midwife, officiated on this occasion also, and according to the story of the nurse there were present at the accouchment but Cornelia, herself and the empress—the commendable custom being then in vogue to not be over-crowded with female assistants

as has become somewhat the fashion in our day; though the repre-
hensible practice of employing *only* women—*a midwife*, and nurse,
was then the invariable rule it seems. as Shakespeare no where
introduces a male accoucheur in any of his obstetric scenes.

We look with wonder upon the picture of depravity drawn from
life at the head of a Roman court, where the empress, fair as
a lily, in lewd embrace clasped to her bosom a murderous and
licentious black-man.   This was in the far-off past, and yet,
through the gloom of twenty hundred years, its horrid details are
sufficient to fill us with loathing.   It seems that these high digni-
taries of earth, whose every walk in life should be an example from
which the lowly might draw lessons of purity and goodness, are the
very first to walk the highways of vice wherein the meanest plebe-
ian should blush to be seen.   Whilst those who lead are blind, we
need not wonder that the led also stumble.

We come again to speak of the nubile age, and give more fully
the matter pertaining to the marriage of Juliet and Romeo.   We
find Capulet making plea that his daughter is too young to marry:

Capulet. " My child is yet a stranger in the world; she hath
not yet seen the change of fourteen years:
   Let two more summers wither in their pride,
   Ere we may think her ripe to be a bride.
Paris. Younger than she are happy mothers made.
Capulet. And too soon marr'd are those so early married."

If all our own authorities are not at fault in observation, this
remark of Capulet's in regard to the pernicious effects of early
marriage is strikingly exemplified in American women.   The custom has obtained in this country for persons of both sexes to enter
the connubial state often at an age when their youth should pre-
clude all thought of such a consummation; and the result is seen
in the wan faces and premature decrepitude of a large majority of
the child-bearing women, even in the rural districts of our country.
The early and long continued procreative effort which results in a
numerous progeny. together with the toil and care incident to the
maintenance of a large family, have become a noticeable fact in
our domestic life : and the burdens entailed upon our females as a
consequence, may justly come in for their share of the censure
which is now coming into vogue upon those who are endeavoring to
adopt some plan for the limitation of offspring.   It is not all to be

laid at the door of a desire for fashionable life, etc.—this growing desire on the part of our females to limit the number of their children; but it has its origin in burdens too grievous to be quietly borne.—Hence the growing sentiment which seeks means,—often illegitimate it may be, to rid them of an evil they know not how else to avoid.

The custom of early marriage, and the rearing of a numerous progeny, as applied specially to the American people, is the result of *natural* conditions. Our country is broad and new, and possessed of resources which invite youths to an early dependence upon their own energies for an independent life, whilst the spirit of our political system, and the often crowded and frugal conditions of the parental home, all exercised a marked influence in directing the minds of our young men to early marriage. Theory prompts to this course in life—a course really the most inviting and acceptable to a large portion of American youths, whilst the practical working of the system has shown it to be fraught with evils which have not been taken into the count—that of an unusual decadence of the physical, *moral* and social life of these young parents, and in a measure that of their offspring also. I emphasize the word moral, for it is asserted by a majority of our best men and women, that in seeking a refuge from the burdens of a large family, our females are not only deteriorating physically but also morally, in the effort. *Mental* degeneracy might also be added to the catalogue.

Whilst it is believed that all the evils herein named do exist to a greater or less extent among our people, I am far from conceding that they exist to an extent sufficient to cause any alarm even among that class of maudlin philosophers who make social science a specialty; therefore, I can calmly recommend to those who feel seriously upon the subject, to possess their souls in peace, as there is little danger at present that the Yankee race will dwindle to exhaustion from excesses in the effort of procreation; or, on the other hand, pass from the stage of living nations in an unholy conflict with non-propagation. We have yet ample elbow-room.

The practice, yet common among nursing women, of applying aloes or some other bitter or nauseous material to the nipple to prevent the babe from taking it at the time of weaning, finds a precedent in the case of the nurse who was so closely identified with Juliet's existence:

Nurse. " On Lammas-eve shall she be fourteen: that shall she: I remember it well. 'Tis since the earthquake now eleven years; and she was wean'd,—I never shall forget it,—of all the year, upon that day; for I had then laid wormwood to my dug, setting in the sun under the dove-house wall: You and my lord were then at Mantua. Nay, I do bear a brain:—but, as I said, when it did taste the wormwood on the nipple of my dug, and felt it bitter, pretty fool, to see it tetchy, and fall out with the dug! Shake, quoth the dove-house; 'twas no need, I trow, to bid me trudge."

How true to the life is this picture of a garrulous nurse, and how true to the welfare of the human family is the principle herein laid down by her, as to the period during which a child should be nursed. The data goes to show that Juliet was nearly three years old at time of weaning, thus making it apparent that the murderous habit of depriving the babe of its natural aliment at an earlier age was not in vogue at that date, even among the fashionable and aristocratic.

The ability to discriminate between the true and the false is no where in the writings of the dramatist more forcibly exhibited than in the few thoughts attributed to this nurse, and the bearing possessed by the nursing period upon the weal or the woe of mankind. This can in no way be better here exhibited than in the quotation presented below: (*Obstetric Gazette*, Vol. 1, No. 2; The Mammary Gland. By J. P. CHESNEY, M. D.)

"To show the wisdom of a lengthened lactiferous period, it is proposed to speak *speculatively* of the female breast, and its relations to the well being of the mother and her offspring.

We shall first notice it in its relations to the child. The milk of the human female in its composition fills more nearly the requirements for tissue building than any other substance with which it is possible to supply the young child. Its tissues require for their development not the substantial elements which give firmness and solidity to its structures, but those which impart to them flexibility, plasticity and a capacity for expansion and growth. I hold it to be a fundamental proposition that no child was ever properly nursed, and I may add properly *nourished*, who did not draw the pabulum for its first two years sustenance from the breast of her who conceived and brought it into existence. Nature does not afford nor can art supply any substitute for this food. Supply the infant with the most perfect wet nurse possible, and you will find there is some incompatibility between her organization and that of the infant of another,—some incomprehensible idiosyncrasy which forever prevents a perfect reciprocity between them. She is not *its* mother. It is not *her* child.

Children who battle with inanition from lack of the mother's milk, are of two classes. Those who starve and those who half starve.

The first emanate from the abodes of luxury on the one hand and from the perlieus of wretchedness on the other; the one goes into the hands of the wet nurse for a few weeks and then to a little gilded tomb; the other is "farmed out" and in the same few weeks its emaciated little form is put silently away. This occurs in large cities where the extremes of society meet face to face. *We* in the country seldom see it.

With the second of the classes, the half starved, we are somewhat more familiar. These children are the offspring of all grades of society, and are to be seen in every community. These are the victims of early weaning. This class is more numerous than the other, and therefore furnishes the man who carries the hour-glass and scythe his most abundant harvest. Those who die at the behest of fashion and of remorseless poverty, die a little earlier; the others, not quite so soon, but equally as sure, from devotion to " custom."

Between those mothers who do not nurse *at all* and those who do not nurse *enough* must be divided the responsibility of our great infantile mortality. Half of mankind dies before the second dentition. Let every mother, from the humblest up to the wife of the President, nurse her own babe; her milk is its life. Let the practice tally with the theory that what we are we suck from our mother's breasts, and we shall regenerate a nation.

As will appear by the foregoing, it is my firm conviction that our teachings and the practice built upon them relative to the proper time at which to wean the infant are fundamentally erroneous. The commencement of, or a reasonable progress in the first dentition is claimed by respectable authors, and agreed to by most mothers and nurses as a safe guide in weaning the babe. This takes the babe from the breast at ten or twelve months of age.

The first dentition I certainly think is such a guide, but its language must not be misinterpreted. It does not necessarily follow that because an infant in utero has a stomach it must therefore receive food, that because it has eyes it must then see. Nor is it essential that because a child is born with legs it must be immediately placed upon them and made to walk. Infants may have teeth

at the age of twelve or fifteen months, but even then they are only
few and rudimentary, and wholly unfit for organs of mastication.
The end of twenty-fourth or thirtieth month completes the deciduous
dentition, and not an hour before the first of these dates can a child
be legitimately weaned.

In reference to the influence exerted by the lacteal functions upon
the well-being of the mother, we may notice it in its bearings upon
her morally, mentally and physically. There seems to be little
doubt but that the peculiar mode of thought which induces a healthy
mother to abandon to another the sacred duty of nursing her child,
has its culmination, in many instances, in a loss of interest in her
family, and a plunge headlong into idleness, extravagance, licentiousness, shame, disease and death.

The babe at its mother's breast is the golden chain which binds
happiness and virtue to the hearth-stone, and the woman who ignores
its dictates is unfit for wife or mother. She who does not nurse her
own infant, and she who is constantly in the hands of the abortion-
ist, are twin sisters, and their works stand side by side as monuments of depravity.

It is, however, more within the province of the physician to view
the mental and physical ills which befall the woman from a quiescent
state of the mammary glands.

When we call to mind the close relations which exist between the
mammary glands and the reproductive organs proper,—remember
that it is through the impressibility of the nervous system alone that
this relation is maintained, we need feel no surprise when we sometimes find these chains of communication themselves becoming the
seat of morbid action ; and while any tissue or organ may perchance
become the focus of disease in this way, yet it is to the brain and
nervous system where we may look with most certainty of recogniz-
ing its manifestations. Disturb the harmonious action of reproductive life, and neuralgia, hysteria, catalepsy, chorea, epilepsy, and the
various forms of insanity arise to tax our professional acumen. The
mammary glands are really annexæ of the female generative organs ;
their sympathies are therefore so closely interwoven, that a disturbance of the functions of the one cannot fail to leave an impression
on the other. It is not my purpose, however, to speak of the pathological conditions of the breast and the disturbances thence reflect-
ed, but my thought is simply to note the pathological concomitants
of a forced or voluntary suppression of the lacteal function. And
first as to the menstrual function.

The two offices are so closely allied that the one may almost perfectly supply to the woman the place of the other. Women whose maternal instincts persuade them to let their babes tug at the breast eighteen, twenty or twenty-four months—"lets them stand on the floor and suck," to use the saying of a wise friend of my own—are

nearly always doing a wise thing unwittingly, both for themselves and their offspring. Wise for themselves, because the lengthened period of lactation gives to the womb and its proper annexæ a period of rest indispensable to the proper performance of their functions. Of the thirty years of procreative life in the human female, not more than ten ought to be devoted to fruitful ovulation.

The life of our women is spent between hemorrhage and gestation; their existence is but a succession of bleedings and pregnancies.

Woman was fashioned by her author to produce and *suckle* children. The gestative period is placed almost specifically at nine months; to this add the nursing period, which is placed with almost the same precision by nature at two years, and we have a period of nearly three years in which the menstrual function of most women will remain passive. This will give eight or ten normal pregnancies during the child bearing period.—a number which very closely coincides with our observations as connected with our most healthy and prosperous rural families.—Families who do not know the definition of " wet nurse," " neuralgia," and " abortion."

I *assume* in this paper what I believe to be true, namely, that if from the first the mothers nurse their babes the full length of time as pointed out by nature as necessary, they will not be likely to menstruate at seven, ten or thirteen months after labor. Work the lacteal glands normally and the womb is not forced into premature activity. Let every mother whose general health will allow her, nurse her babe twenty-two, twenty-four or thirty months, in place of the eight, ten or twelve, as is now the custom, and we shall hear much less of menorrhagia, leucorrhœa, sub-involution, procidentia and the other ten thousand ills to which she is now a prey.

And so, in like manner, we may often trace a clear connection between the uterine congestions consequent upon a repeated ovular nisus, and the many inflammatory conditions which beset the womb ; I am impressed with the belief that to this cause can be traced most of the ulcerations, erosions, endometritis, cellulitis, pelvic abscesses, etc., to which our notice is so frequently called. We must give the womb and ovaries ample rest if we will have them do their work well.

I use the term "ovulation" to imply the irruption of matured " germ cells," meaning of course to exclude all of that vast crop which aborts during the periods of lactation and pregnancy. The fact is remarked by all medical authorities that it is at the close of menstrual life in married women that malignant maladies are most likely to assail them ; more particularly their generative system. Cancers of the ovaries, womb and breasts are likely to occur, while with matured females who have never given milk at all, the same maladies occur earlier, in a greater proportion of such women, and are none the less surely and speedily fatal. In this latter class particularly is it that a crop of fibroids is likely to be developed to the full. The uterus in its effort to do its office of reproduction,— never having received and been rendered satisfied by the normal stimulation of impregnation, makes a futile attempt to do its natural function without assistance, and the effort results in an abortion—a failure—or what is infinitely worse, the production of a crop of parasites, which sap the foundations of life and hurry the woman to an earlier grave.

Without a healthy parentage we cannot hope for a normal conception, a healthy gestation or a robust progeny. The early cessation of the lacteal function whether from design or accident I believe forms no small factor in the production of abortions. I think we need not invoke that very unsatisfactory explanation, the "abortive habit," to meet the difficulty. The compensatory balance which should exist between the generative and lacteal organs is disturbed by the lack of mammary activity; and, to fulfill a law of the economy, the procreative centers are called into play, "come to the rescue," it may be—at a time when they are not recuperated sufficiently, from recent gestation, to admit of the nutrition proper for a normal ovum. The force is equal to the germination of the seed, but *insufficient* to carry it to maturity.

As to the effects of lactation upon *reproduction* it is barely necessary to speak farther.

The term "reproduction" cannot properly be confined in its signification to the periods of conception, gestation and parturition, but it must be made to include the period during which the new being is dependent upon the elaborative offices of its mother for its sustenance also. Therefore the work of the whole machinery is necessary to a perfect finish. To *perfect* the act of propagation the mammary glands are as essential as the womb and ovaries themselves. Of course it should be the desire of every individual, community and nation that none but healthy offspring be propagated. To accomplish this successfully the mother must of necessity bring to her aid all the resources with which the Creator has endowed her. Her instincts, her reason, and her moral training must point out to her the most perfect application of these means to the purposes for which each was designed. Each of these resources has a law which governs it with almost specific certainty, and to learn their interpretation and act upon them in good faith is the office of the wife and mother."

Capulet, as already seen, opposed the marriage of his daughter whilst yet so young, while on the other hand, her mother argued thus:

"Well, think of marriage now; younger than you, here in Verona, ladies of esteem, are made already mothers."

Juliet was not yet fourteen, and if younger than she were made already mothers, that would presuppose the menstrual function to have been established near upon the twelfth year,—an age much too early as appears in the argument put forth in the earlier pages of this chapter.

In our country, where fourteen is about the period at which a majority of our girls take on menstrual life, out of some hundreds of obstetric cases, the writer of these lines has attended but one patient under the age of fourteen, and she was a girl of more than ordinary physical development, and is now, though comparatively young, at least ten years in advance of her real age.

The same talkative nurse, whilst plotting and working in the interests of Juliet and Romeo, thus remarks:

> " I am the drudge, and toil in your delight,
>   But you shall beare the burden soon at night."

It is uncertain whether we are to infer that copulation or parturition is meant in this language, but more probably the latter, as common observation has taught mankind in general that child-birth is more common at night ;—the other, also, perhaps ; but burden would come in therewith as a misnomer as applied to the former it is thought.

Capulet, in his anger against Juliet for not wishing to be married to Paris, uses the term "green sickness" in his abuse of her. How well Shakespeare kept to his physiology and pathology, will be observed even here, where he makes his charge of chlorosis coincide exactly with the age and non-menstrual condition of little Juliet : though "beauty too rich for use, for earth too dear," as is also declared of her, would hardly have been found coupled with a pale chlorotic face. The term "green sickness" is also used in connection with Marina. the young girl in *Pericles*. whose virtue saved her, though she was quartered in a bawdy-house. In "Antony and Cleopatra," it is asserted that Lepidus, a companion of Cæsar, had "green sickness ;" which makes it conclusive that a condition analogous to chlorosis in girls was recognized as sometimes afflicting males, even at that early date. When Lady Macbeth was informed of the purpose of Duncan, King of Scotland, to pass the night at her mansion, she, after having given her husband a curtain-lecture as to how to "catch the nearest way," thus soliloquis'd : "Come, you spirits that tend on mortal's thoughts, unsex me here, and fill me from the crown to the toe, top-full of the direst cruelty : make thick my blood stop up th' access and passage to remorse ; that no compunctious visitings of nature shake my fell purpose, nor keep peace between th' effect and it. Come to my woman's breast, and take my milk for gall, you murdering ministers, wherever in your sightless substances you wait on nature's mischief."

The milk of a woman in the condition of mind in which Lady Macbeth was at the time of this self-communion, would not only often prove gall and wormwood to the unfortunate infant that imbibed it, but might, mahap, more forcibly represent nicotine, or prussic acid. Failing in that as respects its action on the physical well-being of the recipient, it would doubtless prove the pabulum for a mental depravity of the darkest and most malignant type. Most great scoundrels suck it from their mothers' breasts. Lady Macbeth whilst upbraiding her husband for his reluctance in despatching the sleeping king, enforces her arguments thus: " I have given suck, and know how tender 'tis to love the babe that milks me; I would, while it was smiling in my face, have pluck'd the nipple from his boneless gums, and dash'd the brains out had I so sworn as you have done to do this."

In this quotation we recognize the unexplainable truth that whether the young be the offspring of the womb of her that nurses it or not, the simple fact of its receiving its sustenance from her blood serves to engender a tie between the nurse and her charge more closely allied in sympathy, and seemingly approaching a condition of actual consanguinity nearer than does any other relations whatever. This is not so strange, after all. If the blood of the female moulds and forms the being in utero, thus impressing upon it her peculiar traits of character and mind, as also its physical contour,—thus laying the groundwork of an attachment which none but a mother may know, why may not she who afterwards supplies from her own body all the material for the development of the new-born dependant being which thenceforth becomes " flesh of her flesh " grow in love and interest as with her own—which it in reality is? We don't know really but that the nipple is a tie of affection harder to be sundered than are the ovaries and womb, and with reason for its foundation. The first attachment has all that endearment of close personal contact and association essential to the generation of our tenderest sympathies, aided by the peculiar instinctive quality which attaches even the animal creation to that object which is their protege and dependant; whilst the being in utero is, by most, looked upon as an inanimate nondescript with few claims for love or sympathy.

However, give me first the mother who generates and nourishes her own child, and I will present you with a mother who has the only proper maternal instincts;—next to her—not she who loves the pleasures incident to the generation of her species, and turns the infant over to the wet-nurse,—but her who suckles it, is more to my liking.

This masculine speech of his wife so impressed Macbeth, that he thought she ought to " bring forth men-children only," and to illustrate the general idea that to propagate progeny of sound physical and mental qualities it is requisite that the parentage be so also, Macbeth avers that if he be a coward, " protest me the baby of a girl ! "

The " finger of a birth-strangled babe " was an ingredient in the witches curious compound, which is pretty good evidence that the crime of infanticide was not a " thing of the future " even in Shakespeare's time. Very much too much is written, and too little *done* in suppressing the practice of the abortionists of our country ; but be the crime as heinous as it may, whilst the scoundrels who practice it are known, and yet have access as practitioners to the best families in the community, how is mere law going to succeed in even mitigating it ? Public sentiment and its verdict of *Guilty* can only eradicate the evil.

Writing homilies, however, nor yet publishing books by the medical profession, nor moralizing, will abridge or curtail very soon the tendency to abortion among the people. We may censure professional abortionists as much as we may, yet who shall say that if people *will* have it done, it is not better done by one accomplished and skilled in its performance than by a novice ?

While the public is *particeps criminis* it is useless to anathematize their willing instruments. Take away the clients and we shall have no shysters. Physician and patient are murderers who go hand in hand.

· The hero of Shakespeare's Cæsarian section was Macduff, the avenger of the death of Duncan. He seemed to possess the iron will and fearless bravery which characterized Cæsar himself. Whether or not this undaunted courage and stern character marks all individuals who are " from their mother's wombs untimely ripp'd," our statistics are not sufficiently elaborate to enable us to determine.

The circumstances under which the Cæsarian section is performed seems not to have been taken into account by Shakespeare in regard to the birth of Macduff. If the delivery occurred at the hands of a professional attendant, then he or she certainly operated too " previously," as there are no indications for making the section before the termination of the full gestative period—even should there be discovered or known beforehand the most serious impediments to delivery at term by the usual route. As the valiant warrior was ushered "untimely" into the open world it may have been that the "ripping" was of an accidental character, or else done by a professional novitiate, or by one who wished to display his "surgical capacity," regardless of consequences. *We know such.*

The next quotation is from "King Lear," and may be seen in its full connection in Act i., Scene 1., in that drama.

Duke of Kent. "Is not this your son, my lord? (*Referring to Edmund the bastard*).

Gloster. His breeding, sir, hath been at my charge: I have so often blush'd to acknowledge him, that now I am brazed to it.

Kent. I cannot conceive you.

Gloster. Sir, this young fellow's mother could; whereupon she grew round-womb'd and had, indeed sir, a son for her cradle ere she had a husband for her bed. But I have (also) a son, sir, by order of law, some years older than this, who is yet no dearer in my account: though this knave came somewhat saucily into the world, before he was sent for, yet was his mother fair, there was good sport at his making, and the whoreson must be acknowledged;" and the same peculiar old king, in heaping curses upon his ungrateful progeny—his daughter Goneril,—puts it in this pointed style:

"Hear, nature hear! dear goddess hear! Suspend thy purpose, if thou didst intend to make this creature fruitful! Into her womb carry sterility! Dry up in her, the organs of increase; and from her derogate body never spring a babe to honor her! If she must teem, create her child of spleen; that it may live and be a thwart disnatur'd torment to her! Let it stamp wrinkles in her brow of youth; with cadent tears fret channels in her cheeks; turn all her mother's pains and benefits to laughter and contempt: that she may feel how sharper than a serpent's tooth it is to have a thankless child." Lear was both *mad* and *insane.* Alas, how many are there, whose experience is a true but sad commentary upon that of the much abused old Lear; well may parents, and with good and sufficient reasons may the toil-worn physician above all others exclaim, "Ingratitude! thou marble-hearted fiend!"

In "Pericles," the genii thus sings:

"Brief, he must hence depart to Tyre:
His queen, with child, makes her desire
(Which who shall cross?) along to go.

Omit we all their dole and woe:
Lychorida, her nurse, she takes,
And so to sea.   Their vessel shakes
On Neptune's billow; half the flood
Hath their keel cut; but fortune's mood
Varies again: the grizzly North
Disgorges such a tempest forth
That, as a duck for life that dives,
So up and down the poor ship drives;
The lady shrieks, and well-a-near
Does fall in travail with her fear."

This it appears was a prophecy, of which the following was the
sequence:—

Pericles (*on shipboard*).   "Thou God of this great vast, rebuke
these surges, which wash both heaven and hell; and thou, that hast
upon the winds command, bind them in brass, having call'd them
from the deep.   O! still thy deafening, dreadful thunders; duly
quench thy nimble, sulphurous flashes! — O! how, Lychorida, how
does my queen?   The seaman's whistle is a whisper in the ears of
death, unheard. — Lychorida! — Lucina, O!   Divinest patroness
and midwife, gentle to those that cry by night, convey thy deity
aboard our dancing boat; make swift the pangs of my queen's tra-
vails! — Now, Lychorida.—(*Enter the midwife with an infant.*)

Lychorida.   Here is a thing too young for such a place, who, if it
had conceit, would die, as I am like to do.   Take in your arms this
piece of your dead queen.

Pericles.   How, how, Lychorida!

Lychorida.   Patience, good sir; do not assist the storm.   Here's
all that is left living of your queen, a little daughter: for the sake
of it, be manly, and take comfort.

Pericles (*to the babe*).   Now, mild may be thy life; quiet and
gentle thy condition; for thou art the rudeliest welcom'd to this
world that e'er was prince's child.

Sailor (*to Pericles*).   Sir, your queen must over-board; the sea
works high, the wind is loud, and will not lie until the ship be
cleared of the dead.

Pericles.   That's your superstition.

Sailor.   Pardon us, sir; briefly yield her, for she must over-board
straight.

Pericles. As you think meet.—Most wretched queen! A terrible child-bed hast thou had, my dear; no light, no fire: the unfriendly elements forgot thee utterly; nor have I time to give thee hallow'd to thy grave, but straight must cast thee, scarcely coffin'd, in the ooze.''

They throw her overboard, and being close upon land, her body is cast ashore where it is found, and the following colloquy occurs between the finders and the persons to whom they give the body in charge:

" How fresh she looks; they were too rough that threw her into the sea. Make fire within: fetch hither all the boxes in my closet. Death may usurp on nature many hours, and yet the fire of life kindle again the overpressed spirits. I heard of an Egyptian once, that had nine hours lain dead, who was by good appliance recovered.

(*Enter servant with boxes, napkins and fire*). Well said, well said; the fire and the clothes; — the vial once more; — I pray you, give her air!

Gentlemen, the queen will live: nature awakes a warm breath out of her: she hath not been entranc'd above five hours. See how she 'gins to blow into life's flower again!

Gentleman. The heavens through you increase our wonder, and set up your fame forever. (It is to be presumed that this fellow turned *doctor* at once, and went forth ' healing and to heal,' preceded by flaming hand-bills setting forth that he made resuscitation a specialty; at least, any boot-black or hostler who might now chance to be thus eulogized, would straightway arm himself with certificates from the queen and the credulous gentlemen who surrounded her, and would ' swing his shingle' in one of the largest hotels or the most populous street in one of the best cities.)

Cerimon (a lord). She is alive! behold her eye-lids, cases to those heavenly jewels which Pericles hath lost, begin to part their fringes of bright gold: the diamonds of a most praised water do appear to make the world twice rich. Live, and make us weep to hear your fate, fair creature, rare as you seem to be! (*The queen moves.*)

Queen. O dear Diana! where am I? Where's my lord? 'What world is this?

2d Gentleman. Is not this strange?

1st Gentleman. Most rare.

Cerimon. Hush, gentle neighbor! Lend me your hands; to the next chamber bear her. Get linen: Now this matter must be looked to, for her relapse is mortal. Come, come; and Æsculapius guide us."

It is not at all impossible or improbable, that the actions of a ship in a severe storm, or even in ordinary weather, would have produced premature labor in a female who had gone to sea for the first time; the sea-sickness alone would, in many, be sufficient to set up uterine action; and there is nothing improbable in the story of her having fallen into eclampsia immediately after delivery, as her perturbed nervous system would have favored such an accident, hence the term "trance" as used by the dramatist. There is nothing inconsistent with the assertion that she had been "entranced" not more than "five hours" and her recovery occur afterwards, as we know that puerperal convulsions may leave the patient unconscious many hours, and yet the patient recover; and if Shakespeare had let the term "scarcely coffin'd" have remained as her only burial appurtenances, we might have supposed that even the casting her overboard into the water had been a means of aiding in her recovery; but he unfortunately spoils this hypothesis and renders his whole story untenable by fabricating the box farther on so "closely caulk'd and bitumed." Even a *leaky* chest would have served the purpose better, had he kept his story in the region of possibility, for his "close" box draws him into an error that is yet common among the community, and upon which many marvelous newspaper horrors are manufactured,—namely, that persons are sometimes found turned in their coffins, thus showing that they have revived after having been fastened in their coffins. These stories are all "stuff" at best, and particularly would it have been so in the case of the queen, as the casket was water-tight, therefore could under no circumstances have admitted air sufficient to supply the requirements of vitality. When the respiratory function has been completely suspended five minutes in the adult, it is seldom that they are ever "blown into life's flower" again even under the most scientific management. In the case of new-born infants, however, the case is quite different, as they may remain not only many minutes, but I fully believe an hour—two hours! without respiring, and then, sometimes, be resuscitated by proper management. The vital powers of these fresh infants is something wonderful, and I am fully persuaded that many, very many, of them die who might be saved if the accoucheur would only make *persistent* efforts in the right direction. I simply inflate the lungs in these cases by applying my own lips closely to those of the infant, at the same time closing its nostrils with thumb and index finger, and forcibly but steadily forcing my expired breath deep into its lungs; I then turn the babe from side to side and compress the chest with my hands. The process is repeated—repeated—repeated—and often under the most unfavorable circumstances the labor is rewarded by the raising a live child instead of the burying of a dead one.

The Egyptian story is all a hoax; he may have been drunk for nine hours and then have recovered, but never dead. Marina, to whom the queen gave birth on the ship, after she was a grown woman fully believed that her mother died the moment she gave her birth; and Pericles himself also declared "at sea, in child-bed died she." As an evidence of his own virility, and that of Ophelia also. Hamlet speaks thus confidently: "To take off my edge would cost you a grunting."

CHAPTER II.

PSYCHOLOGY.

Definition—Shakespeare's profound knowledge of the subject—Bucknill's eulogium—"It is *all the best*"—Shakespeare's special study of insanity an absurdity—His intuition—Scene before an Abbey—Jealousy versus sanity—A foul conspiracy—A psychological charlatan—Sleeplessness but a symptom—Shakespeare draws on his own domestic experience—*Now* not a joke, but a dark reality—Thrown into a "dankish" vault—The cell of Foscari—Public institutions need surveillance—Preliminary abuses—Probate courts and examinations in lunacy—Monkey and medical expert—A ten-dollar fee—Charles Reade—"Why hast thou put him in such a dream?"—No darkness but ignorance—Make the trial of it in any constant question—Erroneous assumption—Bucknill on memory—What at any time have you heard her say?—"Out damned spot"—Here's the smell of blood still—Will she go now to bed?—Cure her of that—"Make thick my blood stop up the access and passage to remorse"—Cases from De Boismont—"He had a large knife in his hand and went straight to my bed"—He returned as he came—"I had so strange a dream"—His services were thereafter dispensed with—Somnambulism and insanity—The pulse as indicative of insanity—Did you nothing hear?—Hallucinations—The ghost—The spectre cat—The doctor's fright—Look! Amazement on thy mother sits—Lesions of structure necessary to lesions of function—I'm a'gwine to die!—One finale awaits the man and all his attributes—Love and sleeplessness—Age—"No man bears sorrow better"—The final cataclysm—King Lear not insane—A dog's obeyed in office—The "Bedlam beggar"—"How does the king?"—"You are a spirit, I know"—Lord Shaftesbury's opinion—The EMOTIONS—Their close relationship to actual mental diseases—Jealousy—With "pin and web"—Othello, the Moor—"O! now farewell the tranquil mind"—Alas the day! I never gave him cause—The ills we do their ill instruct as to—Ninety children the utmost limit—The relative procreative capacity of the sexes—Monogamistic relations—Abortion and polygamy—Love—All lovers swear more performance than they are able—Love-marks—"Did you ever cure any so?"—The pale complexion of true love—"He took me by the wrist and held me hard"—Mine eyes were not at fault, for she was beautiful—Lust—Not from Shakespeare—One man in every five—Love powders—My daughter! O my daughter!—Lucretius, the poet—A veritable letter—Venereal excitement not love—Let not the creaking of shoes—The will and conception—"Could I find out the woman's part in me"—Painful copulation (Dyspareunia)—Anger—Envy.

In the broadest acceptation of the term, Psychology means the science of the intellectual and moral faculties. More recently, however, the term has been so freely used to denote aberrant phenomena

70

in connection with mental conditions, that its definition can now hardly be connected with healthy intellectual operations, or at least, it cannot be thus restricted in its significance.

I find, in looking over the material collected for this chapter, that to arrange it in an appropriate form is no inconsiderable task. In the first place, we have entire dramas in which the most salient feature of the plot and the pith of the whole play hinges upon the character of an insane actor; while in others the insanity is only counterfeited by the individual himself, or assumed to be so for him. Of the former kind we find most prominent Hamlet, King Lear, Timon of Athens, etc., while of the other a very good illustration is seen in the "Comedy of Errors." Other references to "thick coming fancies," which are so near akin to mental alienations that it is hard to distinguish the line of separation between the sane and the insane, are very numerous, and will all be found referred to in the chapter. Shakespeare has written most learnedly upon this subject. More profoundly it is thought, by good judges, than perhaps upon anything else connected with medicine. So thoroughly and skillfully has he portrayed the various phases of insanity, that Bucknill, a very high English authority upon the subject, says:

"Shakespeare not only possesses more psychological insight than all other poets, but more than all other writers." The extent and exactness of the psychological knowledge displayed (in his writings) has surprised and astonished him, and he can only account for it on one supposition, namely, that "abnormal conditions of the mind had attracted Shakespeare's diligent observation, and had been a favorite study. This would seem to be evident from the mere number of characters to which he has attributed insanity, and the extent alone to which he has written upon the subject."

Anyone, however, who *studies* Shakespeare's writings will be likely to think he has written the *best* on the last portion he has read; and at the conclusion of the reading of the entire work, he is ready to aver that *it is all the best!* I suppose that that was the state of mental admiration which actuated Dr. Bucknill when he penned the lines just quoted. He was a specialist, and could see more of the powers of the great dramatist as connected with his own department of science than with that of any other. We will make allowance for his strong language accordingly. That he should presume, however, that Shakespeare had given special study to aberrant mental phenomena in any thing like a scientific way is rendered utterly absurd even by data furnished from his own pen. He tells us that there was but one small and poorly ordered insane charity then in all England; though he makes excuse that there were plenty of *roving* mad people, and those who lived in the family circle, with whom Shakespeare might have fallen in contact and thus have acquired his wonderful fund of knowledge from actual observation. If we are to grant the truth of this supposition in regard to his knowledge of insanity, then we will be called upon to admit as much in regard to all other subjects upon which he has written. Such an admission is wholly inadmissible—more particularly without better grounds for facilities of studying his various themes can be shown to have existed than is presented in connection with his study of this. The theory therefore still remains, that Shakespeare *learned* few things: he *knew* them *intuitively.*

We will then come directly to our subject, Psychology, or mental perturbations, as found in the "Comedy of Errors," Act v., Scene i., where the following conversation occurs in front of an Abbey:

Abbess. "Be quiet, people. Wherefore throng you hither?

Adriana. To fetch my poor distracted husband hence. Let us come in, that we may bind him fast, and bear him home for his recovery.

Angelo. I knew he was not in his right mind.

Abbess. How long hath this passion held the man?

Adriana. This week he hath been heavy, sour, sad; and much different from the man he was: but till this afternoon, his passion ne'er broke into extremity of rage.

Abbess. Hath he not lost much wealth by wreck of sea? buried some dear friend? hath not else his eye stray'd his affection in unlawful love?—a sin prevailing much in youthful men who give their eyes the liberty of gazing. Which of these sorrows is he subject to?

Adriana. To none of these, except it be the last; namely, some love that drew him oft from home.

Abbess. You should for that have reprehended him.

Adriana. Why, so I did.

Abbess. Ay, but not rough enough.

Adriana. As roughly as my modesty would let me.

Abbess. Haply, in private.

Adriana. And in assemblies too.

Abbess. Ay, but not enough.

Adriana. It was the copy of our conference; in bed he slept not, for my urging it; at board he fed not, for my urging it; alone, it was the subject of my theme; in company, I often glanc'd at it; still did I tell him it was vile and bad.

Abbess. And thereof come it that the man was mad: the venom clamors of a jealous woman poison more deadly than a mad dog's tooth. It seems his sleep was hind'red by thy railing, and thereof comes it that his head is light. Thou say'st his meat was sauc'd with thy upbraidings: unquiet meals make ill digestions; thereof the raging fire of fever bred: and what's a fever but a fit of madness? Thou say'st, his sports were hind'red by thy brawls: sweet recreation barr'd, what doth ensue, but moody and dull melancholy, kinsman to grim and comfortless despair, and at her heels a huge infectious troop of pale distemperatures and foes to life?

> In food, in sport, and life preserving rest,
> To be disturb'd, would mad or man or beast."

"His sleep was hind'red by thy railings, and thereof comes it that his head is light." This is used synonymously with "crazy" or "distracted," and in idea coincides very closely with popular professional notions of to-day—namely, that loss of sleep is a very prolific source of insanity, when the fact is the actual pathological condition upon which the morbid mental manifestations depend have precedence, perhaps always, to the morbid vigilance—the sleeplessness being but a *symptom.*

"Unquiet meals make ill digestions; thereof the raging fire of fever bred: and what's a fever but a fit of madness?" The dramatist doubtless used less precaution in regard to accuracy of idea in this farcical delineation than he would have done had the whole matter not have been one of jest. That the first clause of the paragraph is true to the letter can be verified by the almost daily experience of almost anybody. There may be, perhaps, a remote smattering of fact in the second proposition, while in the last there is no logic at all—an assertion that cannot be truthfully said often of Shakespeare.

"Thou say'st his sports were hind'red by thy brawls; sweet recreation barr'd, what doth ensue, but moody and dull melancholy, kinsman to grim and comfortless despair, and at her heels a huge infectious troop of pale distemperatures and foes to life?"

This quotation shows us that its author appreciated the situation to repletion, and perhaps had *learned* this from his own somewhat strange domestic situation; but while it would do very well to denominate the restraints as irksome, the condition could not be thought a particular "foe to life." If long endured, "moody and dull melancholy," and even actual "grim and comfortless despair," would doubtless beset the victim; but such an extreme instance as is pictured in the text is, it is presumed, beyond the confines of actual experience, and belongs only to the realms of fiction.

But in the case under consideration the individual was not mad at all, as appears from his own story,—a story, by the way, the counterpart of many which happen daily even in this enlightened country,—the counterpart of many such cases in every feature, save one—the motive—which is not usually a joke, but a deep, shameless, damnable, murderous conspiracy to do to some one a dark and murderous wrong. But hear what the much abused husband has to say:

"My wife, her sister, and a rabble more of vile confederates. along with them they brought one Pinch, a hungry, lean-fac'd villain, a mere anatomy, a montebank, a thread-bare juggler, and a fortune-teller, a needy, hollow-eyed, sharp-looking wretch, a living dead man. This pernicious slave, forsooth, took on him as a conjurer, and gazing in mine eyes, feeling my pulse, and with no face as't were, out facing me, cried out I was possess'd. Then, altogether, they fell upon me, bound me, bore me thence, and in a dark and dankish vault at home they left me and my man, both bound together; till, gnawing with my teeth. my bonds in sunder, I gained my freedom and immediately ran hither to your grace, whom I beseech to give me ample satisfaction, for these deep shames, and great indignities."

From the known integrity of the managers of some of our "Private Insane Hospitals," it is presumed that they are conducted on a plan of the first character as to their qualities as a home, and in the advantages they offer as to skilled treatment of their patrons; but that abuses hover about some of them of an order illustrated by the above case, we do not hesitate to believe. "Dankish vaults" conceal within them scenes of horror and tales of woe only equalled by that of the cell of Fascari, "which never echo'd but to sorrow's sounds, the sigh of long imprisonment, the step of feet on which the iron clank'd, the groan of death, the imprecation of despair!" Glimpses of this life of forced imprisonment in so-called "Inebriate Homes," and like institutions, occasionally leak out through the public prints and by other means—tales of horror which make us shudder at their bare recital—many of which are false in toto no doubt, while many of them are, it is to be feared, but too true. These grave apprehensions do not alone apply to "Private Retreats," etc., but our public institutions need the surveillance of close inspection as well. Ordinary individuals can do nothing towards correcting abuses in high places. To one invested with less authority than had Governor Butler when conducting his Tewkesbury investigations, or possessed of less pertinacity and will-force, it would be but folly to even insinuate that there is a probability of something wrong in the management of any of these institutions, either private or public. It is not however exclusively to the abuses of persons *inside* of hospitals that we may refer. Abuses occur which are done in broad daylight, and are open to the inspection of any one who will take the time to look. I have in mind the proceedings preliminary to placing a person in an insane asylum. Who ever heard of one *accused* of being insane, that, when carried before a court of enquiry, come off *cleared* — that is, to be adjudged sane ? I have never been made cognizant of such an occurrence. There are abundant reasons for this. In the first place there are personal favorites of the court officers among the medical men—medical men who dabble in politics, who are by some means (collusory ones commonly) apprised of the fact that an examination in lunacy is to be made, and that their particular erudition is required in the premises. These professional gentlemen are the counterpart of the good citizens who make themselves conveniently near so as to receive a summons to sit on all the juries. Many of these

A Victim of the "Certificate" Process.

professional insane examiners are possessed of little more real
knowledge of the cases they are called to investigate and to
certify to than the monkey—in fact, differ little from the veritable
ape, except in the repudiation of the punchinello cap and the sub-
stitution therefor of the plug-hat.   The fee of ten dollars allowed
for the services of the brace of experts is sufficient to procure an
affirmative certificate which will incarcerate a person, sane or insane, in a limitless imprisonment.   Read the work of Charles
Reade, entitled "A Terrible Temptation," for a pretty fair picture of this subject.   The "lean, hungry, villainous" sort of humanity in physicians' garb are the ones, even in our day, who go
about to "Conjure and gaze in people's eyes, feeling their pulse,
and crying out 'you are possess'd.'"   What show then for justice
has either man or woman who may be singled out by the designing
and crafty with a view to imprisonment under this guise?

   In "A Midsummer Night's Dream," A. iii., S. ii., we find the
fo lowing lines:

        "All fancy-sick she is, and pale of cheer,
          With sighs of love, that cost the fresh blood dear."

Truly, disquietude of mind from any cause will tax the " fresh blood " equal to the severest physical labor ; and of the two, mus-cular exertion is much less destructive of the vital forces. Cæsar's picture of Cassius illustrates this proposition. " Lunatic " is spoken of in "Taming the Shrew," and also in A. ii., S. v., in "Twelfth Night:"

Sir Toby Belch. " Why, thou hast put him in such a dream, that when the image of it leaves him he must run mad.

Maria. Nay, but say true ; does it work upon him?

Sir Toby. Like aqua-vitæ with a midwife."

This dialogue had reference to the trick which the fun-loving maid played at the expense of that self-sufficient gentleman, Mal-volio, who had a great wish to make favor with the affections of his mistress with a view to ultimate marriage. He really loved her, and the jovial Sir Toby compares its hopelessness to a dream, and true to human nature suggests the possibility of his going mad when he is fully undeceived. This was not likely to happen in the case of Malvolio, who, no doubt whilst he loved, also had more or less mercenation coupled with his other motives—a sentiment which would have saved him.

The good lady, Olivia, the subject of poor Malvolio's "flame," was herself " addicted to a melancholy," if we may believe the laughing Maria ; though she was after cured by marriage. The saucy maid and bacchanalian " Sir Toby" were not content to make the poor steward a victim to the cultivation of a delusive hope, but heartlessly carried the joke to the point of declaring that he was " tainted in his wits ; come, we'll have him in a dark room and bound," which they did, as the after conversation will explain : *(Here a clown enters his prison in the guise of a curate.)*—A. iv., S. ii.

Malvolio. " Who calls there?

Clown. Sir Topas, the curate, who comes to visit Malvolio, the lunatic.

Malvolio. Sir Topas, Sir Topas ; good Sir Topas, go to my lady.

Clown. Out, hyperbolical fiend! how vexest thou this man. Talkest thou of nothing but ladies?

Sir Toby Belch. Well said, Master Parson.

Malvolio. Sir Topas, never was man thus wronged.—Good Sir Topas, don't think I am mad: they have laid me here, in hideous darkness.

Clown. Fie! thou dishonest sathan! I call thee by the most modest terms; for I am one of those gentle ones that will use the devil himself with courtesy. Say'st thou that house is dark?

Malvolio. As hell, Sir Topas.

Clown. It hath bay windows transparent as barricadoes, and the clear stories toward the south north are lustrous as ebony; and yet complainest thou of obstruction?

Malvolio. I am not mad, Sir Topas; I say to you this house is dark.

Clown. Mad man, thou errest: I say there is no darkness but ignorance, in which thou art more puzzled than the Egyptians in their fog.

Malvolio. I say, that this house is dark as ignorance, though ignorance was as dark as hell; and I say, there was never man thus abused. I am no more mad than you are; make the trial of it in any constant question.

Clown. What is the opinion of Pythagoras concerning water-fowl?

Malvolio. That the soul of one generation might haply inhabit a bird.

Clown. What think thou of his opinion?

Malvolio. I think nobly of the soul, and no way approve his opinion.

Clown. Fare thee well; remain thee still in darkness. Thou shalt hold the opinion of Pythagoras, or I will allow of thy wits, and fear to kill a wood-chuck, lest thou dispossess the soul of thy gran-dam; fare thee well.''

In the position assumed by Shakespeare when he undertakes to establish the fact of the sanity of an individual by the connected manner in which he can answer a line of questions, we see but the expression of popular opinion. Nothing could be more fallacious than such an idea. Alienists tell us that in '' making trial of it,'' '' in any constant question,'' might serve to disclose aberrations of the mind in those who are afflicted with any form of acute mania, but it would not hold good in numberless instances in chronic mania, nor in melancholia, or partial insanity. Indeed, says Bucknill, '' the possessor of the most brilliant memory we ever met with was a violent and mischievous maniac. He would quote page after page from the French, Latin and Greek classics, and the Iliad and the best plays of Molière in particular he seemed to have at his finger's ends.''

The following graphic description is found in "Macbeth," A. v., S. 1.:

Doctor. " I have two nights watched with you, but can perceive no truth in your report. When was it she last walked?

Gentleman. Since his majesty went into the field, I have seen her rise from her bed, throw her nightgown upon her, unlock her closet, take forth paper, fold it, write upon it, read it, afterwards seal it, and again return to bed; yet all this while in a most fast sleep.

Doctor. A great perturbation in nature, to receive at once the benefit of sleep, and do the effects of watching. In this slumbering agitation, besides her walking and other actual performances, what at any time have you heard her say?

Gentleman. That, sir, which I will not repeat after her.

Doctor. You may, to me; an'ts most meet you should.

Gentleman. Neither to you, nor to any one, having no witness to confirm my speech.

(*Enter Lady Macbeth with a light.*)

Look you! here she comes. This is her very guise, and upon my life fast asleep. Observe her: stand close.

Doctor. How came she by that light?

Gentleman. Why, it stood by her; 'tis her command.

Doctor. You see her eyes are open.

Gentleman. Ay, but their sense is shut.

Doctor. What is it she does now? Look, how she rubs her hands.

Gentleman. It is an accustomed action with her to seem thus washing her hands; I have known her continue in this a quarter of an hour.

Lady Macbeth. Yet here's a spot.

Doctor. Hark! She speaks. I will set down what comes from her, to satisfy my memory the more strongly.

Lady Macbeth. Out, damned spot! Out, I say.—One, two: why, then, 'tis time to do it.—Hell is murky!—Fie, my lord, fie! a soldier and afraid? What need we fear who knows it, when none can call our power to account? Yet who would have thought the old man to have had so much blood in him?

Doctor. Do you mark that?

Lady Macbeth. The thane of Fife had a wife: where is she now? What, will these hands ne'er be clean?—No more o' that, my lord; no more o' that; you mar all with this starting.

Doctor. Go to, go to; you have known what you should not.

Gentleman. She has spoken what she should not, I am sure of that; Heaven knows what she has known.

Lady Macbeth. Here's the smell of the blood still; all the perfumes of Arabia will not sweet these little hands. Oh! Oh! Oh!

Doctor. What a sight is there! The heart is sorely charged.

Gentleman. I would not have such a heart in my bosom, for the dignity of the whole body.

Doctor. Well, well, well.—

Gentleman. Pray God it be, sir.

Doctor. This disease is beyond my practice; yet I have known those who have walked in their sleep, who have died holily in their beds.

Lady Macbeth. Wash your hands; put on your night-gown; look not so pale.—I tell you yet again, Banquo's buried; he cannot come out on's grave.

Doctor. Even so?

Lady Macbeth. To bed, to bed; there's knocking at the gate. Come, come, come, come, give me your hand. What's done, cannot be undone: to bed, to bed, to bed.

Doctor. Will she go now to bed?

Gentleman. Directly.

Doctor. Foul whisperings are abroad. Unnatural deeds do breed unnatural troubles; infected minds will to their deaf pillows discharge their secrets. More needs she the divine than the physician. Look after her; remove from her the means of all annoyance, and still keep eyes upon her."

Farther on in the same tragedy :—

Macbeth. " How does your patient, doctor?

Doctor. Not so sick, my lord, as she is troubled with thick-coming fancies, that keep her from her rest.

Macbeth. Cure her of that. Canst thou not minister to a mind diseas'd, pluck from the memory a rooted sorrow, raze out the written troubles of the brain, and with some sweet oblivious antidote cleanse the stuff'd bosom of that perilous grief which weighs upon the heart?

Doctor. Therein the patient must minister unto himself.

Macbeth. Throw physic to the dogs; I'll none of it. Doctor, if thou could'st find her disease, and purge it to a sound and pristine health, I would applaud thee to the very echo, that should applaud again."

Now, in the analysis of the above quoted matter we find that the good doctor who attended Lady Macbeth did not deem her really sick; but in this he was no doubt mistaken. In the first place, she had been the subject of sleep-walking before the occurrence of the murder of Duncan, and the excitement incident to that occasion had no doubt aggravated the *tendency* into actual insanity, as the doctor says her "thick-coming fancies keep her from her *rest*," a symptom *always* present in acute mania. I say that she had been somnambulistic *before* the murder, from the fact that neither remorse, grief, or indeed any emotional perturbation, is sufficient to start suddenly into existence this form of mental aberration, That when it exists it is of slow and gradual growth—but liable to be excited into active insanity by any circumstances which force a strain upon the mind. Were I called upon to investigate a case analogous to that described as connected with the murder of the sleeping Duncan, and knowing all the facts as therein detailed, I should have no hesitation in expressing the opinion that Lady Macbeth with her own hand committed the deed in her sleep. We have proof that Macbeth was first urged to the commission of the deed by the wife, whose heart was set upon rising to fame and power; she herself says "he is too full of the milk of human kindness to catch the nearest way." Her waking contemplations in regard to the consummation of her wishes could easily have stimulated her sleep-walking propensities into the certain performance of the very act, herself. Lady Macbeth had it in her heart to do the murder with her own hand if need be, as the following will show:

"*(Enter an attendant.)*
Lady M. What is your tidings?
Attendant. The king comes here to-night.
Lady M. Thou'rt mad to say it. Is not thy master with him? who, were't so, would have inform'd for preparation.
Attendant. So please you, it is true; our thane is coming. One of my fellows had the speed of him; who, almost dead for breath, had scarcely more than would make up his message.
Lady M. Give him tending; he brings great news. *(Ex. attendant.)* The raven himself is hoarse, that croaks the fatal entrance of Duncan under my battlements. Come, you spirits

that tend on mortal thoughts, unsex me here, and fill me, from the
crown to the toe, top-full of direst cruelty; make thick my blood
stop up th' access and passage to remorse; that no compunctious
visitings of nature shake my fell purpose, nor keep peace between
th' effect and it. Come to my woman's breasts, and take my milk
for gall, you murdering ministers, wherever in your sightless sub-

stances you wait on nature's mischief. Come, thick night, and pall
thee in the dunnest smoke of hell, that my keen knife see not the
wound it makes, nor heaven peep through the blankness of the
dark to cry, "Hold, hold!"

Of this kind of cases we find ample records. I will quote from
Deboismont: "Dom. Duhaget was of a good family in Gascony;
he had been a captain in the infantry for twenty years; I never
knew any one possessing any more amiability or piety. We had,"
he related, "a friar at ——, where I was before I came to Pierre
Châtel, of a melancholy disposition and a gloomy character, who
was known to be a somnambulist. Sometimes, during the parox-
ysms, he would leave his cell, and re-enter it alone; at others, he
would lose himself, and have to be brought back.

His case had been treated, and as the returns were very rare, it had ceased to attract attention. One night, I was sitting up beyond my usual hour for retiring. I was engaged in looking over some papers in my desk, when I heard the door open, and saw the friar enter, in a complete state of somnambulism. His eyes were open, but fixed (How truthfully Shakespeare notes this fact in the case of Lady M.); he had on only the garments in which he slept, and held a large knife in his hand. He went straight to my bed; appeared to satisfy himself by feeling, that I was really there; after which he struck three heavy blows so powerfully, that the blade, after piercing the clothes, entered deep into the mattress, or rather the mat, which I used in its stead. When he first entered, his brow was frowning and the muscles of his face contracted. Having struck, he turned round, and I observed that instead of the frowning and distorted features, his countenance was overspread with an air of great satisfaction. The light from two lamps that were on my desk had no effect on his eyes; he returned as he came, opening and shutting quietly the two doors that led to my cell.

The next day, I summoned the somnambulist, and asked him quietly of what he had dreamed the previous night. At the question he was agitated. ' Father,' said he, ' I had so strange a dream that I do not like to tell you of it; it is, perhaps, the work of the evil one, and—' ' I command it.' replied I: 'a dream is always involuntary, and is but an illusion.' ' Father.' said he, ' I was hardly asleep before I dreamed that you had killed my mother; that her bleeding shade appeared and demanded vengeance; at this sight I was so enraged that I flew like a madman to your apartment and stabbed you.' I then related to him what had occurred, and showed him the evidence of the blows he had dealt, as he thought, upon me. His services, at night, were thereafter dispensed with.''

It is evident that the symptoms manifest in the conduct of Lady Macbeth were placed to the credit of insanity, and that the treatment in vogue for that malady was perhaps invoked for her cure,— as this phraseology. '' find her disease, and purge it to a sound and pristine health,'' etc., will make apparent: it is certain, however, that we would in diagnosing a case manifesting symptoms as in that of the Prior, have to be cautious in the expression of an opinion, because such freaks may occur in *physiological* conditions. as in dreams, reveries, etc.

It is quite probable, however, that we would always find undoubted insanity in cases so far progressed as that of the two cases mentioned; indeed that is a common sequel to a vast majority of insidious mental disturbances. I have known, however, within the bounds of my own limited observation, somnambulistic conditions of the most confirmed type which never produced, seemingly, anything like a pathological condition, though present in the parties for many years. Judicial decision has, in cases involving offences committed in a state of somnambulism, placed it on a par with insanity,—thus declaring the irresponsibility of a person for acts committed whilst in this state of mind.

In reasoning upon these cases, it certainly would appear that however normal the mind may act during the state of wakefulness, that yet the recumbent position of the body, or some condition resulting from the process of sleep, must, for the time, produce a transient morbid process in the cerebrum which is the starting point for its morbid action. It is scarcely reasonable that we have morbid ideas leading to morbid actions, emanating from a purely physiological source.

The remarkable fact is again apparent in the foregoing quotation of the accuracy of Shakespeare's therapeutics. He would use some " sweet oblivious antidote" just as would the medical man this hour, under like circumstances; though doubtless the modern psychologist has remedies at command which more nearly come up to the idea of " sweet and oblivious " than had the practitioner of 1483. Bromide of potassium, chloroform, hydrate of chloral, etc., were not then known to the profession—except, may be, the latter, or some drug analagous to it in action as used by Friar Lawrence, and noted further on in this volume. Opium and its preparations have always been the " antidotes" (in the Shakespearean sense) to mental troubles,—hold the front rank yet and perhaps always will, though it seems not to be as well borne now as in former times. It is no doubt the remedy referred to in the text.

The doubt and distrust in regard to the potency of medicine, and yet the clinging to the idea that *something* could be done, is clearly manifest in the remarks of Macbeth when he wishes physic to be thrown to the dogs but asks half beseechingly if the doctor cannot find her disease and *purge* it to health. He also is aped by the public to-day in the manner most congenial in compensating the physician for his services—would "applaud him to the very echo." Many people prefer this method of liquidating their doctor's bill rather than by paying cash.

We read the following profound thought in Hamlet:

Queen. "This is the very coinage of your brain: this bodiless creation ecstacy is very cunning in.

Hamlet. Ecstacy! My pulse, as yours, doth temperately keep time, and makes as healthful music. It is not madness that I have utter'd: bring me to the test and I the matter will re-word, which madness would gambol from. Mother, for love of grace, lay not that flattering unction to your soul, that not your trespass, but my madness speaks: it will but skin and film the ulcerous place, whilst rank corruption, mining all within, infects unseen."

This conversation occurred between Hamlet and his mother relative to a declaration on the part of the former that he had seen and conversed with the ghost of his father—the king, whom his mother and her paramour had secretly murdered.

Hamlet's defence of his own sanity is a pretty thorough one. He claims that he had no ecstacy from the fact that he had no lesion of the circulation, and that he maintained ability to recount all that occurred in conversation with the ghost. The first of these pleas had some foundation in fact; as it is known that in ecstatic conditions external sensations are suspended, and all the vital functions retarded and sluggish, whilst voluntary movements are arrested and held in complete abeyance, the pulse therefore not keeping step to "healthful music," but doubtless being less frequent than normal; during this time, however, the mental faculties are not necessarily suspended.

Upon this point so eminent an authority as Bucknill also says, as was said in a previous chapter of Malvolio, who wished his sanity tested "by any constant question"—a maniac may gambol from reproducing in the same words any statement he has made when he is affected with *acute* mania, but in some *chronic* forms he may keep up a line of coherent conversation as well as those of the soundest minds;—and as to the condition of the pulse as an index to the true mental condition, the same writer thinks Shakespeare's conclusions, from the words he places in the mouth of Hamlet, at least doubtful as to accuracy.

The pulse in mania averages about fifteen beats above that of health; that of the insane generally, including maniacs, only averages nine beats above the healthy standard, while the pulse in melancholia and monomania is not above the average.

There had been an interview between Hamlet and his mother before the passage before quoted, and which gave rise to it—namely, the times at which he professed to have talked with the ghost as below detailed:

Hamlet. "A king of shreds and patches.—Save me, and hover o'er me with your wings, you heavenly guards!—What would you, gracious figure?

Queen. Alas! he's mad.

Hamlet. Do you not come your tardy son to chide, that, laps'd in fume and passion, lets go by th' important acting of your dread command? O, say!

Ghost. Do not forget. This visitation is but to whet thy almost blunted purpose. But, look! amazement on thy mother sits: O. step between her and her fighting soul; conceit in weakest bodies strongest works. Speak to her, Hamlet.

Hamlet. How is it with you, lady?

Queen. Alas! how is't with you, that you do bend your eyes on vacancy, and with th' incorporal air do hold discourse? forth at your eyes your spirits wildly peep; and, as the sleeping soldiers in th' alarm, your bedded hair, like life in excrements, starts up, and stands on end. O gentle son! Upon the heat and flame of thy distemper sprinkle cool patience. Where on do you look?

Hamlet. On him, on him! Look you, how pale he glares! His form and cause conjoin'd, pleading to stones, would make them capable.—Do not look upon me; lest with this piteous action you convert my stern effects: then, what I have to do will want true color; tears, perchance, for blood.

Queen. To whom do you speak thus?

Hamlet. Do you see nothing there?

Queen. Nothing at all; yet all that is, I see.

Hamlet. Did you nothing hear?

Queen. No, nothing but ourselves.

Hamlet. Why, look you there! look how it steals away! My father, in his habit as he liv'd! Look, where he goes, even now, out at the portal!" *(Exit Ghost.)*

Hamlet had doubtless been greatly excited by his father's death; doubly so, perhaps, by the "deep damnation of his taking off," and was, therefore, in a fit mental capacity to "see visions and dream dreams," and his scene with his father's ghost is but an example of thousands of occurrences which have taken place in all periods of the world's history, and of the realities of which the beholders have never entertained a doubt.

Hippolyte in "A Midsummer Night's Dream" assures us, that the "lunatic, the lover and the poet are of imagination all compact: one sees more devils than vast hell can hold; that is the mad man." These devils were seen particularly by those religious fanatics and mad men so common to the historic period not very remote from the days in which Shakespeare wrote. Spectres of this character are not now so common among the insane.

The following narrative from DeBoismont is analogous to the vision of Hamlet. He says: "we owe to a very eminent physician of acknowledged reputation, and intimate with Sir Walter Scott, the recital of a fact, that once occurred to a well known personage, which is, without contradiction, one of the most curious examples that can be offered in the history of hallucinations.

The physician was, by chance, called on to attend a man, now long deceased, who, during his life, filled an important office in a particular department of justice. His functions made him frequently an arbiter of the interests of others; his conduct was therefore open to public observation, and for a series of years he enjoyed a reputation for uncommon firmness, good sense, and integrity.

At the time when the physician visited him, he kept his room, sometimes his bed, and yet he continued, now and then, to engage in the duties of his office; his mind displayed its usual force and habitual energy in directing the business which devolved on him. A superficial observer would not have noticed anything indicative of a weakness or oppression of mind.

The external symptoms announced no acute or alarming illness; but the slowness of his pulse, the failure of his appetite, a painful digestion, and an unceasing sadness, appeared to have their source in some cause which the invalid was resolved to conceal. The gloomy air of the unhappy man, the embarrassment which he could not disguise, the constraint with which he replied briefly to the questions of the physician, induced the latter to apply to his family, who could not give him any satisfactory information. The physician then had recourse to arguments calculated to make a strong impression on the mind of the patient. He pointed out the folly of devoting himself to a slow death rather than communicate the secret of the grief which was dragging him to the grave. Above all, he represented the injury he was inflicting on his own reputation, by creating a suspicion that the cause of his affliction, and the consequences resulting, were of too disgraceful a nature to be owned;

and added, that he would bequeath to his family a suspected and dishonored name, and leave a memory to which would be attached the idea of some crime, which he dared not own, even in his dying hour.

This latter argument made more impression than any which had been previously started, and he expressed a desire to unbosom himself frankly to the doctor. They were left together, the door of the sick man's room was carefully closed, and he began his confession in the following manner:—

"You cannot, my dear friend, be more convinced than myself, of the death that threatens me; but you cannot comprehend the nature of the disease, nor the manner in which it acts upon me; and even if you could, I doubt if either your zeal or your talents could cure me."

"It is possible," replied the physician, "that my talents would not be equal to the desire I have to be useful to you, but medical science has many resources, which only those who have studied can appreciate. However, unless you clearly describe your symptoms, it is impossible to say whether it is in my power, or in that of medicine, to relieve you."

"I assure you," replied the patient, "that my situation is not unique, for there is a similar example in the celebrated romance of Le Sage. Without doubt, you remember by what disease the Duke of Olivares died? He was overcome by the idea that he was followed by an apparition, in whose existence he did not believe; and he died because the presence of this vision conquered his strength and broke his heart. Well, my dear doctor, mine is a similar case; and the vision that persecutes me is so painful and so frightful, that my reason is quite inadequate to combat the effects of a frenzied imagination, and I feel that I shall die, the victim of an imaginary malady."

The physician attentively listened, and judiciously abstained from any contradiction; he contented himself with asking for more circumstantial details of the nature of the apparition that persecuted him, and the manner in which so singular an affection had seized on his imagination, which, it would appear, a very moderate exercise of understanding would have succeeded in destroying.

The patient replied that the attack had been gradual, and that, in the commencement, it was neither terrible nor very unpleasant; and that the progress of his sufferings was as follows:—

"My visions," said he, "began two or three years ago. I was then annoyed by the presence of a great cat, which came and disappeared I knew not how; but I did not continue long in doubt, for I perceived that this domestic animal was the result of a vision produced by a derangement in the organs of sight, or of the imagination. At the end of a few months, the cat disappeared, and was succeeded by a phantom of a higher grade, and whose exterior was, at least, more imposing. It was no other than a gentleman usher, dressed as though he was in the service of the Lord-Lieutenant of Ireland, or of a great functionary of the church, or of any other person of rank or dignity. This character, in a court-dress, with big bag wig, a sword by his side, a vest worked in tambour, and a chapeau-brass, glided by my side like the shade of beau Nash. Whether in my own house, or elsewhere, he mounted the stairs before me, as if to announce me. Sometimes he mixed in with the company, although it was evident no one ever remarked his presence, and that I alone witnessed the chimerical honors he paid me.

This caprice of imagination did not make a strong impression on me; but it raised a question as to the nature of the disease, and I began to fear the effects it might have on my senses. After a few months, my gentleman-usher was no more seen, but was replaced by a phantom horrible to the sight, and disgusting to the mind,—a skeleton."

"Alone, or in society," added the unfortunate man, "this apparition never leaves me. It is in vain that I repeat to myself that it has no reality, that it is but an illusion caused by the derangement of my sight, or a disordered imagination. Of what use are such reflections, when the presage and the emblem of death is constantly before my eyes? when I see myself, although only in my imagination, forever the companion of a phantom representing the gloomy inhabitant of the tomb, whilst I am still upon earth? Neither science, philosophy, nor even religion, has a remedy for such a disease; and I too truly feel that I shall die this cruel death, although I have no faith in the reality of the spectre that is always present."

"It would appear then," said the physician, "that this skeleton is ever before you."

"It is my hapless destiny to see it always," replied the sick man.

"In this case," continued the doctor, "you see it now?"

"Yes."

" In what part of the room does it appear to you?"

" At the foot of my bed; when the curtains are a little open, it places itself between them, and fills the opening."

" You say that you understand it to be only an illusion?—In dreams we are frequently aware that the apparition that freezes us with fear is false; but we cannot, nevertheless, overcome the terror that oppresses us. Have you firmness enough to be positively convinced? Can you rise, and take the place which the spectre appears to occupy, in order to assure yourself that it is a real illusion?"

The poor man sighed and shook his head.

" Well, then," said she doctor, " we will try another plan." He quitted the chair on which he had been seated, at the head of the bed, and placing himself between the open curtains, in the spot pointed out as being the place occupied by the apparition, he enquired if the skeleton was yet visible.

"Much less, because you are between it and me, but I see the skull over your shoulder."

It is said that, in spite of his philosophy, the learned doctor shuddered at the thought of an ideal spectre behind him.

The patient perished, a victim of this hallucination.

I quote this lengthy paper to show with what fidelity Shake-

speare drew the picture of hallucination in the case of Hamlet.
Whether his intuitive perceptions gave him the power of description,
or did personal observation, or an idea gained from reading the
details of an analogous case, I am at a loss to conjecture ; certain it
is, however, that it is masterly in its portraiture, be the origin what
it might. The analogy is even borne out in the similarity of the
vague fear which haunted the Queen, even in the presence of Hamlet, and that which startled the learned doctor when the skeleton
peeped over his shoulder. *Ghost.* "But, look! Amazement on
thy mother sits: O, step between her and her fighting soul."
(*Frightened* soul.)

It appears from the observations of high authority upon hallucinations that they are " never an expression of an aroused activity
of the psychic sphere, but on the contrary are indications of the
exhaustion of the same. i. e.. of the cortex of the anterior part of
the brain."

This was eminently the condition of the overworked patient of
which mention is made by De Boismont. Hamlet's mental condition
was also no doubt one in which exhaustion played an important part.
as the exciting incidents connected with the murder of his father
were sufficient to make apparent.

The passage in regard to the illness of King John so often quoted
by medical writers — "It is too late; the life of all his blood is
touch'd corruptibly; and his pure brain (which some suppose the
soul's fair dwelling-house,) doth by the idle comments that it makes.
foretell the ending of mortality," is inimitable—unsurpassed, as a
description of the muttering delirium common to low forms of
fever, etc., but its notice belongs more to the physician than to the
psychatriatist proper. It appears that when we regard mind as
only the offspring or result of matter possessing certain properties
of composition, consistence, form, etc., that we must expect that
when these are in any way changed we must have change also in the
thing which is produced—a change in the mental phenomena.

If the muscular and nervous mechanism of the arm is impaired.
motion (the *results* of the mechanism) is also impaired. If the
lesion in either the brain or in the arm is susceptible of repair and
their mechanism is made good in all its parts. then the work performed must be normal. One broad line of distinction then between
delirium and acute mania, etc., and the other forms of insanity, rests
in the fact that the brain is only temporarily embarrassed in its work-

ings, by agents acting through the general system, in the one case, while in the other the lesion is specifically organic. Of course there are many of the former class of cases which go still farther—farther than a mere limited intoxication of the senses,—as in mania a potu, for example. When these cases go to the extreme, then of course they are subjects of proper psychological research. The assertion however of the king's attendant that it was " too late " was not well founded when predicated upon the fact of the " idle comments " alone, because although always a grave symptom if it occurs early and is persistent, yet it is not accompanied in the mind of the physician with that absolutely fatal prognostication entertained by those who surrounded the king. Shakespeare makes a mistake also, it is thought, in attributing this kind of mental aberration to King John, because delirium is not commonly present in the malady of which he was dying. *Typhoid* and typhus fevers are the maladies in which such delirium is most prominently and commonly noticed. In pernicious fever, from which King John must have died, as the symptomotology as given in another chapter clearly points, there is sometimes, at the very close, a muttering of many words, but they are commonly coherent and the offspring apparently of an unclouded intellect. I recall to mind the death of a very old man with a congestive chill, who at the last moments repeated in a prayerful, chanting tone common to the church service of the sect to which he belonged, the words, "I'm a g'wine to die. O! my friends, in youth is the time to prepare! "—the peculiar intonation of which might readily have lead a non-professional person to have said he was " not in his right mind." It is claimed by the dramatist also, as will be seen in the chapter referred to further on in this work, that the king had been poisoned — a conclusion it is thought wholly untenable. (See King John, A. v., Sc. vi.)

It is however indeed wonderful to note the accuracy of Shakespeare's knowledge even in the medical thought contained in the above short quotation. " The life of all his blood is touch'd corruptibly," and from this fact (constitutionally, and not from a local brain lesion) makes he the muttering and illogical talk! Who besides this master intellect could have so accurately deduced proper symptoms from such hypothecated premises? He was even versed in the *scientific* use of the imagination.

The parenthetical clause " and his pure brain (which some suppose the soul's frail dwelling-house)," contains too much of the profoundly metaphysical to admit of ordinary minds descanting profitably upon it. Briefly, however, it may be said that from our materialistic views we see therein as much logic, and a doctrine which to us offers as much consolation, as any ever advanced upon the subject of the soul. We can see nothing in man—no trait or attribute which answers to the principle of what people call "soul" except the attribute—mind.

As to the *immortality* of that manifestation, I think the *motion* of my arm just as probable of everlasting preservation. Indeed this is the doctrine of the age—force is eternal.

One finale awaits the man and all his attributes.

"Romeo and Juliet," A. ii., S. iii., has this language:

Romeo.   " Good-morrow, father.
Friar.   *Benedicite!*
    What early tongue so sweetly saluteth me?—
    Young son, it argues a distemper'd head,
    So soon to bid good-morrow to your bed:
    Care keeps his watch in every old man's eye,
    And where care lodges, sleep will never lie;
    But where unbusied youth, with unstuff'd brain
    Doth couch his limbs, there golden sleep doth reign."

The observation of Friar Laurence in the present case is very accurate indeed as to the first paragraph, for it is a fact borne out by observation, that of all the passions, love is most potent to cause sleepless nights. A man may hate, but he will sleep to-night and hate again to-morrow: he may get angry or sorry, and yet tired nature's sweet restorer folds him in her embrace, and woos him to present forgetfulness; grief, remorse, despair, envy, jealousy, all find repose in balmy sleep; but a bad case of "mash" never!

It does not occur to us, however, that the residue of the good Friar's philosophy is of that profound quality which engenders unbounded admiration in us. It is not *care* which renders the old man sleepless, but a true pathological change in the structure of the brain—in the vessels particularly,—and perhaps also to a greater or less degree in all the tissues of the organ. The lack of tonicity in the vascular walls allows the blood currents to become sluggish—the brain never becoming emptied sufficiently to approach the anæmic condition essential to normal sleep. In the concluding lines of the quotation, where he speaks of the unstuff'd brain of youth, he undoubtedly in his *language* strikes the true physiological condition of the brain in sleep with all the accuracy incident to the most advanced investigation ; but unfortunately his *ideas* applied to the *thought* which stuffed the organ and not to the blood that loaded its vessels. Yet it must be admitted that the two conditions are inseparably associated. The picture is very skillfully drawn, however, if we look at it even through professional spectacles alone. In the aged, besides the change in the vessels of the brain and the hyperæmia incident thereto, we have a lack of activity in the whole system which favors the local stasis in the brain—the blood not being called away from that organ. The organic functions are apathetic and need only a limited and passive supply for their slowly moving existence. Typical of this fact, let us take the stomach and note what an influence it has upon this brain function—upon sleep. Immediately after a hearty dinner we feel sleepy, because the unusual blood supply necessary to aid the stomach in the performance of its task of digestion unloads the brain. In the old even this function is so impaired, commonly, that its beneficial effects are measurably lost.

The following conversation between Brutus and Cassius explains itself :

Cassius.   " I did not think you could have been so angry.

Brutus.   O, Cassius! I am sick of my many griefs.

Cassius.   Of your philosophy you make no use, if you give place to accidental evils.

Brutus.   No man bears sorrow better.—Portia is dead.

Cassius.   Ha! Portia?

Brutus.   She is dead.

Cassius.   How 'scap'd I killing, when I cross'd you so?—O, insupportable and touching loss!—Upon what sickness?

Brutus.   Impatient of my absence, and grief that young Octavius with Mark Antony have made themselves so strong ;—for with her death that tidings came. — With this she fell distract, and, her attendants absent, swallow'd fire.

Cassius.   And died so?

Brutus.   Even so.

Cassius.   O, ye immortal gods ! "

The period in Roman history in which the above purports to have occurred is known as " the period of civil wars"—an era in which domestic strife, rapine and bloodshed held high carnival. Cæsar had been assassinated in the Senate chamber by the conspirators headed by Cassius and Brutus, and they in turn were pushed to the wall by young Octavius, nephew of the murdered Cæsar, all of which no doubt told fearfully on the body and mind of Portia, the wife of Brutus,—she seeming to entertain for him the most ardent affection. The mental organization of women makes them mostly subject to that form of insanity known as "emotional," and the strange freaks which sometimes seize upon their crazied imagination will cause them to attempt to "eat fire" or do any other unaccountable thing. This is certainly an original way, however, of committing suicide. Some of these poor creatures have curious notions of ways in which to "shuffle off this mortal coil,"—the leaping into the fathomless mass of seething lava which constitutes the terrors of Vesuvius, or the fearful plunge over the falls of Niagara, seem to meet the fastidious notions of some of these unfortunates, whose life has proven a failure. What is the difference, after all, between either of these modes, on the one hand, or by the explosion of an oil can or the drowning in a duck puddle on the other?

The final cataclysm in which the universe goes to wreck, if such an occurrence should ever occur, will be no worse to bear by the single individual than is the death in a rail-road horror.

We find some thoughts on normal mental phenomena in various places in Shakespeare's writings, among others the boastful language of the pedagogue Holofernes, in "Love's Labor's Lost," in which instance he enumerates his special talents, and claims that "these are begot in the ventricle of memory, nourished in the womb of *pia mater*, and delivered upon the mellowing of occasion."

The term "begot in the ventricle of memory" is not scientifically correct;—the conception as to the locality of the registering portion of the brain being at fault;—as is also the idea that "memory" is "begot" in the brain. Strictly speaking, memory is *originated* outside of the brain—that is, it is a recurrence of the mind to an *external* fact, the recognition of which has at some time in the past been registered in the ganglia, and has, perhaps, remained dormant until some similar fact or circumstance brushed the dust of time from the record, and presented it again to the eye of the mind.— When, in reality, it is "delivered upon the mellowing of occasion."

The dramatist came very near the truth however, in the place where he says of *thought* that it is nourished in the womb of pia mater. Modern research has established it as a fact that the portion of the brain in immediate proximity to the pia mater—the convolutions—are really the seat of intellection,—thus rendering it probable that the pabulum from which thought or the power to think is furnished is derived from the pia mater, at least, in part.

"Not sick, my lord, unless it be in mind," says Salanio in "The Merchant of Venice." Sick in mind! I am persuaded that mental suffering in this world greatly over aggregates that of physical; and he who has not chanced to experience their relative powers, has so far escaped misfortune. "Too much sadness hath congealed your blood," and "melancholy is the nurse of frenzy," are found in the same drama. It is true that melancholy does often precede active mania, but that sadness lowers the temperature of the blood is only true figuratively. The power that mental suffering has over the physical well-being of an individual is very well pictured in "The Winter's Tale."

"Conceiving the dishonor of his mother, he straight declin'd, droop'd, took it deeply, fasten'd and fix'd the shame on't in himself, threw off his spirit, his appetite, his sleep, and downright languish'd." Here we have another excellent pen-picture of a troubled mind, where "thick-coming fancies kept him from his rest." As William Cullen Bryant said some years ago, in his address at the unvailing of the statue of the "bard of Stratford" in Central Park, New York.—"What a physician might he not have made to an insane asylum!"

Bearing upon the same point as the matter quoted last above, we find numerous lines and phrases:

"Thy father's beard is turned white with the news," in Henry the Fourth; while in Henry the Sixth we find the mental infirmities of senility compared to mania,—evidently an assertion of the right to latitude which is always granted to fictionists.

The enquiry "what madness rules in brain-sick men," "sure the man is mad," "brain-sick duchess," etc., is also found in the sixth Henry, part second. "My hair be fix'd on end as one distract," is also used in same;—an idea, by the way, that is universal. How often do we hear the term—"My hair lifted my hat from my head," as descriptive of horror or excessive fright. There is certainly some foundation for the sensation—possibly a contraction of the muscular structures of the scalp, or may be a congestion of its capillary circulation, or some other condition made upon the parts through the medium of the nervous apparatus—analogous to that of suffusion of the face in blushing for example. The hair does really assume a more or less erectile condition; we see its analogue in animals—the dog and cat especially, when they turn their hair the wrong way, in the condition of affright, and also of anger.

The term "brain-sick" is also used in "Troilus and Cressida" and in "Titus Andronicus," whilst in the former it is asserted that "extremity of griefs do make men mad"—a declaration which it has been the misfortune of thousands to see verified. A graphic description of a "tainted" mind is given by Lady Percy, in Henry IV., A. ii., S. ii.: "O, my good lord, why are you thus alone? For what offence have I this fortnight been a banish'd woman from my Harry's bed? Tell me, sweet love, what is 't takes from thee thy stomach, pleasure and thy golden sleep? Why dost thou bend thine eyes upon the earth, and start so often when thou sit'st alone? Why hast thou lost the fresh blood in thy cheek, and given my treasure, and my right of thee, to thick-ey'd musing and curs'd melancholy?"

Percy was a political and military schemer, and scrupled not, like all of his class, to go into any game, however hazardous, provided he had a show to win. It was upon the eve of an important enterprise that his wife addressed him in the language above.

In "Troilus and Cressida" it is said that "with too much blood and too little brain these two may run mad; but if with too much brain and too little blood they do, I will be a curer of mad men." Here we have an error in supposition, as it is not "little" brains that "run mad," though "plethora" be present by the barrel. Too much brain and too little blood are much more favorable conditions for such an occurrence, though Shakespeare seems not to so regard it; it seems that to the feeble intellect and plethora he looks for his causation in the instance before us. He tells us himself in "Cymbeline" that "Fools are not mad folks."

As to the mental condition of King Lear, I cannot view his eccentric railings as the acts of a mad man, but rather as freaks in the harrassed mind of one possessed naturally of a large degree of senile asceticism. He was by nature a cynic.

This is evidently the view taken of the father's condition by both Goneril and Regan. The latter says to him on an occasion of his having had some harsh language toward her sister: "O, sir! you are old; Nature stands in you on the very verge of her confine: you should be rul'd and led by some discretion, that discerns your state better than yourself," while the former at another time tells him: "All's not offense that indiscretion finds, and dotage terms so." Though later on in their relations, and when their intolerance of their father and his retinue of an hundred revelous retainers had rendered their quarrel with him very bitter, they do not hesitate to use such terms toward him as " to whose hands have you sent the lunatic king," and even his own friends who were often witnesses of his maledictions could not, sometimes, but think him mad.   He *was* ANGRY, but not insane; and these declarations of his daughters were not their real sentiments, but were only used by them to show the extremity of their bitter resentment toward him.   We note this idea of morbid-mind in the language of *Gloster:* "Come hither, friend: where is the king, my master?" *Kent:* "Here, sir; but trouble him not; his wits are gone;" and Cordelia also says on meeting him after her short stay in France: "Alack! 'tis he: why, he was met even now as mad as the vex'd sea: singing aloud," etc., while, in description of some of his sarcastic philippics, Edgar, another of his friends, says: "O, matter and impertinency mix'd; reason in madness!"

Lear was old—eighty years and more, according to his own declaration, and to one who will study closely all he says it will be seen that much of profound thought and little of mental alienation is apparent in what he says.   Take this passage for example, which occurs toward the close of his life, and judge whether it sounds like the utterance of one whose mind is in abeyance: "A dog's obey'd in office." "Through tattered clothes small vices do appear; robes and furr'd gowns hide all.   Plate sin with gold, and the strong lance of justice hurtless breaks: arm it in rags, a pigmy's straw doth pierce it."   His integrity of purpose as is manifested in all he says and does, and the clear conceptions he has as to the great ingratitudes and lack of filial duties on the part of his daughters, is never lost sight of even in his wildest and most extravagant moments.   The " stings and sorrows of outrageous fortune " could not drive these thankless deeds from his mind, but presented them to him at all times in their real character of undiluted diabolism.   He was indeed but a " poor old man, full of grief and age," and any one of us burdened even with fewer of the snows of life's winters, placed under like circumstances would need more than " an ounce of civet" to sweeten our imaginations, and we needn't be crazy either.   In his most irrelevant language he is much less the madman than is Edgar, who openly declares that he has assumed the character of a Bedlam beggar—one just out of a mad-house,—for a purpose. Lear's distemper was but the "unruly waywardness that infirm and choleric years bring with them. The best and soundest of his time had been but rash."

After Lear had been refused lodging by his daughters, and had been by them turned adrift into the night of relentless storm, his sense of outraged justice reached its climax; and from the hour in which he was again brought into the presence of the sympathetic soul of Cordelia he calmly resigns himself to quietude—resolved, as I can see, to bother himself no more over grievances he is powerless to amend. Hence we find him enjoying the long and refreshing sleep as appears in the quotation below:

"*Cordelia.* (*To the physician.*) How does the king?
Doctor. Madam, sleeps still.
Cordelia. O, you kind gods, cure this great breach in his abused nature! Th' untim'd and jarring senses, O, wind up of this child-changed father!
Doctor. So please your majesty that we may wake the king? he hath slept long.
Cordelia. Be govern'd by your knowledge, and proceed i' the sway of your own will. Is he array'd?
Doctor. Ay, madam; in the heaviness of his sleep we put fresh garments on him.
Kent. Good, madam, be by when we do awake him—I doubt not of his temperance.
Cordelia. Very well. (*Music.*)
Doctor. Please you, draw near.—Louder the music there.
Cordelia. O my dear father! Restoration, hang thy medicine on my lips; and let this kiss repair those violent harms, that my two sisters have in thy reverence made!.
Kent. Kind and dear princess.
Cordelia. Had you not been their father, these white flakes had challeng'd pity of them. Was this a face to be expos'd against the jarring winds? to stand against the deep dread-bolted thunder? in the most terrible and nimble stroke of quick, cross lightning? to watch with this thin helm? Mine enemies' dog should not——
Alack, alack! 'Tis a wonder that thy life and wits at once had not concluded all.—He wakes; speak to him.

Doctor. Madam, do you; 'tis fittest.

Cordelia. How does my royal lord? How fares your majesty?

Lear. You do me wrong, to take me out of the grave.—Thou art a soul in bliss, but I am bound upon a wheel of fire, that mine own tears do scald like molten lead.

Cordelia. Sir, do you know me?

Lear. You are a spirit, I know. Where did you die?

Cordelia. Still, still, far wide.

Doctor. He's scarce awake: let him alone awhile.

Lear. Where have I been? where am I? fair daylight?—I am mightily abus'd.—I should even die with pity to see another thus. I am a very foolish, fond old man, four-score and upward, and, to deal plainly, I fear I am not in my perfect mind. (*Cordelia weeps.*)

Doctor. Be comforted, good madam: the great rage, you see, is cur'd in him; and yet it is danger to make him even o'er the time he has lost. Desire him to go in: trouble him no more, till farther settling.

Cordelia. Will't please your highness walk?

Lear. You must bear with me: pray you now, forget and forgive. I am old and foolish."

It is perceived throughout the whole of the foregoing extract that the paramount idea of every one—doctor, Cordelia, and even the old king himself, is that "mental worry," occasioned by the ill usage received at the hands of his daughters, constituted the sum total of this brain malady—merely extreme excitement, relieved as it always is by a quiet sleep—the physical "tire" occasioned by his night of exposure and a dose of opium doubtless contributing to that end. Refreshing sleep is always a favorable sign in the insane, but does not by any means always argue a complete subsidence of the malady.

In none of the other characters of Shakespeare who are by writers considered in some degree insane, namely — Timon of Athens, Ophelia, Constance, Jaques, Melvolio, etc., can I see actual insanity, except, perhaps, in the case of Ophelia. A close study of these characters will reveal the fact that Shakespeare did not intend or essay the description of insane persons in the delineation of their characters through their own mouths. In Timon we certainly find an individual possessing a mental organization very nearly akin to that of Lear, and in whose freaks we see but the form of continued anger which renders men misanthropes. If mere eccentricity and oddity of character be placed as insanity, we need hardly search for the sane. Shakespeare's characters named above very clearly belong to the class of characters named by Lord Shaftesbury as quoted by Bucknill: "There is also among these a sort of hatred to mankind and society; a passion which has been known perfectly reigning among some men, and has had a peculiar name given to it —misanthropy. A large share of this belongs to those who have habitually indulged themselves in moroseness, or who, by force of ill-nature and ill-breeding, have contracted such a reverse of affability, and civil manners, that to see or meet a stranger is offensive. The very aspect of mankind is a disturbance to them, and they are sure always to hate at first sight."

In introducing into the pages of this book those portions of Shakespeare's writings which pertain exclusively to the emotions, it is done from consideration of the fact that in their extremes, as we here find them, it is difficult to say just where the purely physiological ends and the psychological begins. Shakespeare himself fully comprehended this fact. He puts the following words into the mouth of Rosalind: "Love is merely a madness, and I tell you, deserves as well a dark-house and a whip as mad men do." In the above position we are sustained by the opinions of Bucknill, from whose writings we have before quoted, as he says " no state of the reasoning faculty can, by itself, be the cause or condition of madness; congenital idiocy and acquired dementia being alone excepted. The corollary of this is, that emotional disturbance is the cause and condition of insanity. In the prodromic period of the disorder the emotions are always perverted, while the reason remains intact. Disorders of the intellectual faculties are secondary; they are often, indeed, to be recognized as the morbid emotions transformed into perverted action of the reason; but in no case are they primary or essential."

Among all the *emotions* which are common to the human mind, there is none which more surely and swiftly preys upon the mental and physical organization of man or woman than the hideous monster jealousy. What other passion of the mind could have stirred with equal force the stern and haughty soul of Othello, or have aroused in an equal degree the revengeful ire of Leontes? If there is one sentiment in the bosom of the human family that is *supremely* selfish, it is found in the emotion known as jealousy.

In "Much Ado About Nothing," Beatrice, in one of her caustic conversational sallies, uses the following language: "The count is neither sad, nor sick, nor merry, nor well; but civil, count, civil as an orange, and something of as jealous a complexion;" whilst in "The Merchant of Venice" the fair Portia is made to say:

> "How all the other passions fleet to air,
>   As doubtful thoughts, and rash embrac'd despair,
>   And shuddering fear, and green-eyed jealousy."

She was comparing the other passions with love, and like the female world in general, made it paramount to all other human attributes. In each of the passages above noticed, we see the notion put forth as to the close connexion of this passion—jealousy—and biliary derangement,—giving origin to the term in such common use, "The green-eyed monster." Indeed, it is a fact admitted by most writers on physiology that this condition of the mind, above all others, has a specific tendency toward deranging the hepatic functions; and melancholia is said also to sometimes produce the same effect. We have never observed either to be causative of such a condition,—although we have known a pang of jealousy, in a person otherwise in excellent health, to so affect the halitus from the pulmonary tissues as to render it insufferably offensive in less than five minutes,—the extremities at the same time passing into an icy coldness. These manifestations are not strange, however, when we remember what power other emotional conditions exert over the various functions of the body—as, for instance, fear over the alimentary and urinary organs, anger upon the mammary secretion, etc., etc.

In "The Winter's Tale" we have the matter between Leontes, his queen, and Polixenes, king of Bohemia.

Leontes, being of a jealous disposition, thinks he discovers a growing intimacy springing up between his guest and his queen, and half to himself, half to his young son, he thus soliloquizes:

"To mingle friendships far is mingling bloods; there have been, or I am much deceiv'd, cuckolds ere now; and many a man there is (even at this present, now, while I speak this) holds his wife by the arm, that little thinks she has been sluc'd in 's absence, and his pond fish'd by his next neighbor, by Sir Smile, his neighbor. Nay, there's comfort in 't, whilst other men have gates, and those gates open'd, as mine, against their will. Should all despair that have revolted wives, the tenth of mankind would hang themselves. Physic for 't there's none: it is a bawdy planet, that will strike wher 't is predominant; and 'tis powerful, think it, no barricado for a belly: know it; it will let in and out the enemy, with bag and baggage; many a thousand on 's have the disease, and feel it not."

His faithful servant Camillo essayed hard to persuade him that his queen was pure as the beautiful snow,—that he was laboring under a perturbed imagination; but all this nice talk was hushed into stillness by the following inexorable logic of the king:

"Is whispering nothing? Is leaning cheek to cheek? is meeting noses? kissing with inside lip? stopping the career of laughter with a sigh? (a note infallible of breaking honesty:) horsing foot on foot? skulking in corners? wishing clocks more swift? hours, minutes? noon, midnight? and all eyes blind with 'pin and web' *(old name for cataract)* but theirs, theirs only, that would unseen be wicked? is this nothing?

Camillo. Good, my lord, be cur'd of this diseas'd opinion, and betimes; for 'tis most dangerous."

Whether "so thick a drop serene had quench'd *their* orbes," or else the good king himself labored under an unusual obliquity of vision, we are certainly unable to say; but without doubt he put up a pretty hard case against the queen. In the meantime, Polixenes having "smelt a rat" endeavored to "pump" the man Camillo in regard to his master's conduct, which brought about this conversation:

Polixenes. "The king hath on him such a countenance, as he had lost some province, and a region lov'd as he loves himself: even now I met him with customary compliment, when he, wafting his eyes to the contrary, and falling a lip of contempt, speeds from me."

Reader, if you have ever had the misfortune to have engendered in the bosom of a friend a sense of jealousy, how do you like his picture? Camillo, in explanation, tells Polixenes that "there is a sickness which puts some of us in distemper; but I cannot name the disease, and it is caught of you that yet are well." But, as suggested at another place in this work, it is left to the part of Othello, the Moor of Venice, to portray to the utmost bounds of possibility the tortures of a jealous soul: the agonies of the doomed, in perdition, cannot surpass in reality what the author puts upon the soul of this black-a-moor. Could we sometimes draw aside the veil, and look for one short hour into the depths of the human heart, what of woe and misery might we not discover there, though it be gilded in its superfices with bright and sunny smiles and shrouded with a merry laugh. After a lengthy talk between the black general and his special pet, the villain Iago, the latter admonished his master thus:

"O! beware, my lord, of jealousy; it is the green-eyed monster, which doth make the meat it feeds on: that cuckold lives in bliss, who, certain of his fate, loves not his wronger; but O! what damned minutes tells he o'er, who dotes, yet doubts; suspects, yet fondly loves! In Venice these women do let heaven see the pranks they dare not show their husbands; their best conscience is, not to leave 't undone, but keep 't unknown.

Othello. O, curse of marriage! that we can call these delicate creatures ours, and not their appetites. I had rather be a toad, and live upon the vapors of a dungeon, than keep a corner in the thing I love, for others' uses."

"Honest Iago," upon possessing himself surreptitiously of his mistress' handkerchief, which he intends placing in the room of the innocent Cassio, thus talks to his noble self:

"I will in Cassio's lodging lose this napkin, and let him find it; trifles light as air, are to the jealous, confirmation strong as proofs of holy writ. This may do something; the Moor is already charged with my poison.

Othello. I swear 'tis better to be much abus'd, than but to know a little. What sense had I of her stolen hours of lust? I saw it not, thought it not, it harm'd not me: I slept the next night well, was free and merry; I found not Cassio's kisses on her lips: he that is robb'd, not wanting what is stolen, let him not know't, and he's not robb'd at all. I had been happy if the general camp, pioneers and all, had tasted her sweet body, so I had nothing known. —O! now, forever, farewell to the tranquil mind; farewell all content; farewell the plumed troops, and the big wars, that make ambition virtue; O, farewell! Farewell the neighing steed, and the shrill trump, the spirit-stirring drum, the ear-piercing fife, the royal banner, and all quality, pride, pomp, and circumstances of glorious war! And O! you mortal engines whose rude throats th' immortal Jove's dread clamors counterfeit, farewell! Othello's occupation's gone.''

In his frenzied despair he goes on (*to Iago*):

'' Villain, be sure thou prove my love a whore, be sure of it: give me the ocular proof, or by the worth of mine eternal soul, thou hadst better have been born a dog, than answer my wak'd wrath. Make me see it; or at least so prove it, that the probation bear no hinge, nor loop to hang a doubt on, or woe upon thy life!''

After this, in company with his greatly wronged Desdemona, Othello nurses his jealous wrath, and accuses his innocent child-wife in this language:

'' This hand is moist, my lady. This argues fruitfulness and liberal heart. Hot, hot and moist: this hand of yours requires a sequester from liberty, fasting and praying, much castigation, exercise devout, for here's a young and sweating devil here that commonly rebels.''

This extract contains the spirit of an idea that retains a hold upon popular credulity up to this day—namely, that a '' moist palm '' foretells '' breaking honesty.'' There is perhaps little foundation for the notion, save possibly the connection such a humidity may have with a vigorous and healthy circulation—that, and not the soft and placid hand, being the progenitor of amativeness.

To illustrate the difficulty with which we recover those who have once had the jealous thorn thrust into their side, we may give the following conversation which occurred between Desdemona and her woman:

Emilia. '' Pray heaven it *(Othello's inquietude)* may be state matters, as you think, and no conception, nor jealous toy concerning you.

Desdemona. Alas, the day! I never gave him cause.

Emilia. But jealous souls will not be answer'd so; they are not ever jealous for a cause, but jealous for they are jealous: 'tis a monster, begot upon itself, born on itself.''

Iago, *honest* Iago, then consoles his master thus:

'' Good sir, be a man; think, every bearded fellow that's but yok'd, may draw with you: there's millions now alive, that nightly

lie in those improper beds, which they dare swear peculiar: your
case is better. O! 'tis the spite of hell, the fiend's arch-mock, to
lip a wanton in a secure couch, and to suppose her chaste.''

Desdemona. `` Mine eyes do itch; doth that bode weeping?

Emilia. 'Tis neither here nor there.

Desdemona. I have heard it said so.—O! these men, these
men!—Doth thou in conscience think,—tell me, Emilia,—that there
be women who do abuse their husbands in such gross kind?

Emilia. There be some such, no question.

Desdemona. Wouldst thou do such a deed for all the world?

Emilia. Why, would not you?

Desdemona. No, by this heavenly light.

Emilia. Nor I neither by this heavenly light; I might do 't as
well i' the dark.

Desdemona. Wouldst thou do such a thing for all the world?

Emilia. The world is a large thing: 'tis a great price for a
small vice.

Desdemona. In truth, I think thou wouldst not.

Emilia. In truth I think I should, and undo 't when I had done.
Marry, I would not do such a thing for a joint-ring, nor for measures of lawn, nor for gowns, petticoats, nor caps, nor any petty
exhibition, but for the whole world, who would not make her husband a cuckold, to make him a monarch? I should venture pur-
gatory for it.

Desdemona. Beshrew me if I would do such a wrong for the
whole world. I do not think there is any such women.

Emilia. Yes, dozens; but I do think it is their husband's faults
if wives do fall. Say, that they slack their duties, and pour out
treasures into foreign laps; or break out into peevish jealousies,
throwing restraint upon us; why, we have galls, and though
we have some grace we have some revenge. Let husbands know
their wives have sense like them; they see and smell, and have
their palates both for sweet and sour, as husbands have. The ills
we do, their ills instruct us to.''

The philosophy of Emilia as to the justice of an equality in regard to the sexual relations is a common one among mankind in
general even at this time; and at first thought would appear to be
founded in an unimpeachable provision of nature—`` what is good
for the gander is also good for the goose;'' but this it is thought,

is not so, either from a moral or scientific stand-point. The sexual appetite in the male and female are quite dissimilar; nature has placed them upon different planes in this respect. While sexual indulgence becomes in some men the ruling passion of existence, in women this is scarcely ever so. While they may consummate the act with equal frequency, it is in a quiescent way — rather one of submission than active, enjoyable participation. Again, woman is only endowed with the capacity of procreating the species to a limited degree. Placing her reproductive life at thirty years, and allowing her to be able to reach the utmost confines of fecundity, she could not become the mother of more than ninety mature children—thus giving her triplets every year during her entire reproductive life—a thing unheard of, but yet possible.

This ought to represent the ratio—the sum total, of her sexual desires and her sexual liberties. On the other hand, man is endowed with procreative capabilities only limited by his existence, be that twenty-five or two hundred and twenty-five years. Limit this period say to one hundred years as the remotest possibility in man at this age of the world, and let his virile life begin at fifteen; allow one copulative act for every twenty-four hours of his life, and we find his fructifying capacity to reach over thirty-one thousand. We need not be accused of exaggeration in the statement of the belief that this number is under the limit of actuality as possessed in the reproductive energies of many men. Measuring, then, sexual licence allowable in man and woman relatively as to their reproductive capacities, we must conclude that in her domestic relations as wife and mother she has what is properly allotted to her, and when she goes outside, even to barter for monarchies and worlds, she is over-stepping the bounds set about her by the hand of nature. Physiological propriety therefore makes it repugnant for the youth to be coupled in marital relations with the aged of the other sex, while the young woman may, without transgressing any law fixed about her in her organization, become consort to one much her senior.

An analysis of the subject from another stand-point would also seem to militate against the views expressed by Emilia, because it is an incontrovertible fact, that the procreative desire and power in man is, as before stated, far beyond that of woman,—and the gratification of the sexual appetite becomes in him a *physiological necessity*—a necessity to the maintenance of the best physical and men-

tal interests of the individual, and therefore necessitating a wider
scope for its indulgence. The regulations of Mormon society fully
illustrate this principle ; whilst the teachings of common sense itself
point unerringly to the fact that nature had a purpose in placing man
in possession of this appetite—and for an end, as nothing was made
in vain. If God gave man any faculty in a measure beyond that
bestowed upon woman, the plan of creation would be a lame one
without the means also being created whereby it is to be exercised ;
and whilst monogamistic relations between the sexes may be best
suited to the advance of morals, it is far from certain that it is best
for the physical well-being of the human race. This view may not
only be applied to man, but also to woman as well ; as it is the
universal belief, not only among individuals and communities, but
also among scientists, that it is the undue sexual labor imposed
upon the wife in our modern society (monogamistic) that is rightly
chargeable with the evident decadence of married females. This
is claimed to be the fault of the husband—and rightly so, *directly;*
but *indirectly* to the erroneous constitution of the sexual relations
of modern society—scientifically considered. The burdens imposed upon the woman in this regard are a fruitful source of the
triple crime of abortion and infanticide, which is said to be so prevalent at this day. Why did this evil not prevail among the poly-
gamic wives of the patriarchs, and why do we not hear of its prev-
alence among the denizens of Utah? There must be a cause for it.
'Tis over-burdened woman that seeks to evade the responsibility
of a numerous progeny—man never. The plea, therefore, of
Emilia, that their husbands set them the example by pouring their
treasures in other laps, is not well founded ; though her argument
is built upon the assumption of Rosalind, that " that woman that
cannot make her fault her husband's accusing, let her never nurse
her child herself, for she will breed it like a fool."

Love will be the next subject to claim our notice.

Speed, in the "Two Gentlemen of Verona," enlightens his
master in regard to the symptomatology of this affection in a lucid
and forcible manner :

Valentine. " How know you that I am in love?

Speed. Marry, by these special marks.—First, you have learn'd,
like Sir Proteus, to wreath your arms like a malcontent ; to relish a
love-song, like a robin-red-breast ; to walk alone, like one that hath
the pestilence ; to sigh, like a school-boy that hath lost his A B C ;

to weep, like a young wench that hath buried her grandam; to fast, like one that takes diet; to watch, like one that fears robbing; to speak puling, like a beggar at Hallowmas. You were wont, when you laugh'd, to crow like a cock; when you walk'd, to walk like one of the lions; when you fasted, it was presently after dinner; when you look'd sadly, it was for want of money; and now you are so metamorphosed with a mistress, that, when I look on you, I can hardly think you my master.''

Falstaff, in his letter to Lady Page, tells it in this natural style: ''Ask me no reason why I love you; for though love uses reason for his physician, he admits him not for his counsellor.'' It would seem that the exalted feelings which a man possesses, and the wonderful things he imagines he could and would perform for the woman he loves, is very fitly expressed in a conversation between Troilus and Cressida:

Troilus. '' When we vow to weep seas, live in fire, eat rocks, tame tigers, think it harder for our mistress to devise imposition enough, than for us to undergo any difficulty imposed. This is the monstrosity in love, lady,—that the will is infinite and the execution confined; that the desire is boundless, and the act a slave to limit.

Cressida. They say, all lovers swear more performance than they are able, and yet reserve an ability that they never perform; vowing more than the performance of ten, and discharging less than the tenth part of one.''

Then comes the coquettish little Dolly Varden of Shakespeare,— Rosalind, in '' As You Like It,'' and shows us that she can diagnose a love fit as well as the best of them; this is the way she says an excess of the endearing passion manifests itself:

Rosalind. ''There is none of my uncle's (love) marks upon you: he taught me how to know a man in love: in which cage of rushes, I am sure, you are not prisoner.

Orlando. What are his marks?

Rosalind. A lean cheek, which you have not; a blue eye, and sunken, which you have not; an unquestionable spirit, which you have not; a beard neglected, which you have not; but I pardon you for that, for, your having no beard is a younger brother's revenue. Then, your hose should be ungarter'd, your bonnet unbanded, your sleeve unbuttoned, your shoe untied, and everything about you demonstrating a careless desolation.

Orlando. Fair youth, I would I could make you believe I love. *(It will be remembered by the reader, that Rosalind was disguised in the habiliments of a shepherd boy.)*

Rosalind. Love is merely a madness, and I tell you, deserves as well a dark house, and a whip as mad men do; and the reason why they are not so punished and cured, is that the lunacy is so ordinary that the whippers are in love too. Yet I profess curing it by counsel.

Orlando. Did you ever cure any so?

Rosalind. Yes, one; and in this manner. He was to imagine me his love, his mistress, and I set him every day to woo me: at which time would I, being but a moonish youth, grieve, be effeminate, changeable, longing, and liking; proud, fantastical, apish, shallow, inconstant, full of tears, full of smiles; for every passion something, and for no passion truly anything, as boys and women are, for most part, cattle of this color: would now like him, now loathe him; then entertain him, then forswear him; now weep for him, then spit at him; that I drave my suitor from his mad humor of love, to a loving humor of madness; and thus I cured him; and this way will I take upon me to wash your liver as clean as a sound sheep's heart, that there shall not be one spot of love in 't.

Orlando. I would not be cured, youth.''

After a long acquaintance, in which Orlando courts the shepherd boy, the young flirt tells him it is '' no use talking ''—she cannot marry him; and in his infatuation he says '' then in mine own person I die.'' She responds, '' No, faith, die by attorney. The poor world is nearly six thousand years old, and in all that time there was not any man died in his own person,—*videlicet*, in a love cause.''

In the same comedy we have another description of the '' symptoms '' which is characteristic of the tender passion. It is in the scene between Silvius and Phebe, and runs thus:

Corine. (To Rosalind and Celia.) '' If you will see a pageant truly play'd, between the pale complexion of true love and the red glow of scorn and proud disdain, go hence a little, and I shall conduct you, if you will mark it.

Rosalind. O! come, let us remove; the sight of lovers feedeth those in love.''

Who, save Shakespeare, ever noted the "*pale*" complexion of true love? Perhaps the "red glow of scorn and proud disdain" had been observed by many a languishing swain long, long before, but the other observation is only original as it is true.

In "Hamlet," A. ii., S. i., Ophelia tells of Hamlet's spasm in this characteristic language:

Ophelia. "Alas, my lord, I have been so affrighted!

Polonius. With what, in the name of God?

Ophelia. My lord, as I was sewing in my chamber, Lord Hamlet,—with his doublet all unbrac'd; no hat upon his head; his stockings foul'd, ungarter'd, and down-gyved to his ankles; pale as his shirt; his knees knocking each other, and with a look so piteous in purport, as if he had been loosed out of hell, to speak of horrors,—he comes before me.

Polonius. Mad for thy love?

Ophelia. My lord, I do not know; but, truly, I do fear it.

Polonius. What said he?

Ophelia. He took me by the wrist, and held me hard; then goes he to the length of all his arm, and with his other hand thus o'er his brow, he falls to such perusal of my face, as he would draw it. Long stay'd he so; at last, a little shaking of mine arm, and thrice his head thus waving up and down,—he rais'd a sigh so piteous and profound, that it did seem to shatter all his bulk and end his being. That done, he lets me go, and with his head over his shoulder turn'd, he seem'd to find his way without his eyes,—for out o' doors he went without their help.

Polonius. Come, go with me: I will seek the king: this is the very ecstasy of love; whose violent property foredoes itself, and leads the will to desperate undertakings, as oft as any passion under heaven, that does afflict our natures."

In this extract we again have reiterated the observation of the pale face of desperate love, and also the repetition of the assertion that Hamlet had ecstasy—a matter noted specially in the earlier portion of this chapter. In this connexion even, we find how admirably Shakespeare keeps to his ideas—the idea in this instance, that the eccentricities of Hamlet are due to perturbed intellection. Polonius evidently feared, what would be likely to happen now, were one of our "blooded" youths placed in Hamlet's predicament; viz.—draw his little revolver and murder either Ophelia herself, or her dear mother, or both, and then make an *unsuccessful* attempt upon his own valuable existence.

We have greatly improved upon the plan of putting one's head over the shoulder, and walking us sideways out of the parlor.

Poor Ophelia had acted the wiser part had she made the matter right then and there, rather than to have pined over the matter later,—and then, to end it, bury her fair form in the dark waters beneath the willows. Woman in love affairs has been an enigma from the first dawn of the creation; and if God Himself understands her, He surely guards His knowledge carefully as one of His inscrutable secrets.

Cymbeline admits the folly of his choice indirectly, in these words: "Mine eyes were not at fault, for she was beautiful; nor mine ears, that heard her flattery; nor mine heart, that thought her like her seeming: it had been vicious to have mistrusted her,"— all of which plainly tells that size, age and royalty have no protection from the machinations of designing women any more than do the young and unwary; neither have they any more discretion in judging of *her* character, though experience may be serviceable to them in all things else.

The next subject demanding notice is Lust, the darkest and most degrading passion of the human heart.

"Say unto wisdom, thou art my sister; and call understanding thy kinswoman: that they may keep thee from the strange woman, from the stranger which flattereth with her words. For at the window of my house I looked through my casement, and beheld among the simple ones, I discerned among the youths a young man void of understanding, passing through the street near her corner; and he went the way to her house, in the twilight, in the evening, in the black and dark night: and, behold, there met him a woman with the attire of a harlot, and subtile of heart. (She is loud and stubborn; her feet abide not in her house: now she is without, now in the streets, and lieth in wait at every corner.)

So she caught him, and kissed him, and with an impudent face said unto him, I have peace offerings with me; this day have I paid my vows. Therefore came I forth to meet thee, diligently to seek thy face, and I have found thee. I have decked my bed with coverings of tapestry, with carved works, with fine linen of Egypt. I have perfumed my bed with myrrh, aloes and cinnamon. Come, let us take our fill of love until the morning: let us solace ourselves with loves. For the goodman is not at home, he is gone a long journey: he hath taken a bag of money with him, and will come home at the day appointed. With her much fair speech she caused him to yield, with the flattering of her lips she forced him. He goeth after her straightway, as an ox goeth to the slaughter, or as a fool to the correction of the stocks; till a dart strike through his liver; as a bird hasteth to the snare, and knoweth not that it is for his life."

My reader, this is not from Shakespeare, but it illustrates very beautifully the condition of things wherein lust makes the chief ingredient.

Shakespeare himself, however, declares that "lust is as near to murder as flame is to smoke."

Lucio, the fantastic, in "Measure for Measure," in conversation with the duke relative to the severity with which Angelo, the deputy, was executing the laws against lewdness, unbosoms himself of his ideas in this wise:

"This ungenitur'd agent will unpeople the province with continency; sparrows must not build in his house-eaves, because they are lecherous. The duke yet would have dark deeds, darkly answer'd; he would never bring them to light: would he were return'd! Marry, this Claudio is condemned for untrussing. Fare well, good friar; yet, and I say to thee, he would mouth with a beggar, though she smelt brown-bread and garlic."

The term "untrussing" used here, perhaps simply means that he had relieved himself of his amatory excitement by the copulative act, or else to relieving himself of his "doublet and hose," preparatory to such an encounter. He *might* certainly have been the victim of a hernial protusion, requiring the use of the surgical appliance implied in the language,—and this would be made the more possible when we remember that it is asserted by good authority that one man in every five has the malady to a greater or less extent.

In "All's Well that Ends Well," Bertram, in his lascivious intrigue with Diana, the widow's daughter, pleads his case in these terms: "Be not so holy cruel: love is holy, and my integrity ne'er knew the crafts that you do charge me with. Stand no more off, but give thyself unto my sick desires, who then recover." And in

"The Winter's Tale," the old Shepherd deprecates the procreative appetite in this way: "I would there were no age between ten and twenty-three, or that youth sleep out the rest, for there is nothing in the between but getting wenches with child." The Shepherd falls into the error of placing the power of procreation at a much earlier age in the male, than the others of Shakespeare's characters do in the female. It is the universally received opinion that the human female acquires the virile power at an age one or two years earlier than the male; but it is also conceded that she loses it at a period at least many years before her male companion, if, indeed, he ever does so. It is probable, however, that it was not intended that the observation of the old Shepherd was to be regarded from a scientific stand-point, but that it was purposely made a little on the extreme the better to illustrate the idea of the lecherous tendency in the youth of the age in which it was written.

There has, perhaps, from time immemorial, been an idea prevalent among the credulous portion of mankind, that there are certain drugs, which, when swallowed, will cause the person to form an amorous desire and attachment for the person who thus administers them. This love specific is often sought from doctors and apothecaries by ignorant and unsophisticated swains, under the name of "love powders," and the delusion is often pandered to by the unprincipled, through a motive of pecuniary gain. Brabantio suspected that Othello had practiced some nefarious art of this character upon Desdemona, as will be fully shown in the following passage:

Brabantio. "O, thou foul thief! where hast thou stowed my daughter? Damn'd as thou art, thou hast enchanted her; for I'll refer me to all things of sense, if she was not in chains of magic bound, whether a maid so tender, fair and happy would ever run from guardage to the sooty bosom of such a thing as thou; thou hast practiced on her with foul charms, abused her youth with drugs or minerals that weaken motion. — I, therefore, apprehend thee for an abuser of the world, a practiser of arts inhibited, and out of warrant. My daughter! Oh, my daughter!

Senator. Dead?

Brabantio. Ay, to me; she is abused, stolen from me, and corrupted by spells and medicines bought of mountebanks.

Othello. I will a round unvarnished tale deliver of my whole course of love; what drugs, what charms, what conjuration, and what mighty magic, I won his daughter with.

Brabantio. I vouch again, that with some mixture powerful o'er the blood, or with some dram conjur'd to this effect, he wrought upon her ;'' and "If the rascal have not given me medicines to make me love him, I'll be hanged," taken from Falstaff, perhaps has its origin in the same perverted idea. There are some remedies certainly, and some special local irritations which act as provocatives to venereal appetite; but none which act in any way to produce the sentiment of affection. That not only the ignorant, but persons in the highest ranks of life, among the nations of antiquity, believed in " love-drinks " we have abundant evidence. Ovid and other early writers described these drinks as sometimes affecting the mind and causing death. Lucullus, a celebrated Roman general, was said to have died thus; and Lucretius, a noted Roman poet, was said to have written one of his most celebrated productions in intervals of delirium occasioned by a "love-drink." To such an extent was this custom of administering remedies of power through the erroneous notion of their erotic powers, that rigid legal enactments were at length resorted to in some countries for its suppression. The remedies in use for this purpose were as numerous and often of as disgusting a nature as the Chinese materia medica of to-day. The delusion held large popular sway until about the middle of the seventeenth century, at which time we find Van Helmont propagating such doctrine as this: "I know a plant, which if you rub in the hand until it becomes warm, and then take the hand of another and hold it until it also becomes warm, that person will forthwith become stimulated with love for you and continue so for several days."

Though, as before suggested, people of sound sense of to-day pay no attention to such nonsense as " love-powders," " love-drinks," or " philters," yet there are very many persons in our enlightened land who yet believe in their existence, as almost every physician can attest. Following is a verbatim copy of a letter received by the writer from a young lady, only a few days ago:

"———, Iowa, June 11, 1883.

Sir :—I take this opportunity (which is to be strictly confidential), from seeing your card in the paper, to write to you. I am the daughter of a once wealthy man, who has failed. In the days of our

riches I kept company with a well-to-do young man who now refuses
to comply with our former engagement, and if you will send me
something to give him (which I know you can), I will pay you
liberally after I have him under my control. You please send it to
me and you will never regret it, as I will see you well paid.

MINNIE MARSHALL."

The name here of course is fictitious, but the letter is genuine
and has a genuine signature. I introduce it to show that while
people may possess intelligence enough to write a letter, the composition, chirography, orthography, punctuation, etc., of which
points to the more than ordinary intelligence of the writer, yet we
find her making a very foolish request—one not at all susceptible of
fulfillment—in real earnest.

To prove that venereal desire is not love, "Timon of Athens"
may be quoted. Here is his conversation with Timandra: "Be a
whore still! they love thee not that use thee: give them diseases,
leaving with thee their lust;" then he resumes the talk in this
strain,—(I have gold) "enough to make a whore forswear her
trade, and to make whores abhorr'd; hold up, you sluts, your
aprons mountant; you are not oathable,—although I know you'll
swear,—speak your oaths, I'll trust to your conditions; be whores
still, and he whose pious breath seeks to convert you, be strong in
whore, allure him, burn him up; let your close fire predominate
his smoke, and be no turncoats." But the most trite passage,
descriptive of the morbid condition of the mind and morals which
leads to the embrace of lewdness, is found in the story of the ghost
of Hamlet's murdered father; he speaks of his brother and his
queen. "Ay, that incestuous, that adulterate beast, with witch-
craft of his wit, with traitorous gifts, (O wicked wit and gifts that
have the power to seduce!) won to his shameful lust the will of my
most seeming virtuous queen. O, Hamlet, what a falling-off was
there! From me, whose love was of that dignity, that it went hand
in hand even with the vow I made to her in marriage, and to decline
upon a wretch, whose natural gifts were poor to those of mine! But
Virtue, as it never will be moved, though Lewdness court it in the
shape of heaven, so Lust, though to a radiant angel link'd, will sate
itself in a celestial bed, and prey on garbage." This is the counterpart to occurrences which fall under our observation in the social
world, every day, and strange as it is true. This "garbage" on
which so many men and women prey is a source of greater evil to

mankind, than all the seething pools of physical corruption com-
bined; the contagion of small-pox, cholera, and the plague united,
are harmless in comparison as the zephyr of a summer's morning.

King Lear. " What hast thou been?

Edgar. A serving-man, proud in heart and mind; that curl'd
my hair, wore gloves in my cap, served the lust of my mistress'
heart, and did the act of darkness with her; swore as many oaths
as I spake words, and broke them in the sweet face of heaven;
one, that slept in the contriving of lust, and waked to do it. Wine
lov'd I deeply; dice dearly; and in woman, out-paramoured the
Turk: false of heart, light of ear, bloody of hand; hog in sloth,
fox in stealth, wolf in greediness, dog in madness, lion in prey.
Let not the creaking of shoes, nor the rustling of silks betray
your poor heart to woman: keep thy foot out of brothels, thy hand
out of plackets, and defy the foul fiend. The gods are just, and
of our pleasant vices make instruments to plague us:" and referring to his father. the same fellow says, "the dark and vicious
place where thee he got, cost him his eyes." Edmund was the
bastard son of old Gloster, "who in the lusty stealth of nature
took more composition and fierce quality, than doth within a dull,
stale, tired bed, go to the creating a whole tribe of fops, got 'tween
sleep and wake." The inference might naturally arise that old
Gloster got gonorrhœal ophthalmia in the place where he got that
bastard son, were we to give weight to the clear significance of the
language in the last line of the extract; but it is not so, as his eyes
were torn out by the cruelty of Regan and Cornwall, as is seen in
Lear, A. iii., S. vii.

Iago gives us the signs of "breaking honesty" in this way; he
is speaking to Roderigo in regard to Desdemona. "Didst thou not
see her paddle with the palm of his hand? didst not mark that?

Roderigo. Yes, that I did; But that was but courtesy.

Iago. Lechery, by this hand; an index, an obscure prologue to
the history of lust and foul thoughts. They met so near with their
lips, that their breaths embraced together." O, the murderous
liar! In "Antony and Cleopatra," it is said, "Nay, if an oily
palm be not a fruitful prognostication, I cannot scratch mine ear,"
—a quotation referred to in a preceding page of this chapter, when
relating the scene between Othello and Desdemona, and of which
enough is there written. The writer has sometimes concluded that

those frigid, pale, hard-hearted specimens of femininity with which
we sometimes meet, and who are barren,—sterile as they are cold,
prevent conception by the very perversity of their wills. Indeed,
I was in conversation with a married lady only a short time ago,
upon the subject of the sterile condition, who informed me that an
intelligent lady friend of her own had assured her that by an effort
of the will alone, she could prevent conception in her own person
with the most unerring certainty. We are all aware, no doubt, of
the very powerful effects mental conditions have over the power of
generation. Who, for example, ever knew conception to follow a
rape? Who has not noted the lack of fruitfulness on the part of the
people during great and depressing calamities?

In Cymbeline, after Posthumus supposed he had lost the wager
made with Iachimo in regard to his wife's constancy, he gives his
apostasy in the following manner:

"Is there no way for man to be, but women must be half workers? We are all bastards; and that most venerable man, which I
did call my father, was I know not where when I was stamped;
some coiner with his tools made me a counterfeit: yet my mother
seemed the Dian of that time; so doth my wife the nonpareil
of this.—O vengeance, vengeance! Me of my lawful pleasure she
restrained, and pray'd me often forbearance; did it with a pu-
dency so rosy, the sweet view on't might well have warm'd old
Saturn; that I thought her as chaste as unsunn'd snow:—O, all the
devils!—This yellow Iachimo, in an hour,—was't not?—or less,—at
first; perchance he spoke not, but, like a full-acorn'd boar, a
foaming one, cry'd 'Oh!' and mounted; found no opposition but
what he look'd for should oppose, and she should from encounter
guard. Could I find out the woman's part in me! For there's no
motion that tends to vice in man, but I affirm it is the woman's
part: be it lying, note it, the woman's; flattering, hers; deceiving,
hers; lust and rank thoughts, her, hers; revenge, hers; ambitions,
coveting, change of prides, disdain, nice longings, slanders, muta-
bility, all faults that may be nam'd; nay, that hell knows, why,
hers, in part, or all; but rather, all; for even to vice they are not
constant, but are changing still one vice but of a minute old, for
one not half so old as that."

There is one point in the foregoing extract that we may say one
word in comment upon, and that is in regard to the wish on the

part of the beauteous wife of Posthumus to abstain from copulation. This has been a source of disquietude in the marital relation
no doubt many thousands of times since the world began — not so
often perhaps from a lack of desire on the part of the wife as from
an excruciating physical suffering—produced by a cause undis-
coverable and irremediable by the parties themselves, and a mystery, many times, even to the medical profession until very lately.
I have reference to the pain given to the female during the act of
coitus by the presence of vaginismus, fissure of the osteum vagina,
vaginitis, cervicitis, metritis, oophoritis, pelvic cellulitis, vulvar
abscess, urethral caruncle, etc., with numerous other causes, which
are the source of dyspareunia, and often lead to the most intense
suffering on the part of the female during the sexual congress.
Women submit to very much more physical pain from this source
than is known of except by those whose business it is to alleviate
as much as may be the ills incident to the condition. It is quite
likely that Posthumus in the above extract had no adequate conception of the real motives which induced his wife to plead for
forbearance; as women will often bear the most excruciating torment in this way rather than give grounds (as they doubtless
imagine) of having themselves suspected of sexual imperfection.
They will freely disclose all, perhaps, to the physician. Women
are, as a general proposition, much more frank and sensible in this
way than men.

As in the case quoted, wives are sometimes made the victims of
false accusations by the ignorant and designing when laboring
under any form of these maladies, and there is none who can or
will more willingly or to her greater profit sympathize with her
than her physician, if he be a gentleman.

Mrs. Ford. "How shall I be revenged on him? I think, the
best way were to entertain him with hope, till the wicked fire of
lust have melted him in his own grease.—Did you ever hear the
like?

Mrs. Page. To thy great comfort in this mystery of ill opinions,
here's the twin brother of thy letter. But, let thine inherit first;
for, I protest, mine never shall; I will find you twenty lascivious
turtles, ere one chaste man." This may be found in "Merry Wives
of Windsor," whilst the term "when my lust has dined," may be
found as the expression of the brutal Cloten in "Cymbeline." All
of which is "respectfully submitted."

Shakespeare makes Hotspur describe the physiognomic expression of *anger* thus: "Then his cheek looked pale, and on my face he turned an eye of death;" whilst to the picture is added, "he hangs the lip at something," in "Troilus and Cressida," and "why gnaw you so your nether lip," in "Othello." The first and last of these tell of intense anger, and a state of mind portentous of danger to he who provokes it; whilst the other tells of a moody disposition, which may be appeased by conciliation.

In moderate anger the color of the cheeks is somewhat hightened and the eyes brighten; while in rage, which is but a greater degree of anger, the face may become deadly pale, the voice become husky and articulation imperfect, while the body at the same time may tremble from head to foot. This tremulousness is not however the result of fear or cowardice.

Of *envy* he calls it "lean-faced," and in an another place he says "no black envy shall make my grave," while yet in another place he uses the line " above pale envy's threatening reach,"—in all of which is shown the acuteness of his observation or else his wonderful intuition.

CHAPTER III.

NEUROLOGY.

Epilepsy—Falling Sickness—"Rub him about the temples"—Playing "wolf"—The prototype of Othello—"What, did Cæsar swoon?"—The epileptic zone—The trade-mark and "plug" hat—Mistaken diagnosis—This apoplexy will certain be his end—Gad's Hill and Sir John—I talk not of his majesty—It is a kind of *deafness*—Croups—Drowning as a consequence of popular delusion—The mad-stone and its votaries—Not known by medical men—The treatment as good as any—"John Jones, of Albany"—Odontology—Set up the bloody flag against all patience—The nurse's head-ache—"Let me but bind it hard"—Varieties of the malady—Sciatica—Syphilis as a complication—Gout—Plays the rogue with my great toe—Anorexia—Paralysis—"My firm nerves shall never tremble."

Under the heading of this chapter it is proposed to group everything found in Shakespeare pertaining to the nervous system, whether physiological or pathological in its nature. Since looking over our notes upon the subject, we find only sufficient matter to make a very brief article;—and such as it is, we present below:

We have epilepsy spoken of twice,—directly in the case of Othello; and, under the name of "falling sickness" in the case of Cæsar, who fell down during his harangue to the Roman populace.

Othello was greatly moved at the statements of Iago as to the faithlessness of Desdemona. The occurrence is thus stated:—

Iago. "My lord is fallen into an epilepsy: this is his second fit; he had one yesterday.

Cassio. Rub him about the temples.

Iago. No, forbear. The lethargy must have his quiet course, if not he foams at mouth; and by and by, break out to savage madness. Look, he stirs: do you withdraw yourself a little while; he will recover straight."

We know that any emotional disturbance, if great, is often an excitant in the production of epileptiform maladies;—exciting

attacks not only in those who have once had them, but also being
in themselves sufficient to set up the morbid phenomena in those
previously to all appearances in good health: thus,—I knew a boy
who had always been hearty, but got epilepsy of the most confirmed type from fright occasioned by a waggish old man playing
"wolf" on him; and a man, the prototype of Othello, who suddenly fell down in an epileptic convulsion through sympathy for
his wife, who was in the throes of child-birth, under my care; and
only yesterday, whilst listening to the recitals of a father in regard
to an epileptic child, he assured me that the least mental or physical
excitement proved of the greatest danger to him. It has been
witnessed in but the above single instance by the writer in the
negro race.

In "Julius Cæsar" we find a paragraph which reads in this way:

Cassius. "But, soft, I pray you; what! did Cæsar swoon?

Casca. He fell down in the market-place, and foamed at the
mouth, and was speechless.

Brutus. 'Tis very like he had the 'falling sickness;' what said
he when he came unto himself?

Casca. Before he fell down, when he perceiv'd the common herd
was glad he refused the crown, he pluck'd me ope his doublet, and
offered them his throat to cut;—and so he fell down."

This was a genuine epileptic seizure no doubt, for Cæsar speedily
recovered, and went about his apology in these words: and if he
had "done or said anything amiss, he desired their worships to
think it was his infirmity."

This Cæsar was a schemer of the first water, and he *could* well
have worked upon the sympathies of his audience through the medium of a bit of Castile soap, as do some of our lawyers with
capsicum. To be ruler of an empire is only to be versed in trivial
chicanery. The malady was, however, not assumed in this instance.

These pictures of epilepsy, though terse, are yet very well
drawn,—even a medical pen well skilled in portraiture could not do
it better in the same number of words.

The frequent occurrence of the seizures of epilepsy had been
well marked by Shakspeare. "He had one yesterday" is conclusive evidence that the phenomena belonging to the malady had
impressed his observation so as to enable him to grasp and describe

its salient features; and again, behold the prophetic declaration as to the location of the point where the disease had its *origin* (if it may be so termed): "*Rub him about the temples.*" Prophetically upon the very site of the epileptic zone of the present day, though unfortunately the rubbing at that point might be the means of producing rather than of removing the malady.

The term "falling sickness" is yet vernacular among the common people, and appears to have been plebian even in the days of Cæsar. It is so called of course from the fact of persons thus afflicted falling suddenly, as if shot or struck down; and in the knowledge of this fact a charlatan and neighbor of my own has fabricated a trade-mark—a man falling backwards, hands outstretched, plug-hat preceding him in his descent, representing indeed very forcibly an *idea*. Out of this the author (if such he really is) has made a fortune, and *spent it also.*

In "King Lear," A. ii., S. ii., we also find the term "epileptic visaged," as applied by Kent to one of the attendants of the king's daughters, thus showing that the peculiar physiognomic expression common to persons thus afflicted did not escape the observation of the acute eye of Shakespeare. I am of the opinion that this dull and apathetic expression of the countenance is now much more marked in the epileptic than formerly, and is due, no doubt, mainly to the excessive use of the bromides.

In Henry IV., A. iv., S. iv., there is a description of the malady of which the king was suffering, wherein the diagnosis of apoplexy was made:

King. "I should rejoice now at this happy news, and now my sight fails, and my brain is giddy.—O me, come near me; now I am much ill. *(He falls back.)*

Prince Humphrey. Comfort, your majesty!

Clarence. O my royal father!

Westmoreland. My sovereign lord, cheer up yourself: look up!

Warwick. Be patient, princes: you do know these fits are with his royal highness very ordinary. Stand from him, give him air. He'll straight be well.

Clarence. No, no; he cannot long hold out these pangs. Th' incessant care and labor of his mind hath wrought the mure, that should confine it in, so thin that life looks through and will break out."

Prince Humphrey and Clarence are talking to themselves in regard to their father's condition, when Warwick thus addresses them :

"Speak lower, princes, for the king recovers.

Prince Humphrey. This apoplexy will, certain, be his end.

King. I pray you, take me up, and bear me hence into some other chamber: softly, pray. *(His attendants do as desired.)* Let there be no noise made, my gentle friends ; unless some dull and favorable hand will whisper music to my weary spirit.

Warwick. Call for the music in the other room.

King. Set me the crown upon my pillow here.

Clarence. His eye is hollow,—and he changes much.

Warwick. Less noise, less noise!

Enter Prince Henry. How doth the king?

Prince Humphrey. Exceeding ill.

Warwick. Not so much noise, my lords.—Sweet princes, speak low, the king, your father, is disposed to sleep."

It seems probable from a close scrutiny of the details of this case, that there was a mistake in the diagnosis ; the history of its symptomatology would go as near to making it one of epilepsy perhaps as of apoplexy ;—the frequency of the occurrence of his "spells," his rapid recovery, the "wearied spirit," his subsequent falling into slumber, his speedy recovery of consciousness, etc., etc., all point to that fact, and all contradict the notion of apoplexy. And the idea is strengthened as to the error, at the conclusion of his life, where he is so clearly conscious as to say, "More would I, but my lungs are wasted so, that strength of speech is utterly denied me." In cases of apoplexy of such severity as to threaten speedy death the coma is too profound to admit of conscious utterances like these, and he probably had no pulmonary lesion, and was only suffering from simple prostration incident to the nervous malady.

After the ludicrous robbery at Gadshill, in which Falstaff and "Hal" figured so noticeably, "Sir John" was brought to account for it ; the following "war of words" ensued upon the occasion between the knight and Chief-Justice :

Falstaff. "An't please your lordship, I hear his majesty is returned with some discomfort from Wales.

Chief-Justice. I talk not of his majesty.—You would not come when I sent for you.

Falstaff. And I hear, moreover, his highness is fallen into this same whoreson apoplexy.

Chief-Justice. Well, heaven mend him. I pray you, let me speak with you.

Falstaff. This apoplexy is, as I take it, a kind of lethargy, an't please your lordship; a kind o' sleeping in the blood, a whoreson tingling.

Chief-Justice. What tell you me of it? be it as it is.

Falstaff. It had its original from much grief; from study, and perturbation of the brain; I have read the cause of its effects in Galen: it is a kind of deafness.

Chief-Justice. I think you are fallen into the disease, for you hear not what I say to you.

Falstaff. Very well, my lord, very well; rather, an't please you, it is the disease of not listening, the malady that I am troubled withal."

Shakespeare has here displayed the commendable and rare faculty of not contradicting himself—calling it in the mouth of Falstaff apoplexy, also, as the malady of which Henry the Fourth was the victim. It will be noted by the reader that Hal, the companion of Sir John Falstaff, was the successor of his father as ruler of Britain and ascended the throne as Henry the Fifth. There is not more laughable material found in the writings of any writer in any language than is found in Shakespeare in the relations between Hal and Sir John.

That very unsatisfactory term, "cramp," is used three times in "The Tempest"—each time, save one, as a punishment to the sour-visaged nondescript, Calaban; in the other, Stephano complains of being not himself, but a "cramp," at the conclusion of his debauch, after the shipwreck. In "As You Like It," Rosalind, in discoursing on the improbabilities of a man's dying in a love-cause, relates a historic reminiscence which illustrates well an idea yet largely prevalent among mankind, namely—that "cramp" is a very fruitful source of danger to those who go into deep water; she says, "Leander, he would have lived many a fair year, though Hero had turned nun, if it had not been for a hot midsummer night; for, good youth, he went but forth to wash himself in the Hellespont, and being taken with the cramp, was drowned." Why the notion prevails so generally, that "cramp" is at the bottom of all these accidents, has long been a mystery to me ; I have never yet seen a person who had been attacked thus whilst in water, nor have I conversed with a person who has. Why do we not see persons who get cramp in shallow water, in a shower-bath, etc., and who come out to tell the story? If all the cases we read of in the public prints are really the result of a mishap of that nature, then "aquatic cramp" is as surely fatal as fully established rabies. It will be seen, therefore, that though danger from this source has age to lend plausibility and dignity to its pretensions,—yet it really deserves a place side by side with the wide-spread mad-stone delusions· It is the proper province of medical men on all occasions to disabuse the public mind of these absurdities, because life is often sacrificed at the shrine of these stupid errors. This is particularly so with the substance which the vulgar know as a mad-stone,—valuable time being wasted in its application which ought to be employed in calling a surgeon. It is singular in the extreme to note the hold this notion has upon the public mind ; and that too upon those whose native intellect ought to be a guarantee of better things ;—read the following from a leading New York Journal, July 3d, 18—. "With this hot weather, and mad dogs, comes the usual complement of wonderful stories of extraordinary cures of hydrophobia by means of mad-stones. In many parts of the country, especially in the West and South, the majority of the people have implicit confidence in the efficacy of these stones in counteracting the effects of wounds inflicted by rabid animals. In some families, stones of this character have been possessed for a great number of years, and have acquired a wide-spread local celebrity. Every summer numerous accounts are published of cures wrought by mad-stones, and these generally give the names of the persons cured, with other circumstances which go to show that the persons printing the accounts have entire faith in the authenticity of the cases which they chronicle. One of the most celebrated of these stones is owned by a Mrs. Chastria, living near Hodgenville, Kentucky. She calls it a Chinese stone. It is said that when applied to a person bitten by a mad dog, or poisonous snake, this stone adheres so firmly that it cannot be drawn off without considerable effort, until it has absorbed all the poison from the wound. This stone is reported to have performed many cures, the last being that of a Miss Prather, to whom it was applied while she was in a state of raging madness. It immediately stuck fast, where it remained four days, when it dropped off, and the patient recovered. Stories of a like nature are told of mad-stones in various parts of the country."

Now, though the foregoing quotation is from one of the leading New York weeklies, not one word is said by the writer to tell us that he too is not a believer in this mad-stone delusion. If there really existed a remedy so potent for good in this terrible malady, why should not a portion of it, at least, be found in the hands of the medical profession? How happens it that articles of such incalculable value should *always* happen to be the property of some dilapidated old crone in some immensely obscure corner of the earth? Who ever met a regular physician who possessed a mad-stone, or had beheld wonders performed by them? It is time *intelligent* people, at least, should realize the fact that there is no such a thing in existence as the thing reputed a mad-stone. No doubt but there are many things called such, as for instance a bit of brick-bat, a lump of hardened clay, chalk, or a bit of calcined bone, etc.,— one as good as the other so long as the delusion is maintained. After all, however, as disgusting as the popular ignorance is in the minds of reflecting persons,—especially so to professional men, it may have a share of bliss in it,—because when we reflect that the mind of him who may be bitten by a dog,—mad, or one supposed to be mad, may by the application of one of these substances be rendered satisfied as to his future security—that certainly is a boon to the nineteen that may be bitten by real rabid animals but who never have symptoms of rabies, whilst the twentieth one, who has it applied, dies;—just the termination of these cases as when left entirely to nature. Viewing it then in this way, we may not consider it such bad treatment after all, as neither medicine nor surgery could make a better exhibit in a malady so dreadful. To be sure surgical attention, timely applied, might have saved the one fatal case; but considering the uncertainties of whether even the most scientific assistance has ever obviated death in rabies, it is questionable whether intense expectancy and place-bos (as the mad-stone) in the conduct of these cases is not, in the present state of our knowledge, about as good a course as any; though one can hardly forbear wishing to be rid of the ignorance which persists in the belief in their reality—more so when it is of that presumptuous kind which prompted the fellow to leave this inscription on my office slate, a short time ago: "Doctor, don't you want to buy a mad-stone? JOHN JONES, Albany, Mo."

I beg the reader's pardon for this long irrelevancy, but the subject forced itself upon me in this connection, and it was thought the space might not be filled with more useful matter. Odontalgia is spoken of under the common term "toothache" twice or more in "Much Ado About Nothing,"—once as a "raging tooth," in A. iii., S. iii., Othello,—and in "Cymbeline" is repeated the old adage that "he that sleeps feels not the toothache." And that popular complaint, palpitation, which often causes so great an alarm and so little harm, among the uninform'd, is noticed as a coincidence of jealousy in the case of Leontes. He is so particular in regard to the friendship between his queen and friend, that he thinks that to "mingle friendships far is to mingle bloods," and he gets *tremor cordis* accordingly; his heart danced, but "not for joy—not joy." He is not the only man, poor soul, whose heart has been made to "palpitate" by the actions of a flirt. Of colic, we find the following in Coriolanus; it is a conversation between Menenius and Brutus,—the latter being one of the "tribunes of the people :"

Brutus. "Come, sir, come ; we know you well enough.

Menenius. You know neither me, yourselves, nor anything. When you are hearing a matter between party and party, if you chance to be pinched with the colic, you make faces like mummers, set up the bloody flag against all patience, and in roaring for a chamber-pot dismiss the controversy."

This was said to illustrate the want of stability in a Roman nobleman,—if such a character as a nobleman could exist in a republic, which I believe Rome was at that time ; and shows the contempt with which they view'd physical sufferings.

In regard to cephalalgia, the good old nurse of Juliet gives us this : "What a head have I ; lord, how it aches : it beats as it would fall in twenty pieces. My back ! o' t' other side.—O, my back, my back ! Beshrew your heart for sending me about to catch my death."

Othello tells Desdemona, "I have a pain upon my forehead here.

Desdemona. Faith, that's with watching ; 'twill away again : let me but bind it hard, within this hour it will be well." Desdemona was domestic. The fashion of compressing the head to relieve pain in the different regions of it has perhaps always been practiced. This is not to be wondered at when we remember how few remedies there are in the way of medicine even in our advanced age, that will afford it relief—some of its forms at least. Indeed the true pathology of headaches is difficult to make out in most cases; therefore our therapeutics have had little basis except empiricism until lately, when the ophthalmoscope has done something to elucidate the uncertainty.

Headaches commonly depend upon some internal cause—some *inter-cranial cause*, though not always. The pain may be continual, or it may be occasional or periodic; it may be aggravated or ameliorated according to the position of the body. This pertains only to the complaint in some of its forms. Headache may occupy one particular region, or it may include the whole of the head. The latter is rare. The pain may have any one of the characteristics, as acute, throbbing, dull, etc., and may have particular hours or days for its recurrence. These varied characteristics of the pain have certain significance attached to them, from the fact of their being indices to the causation of the malady. Thus, the periodic variety pointing nearly always to a sympathetic or constitutional origin, while the continuous or persistent form more commonly has as its etiological factor some morbid process connected directly with the head—(brain, membranes, etc.)

Some constitutional diseases manifest themselves particularly in the way of localizing their ravages upon the organs of mentation, and thus producing pain in the part. Of these, tubercle and syphilis are examples. The pain in these, particularly the last, may have something of a periodicity attached to it, but not the regularity which marks those cases of brow ague, etc., which have a malarial origin.

It would commonly be as well in our divisions as to the pathological status of headaches to say that they are always accompanied by, and depend largely for their characteristic symptoms upon, one of only two pathological conditions—anemia or hyperemia. Of course, in determining to which of these varieties a given case belongs we have to weigh well the accompanying conditions,—and here the ophthalmoscope will always be found a valuable aid in making the diagnosis. Unfortunately, its use is now restricted to the hands almost exclusively of the specialist; but it will in time find a broader field in general practice.

Of the medicines which do most for headaches, morphine is certainly most indispensable in the more usual forms. Arsenic, in the form of Fowler's solution, as a remedy in the yet more persistent cases, while iodide of potassium is indispensable to the treatment of many forms,—of course more so in the specific varieties, as above named.

Othello's headache was, it seems, of a transitory character, and would have yielded to a dose of morphine.

In "Measure for Measure," and also in "Timon of Athens," sciatica is spoken of;—in the latter the language is as follows: "Plagues, incident to men, your potent and infectious fevers heap on Athens! thou cold sciatica, cripple our senators, that their limbs may halt as lamely as their manners." Sciatica, in the drama first referred to, was located in the "hip" of course, and was in the person of a character said to be also syphilitic,—a complexity in these cases quite common now, and common enough then it seems to fall under the non-medical notice of Shakespeare.

Titania, in "A Midsummer Night's Dream," thus muses: "The moon, the governess of floods, pale in her anger, washes all the air, that rheumatic diseases do abound," whilst the term "rheumatic" is used twice to illustrate the little querulous bouts between Falstaff and his "Doll." Venus even allows that she is neither "rheumatic" nor "cold" in her efforts to arouse her bashful boy Adonis to the "sticking point."

Now for the gout:

"A Midsummer Night's Dream." "Friend has thou none; for thine own bowels, which do call thee sire, the mere effusion of thy proper loins, do curse the gout," whilst the little vixen, Rosalind, who had a very old head on a very pretty body doubtless, talks thus:

Orlando. "Who ambles time withal?

Rosalind. With a priest that lacks Latin, and a rich man that hath not the gout: for the one sleeps easily because he cannot study, and the other lives merrily because he feels no pain."

Falstaff even knows a "thing or two" about it also:

Falstaff. "I can get no remedy against this consumption of the purse: borrowing only lingers and lingers it out, but the desire is incurable; go bear this letter to my lord of Lancaster; this to the prince; this to the earl of Westmoreland; and this to old Mistress Ursula, whom I have weekly sworn to marry since I perceived the first white hair on my chin. About it: you know where to find me. *(Exit Page.)* A pox of this gout! or, a gout of this pox! for the one or the other, plays the rogue with my great toe! 'Tis no matter, if I do halt; I have the wars for my color, and my pension shall seem the more reasonable."

It seems probable that a "gout of this pock" was much the more reasonable exclamation for Sir John to make, as the easy virtue of Mrs. Tear-sheet, and others perhaps of the knight's female friends, rendered its acquirement much easier than that of the other. It certainly is not a common point—the "great toe," in which to locate a local syphilitic lesion; but yet, it presents itself under such varied forms, that we need not be at a loss to find it cropping out at any place in the person of such an old sinner as he.

The term "gouty" is used incidentally in "Timon of Athens," and in "Cymbeline," thus:

Scene: a Prison.

Jailer. "You shall not now be stolen; you have locks upon you, so graze as you find pasture.

2d Jailer. Ay, or stomachs.

Posthumus. (In Jail.) Most welcome, bondage, for thou art a way, I think, to liberty. Yet am I better than one that's sick o' the gout; since he had rather groan so in perpetuity, than be cured by the sure physician, death, who is the key t' unbar these locks." ·This extract shadows the obstinate nature of gout,—points to the trouble of both physician and patient, and is altogether a good simile.

Anorexia, which, like thirst, may be classed among the nervous phenomena, is mentioned definitely but once in Shakspeare:

"To her, my lord, was I betroth'd ere I saw Hermia! but, like in sickness, I did loath this food; but as in health, came to my natural taste."—"A Midsummer Night's Dream," A. iv., S. i.

Paralysis is spoken of three times; once by the duke of York in "Richard the Second," who would have chastis'd Bolingbroke had his arm not been "prisoner to the palsy;" and again Lord Say, when brought before Jack Cade, when accused of trembling, denied it, saying "the palsy and not fear provoketh me." It is also noted in "Troilus and Cressida," where Ulysses describes the jests of Patroclus—the latter personifying old Nestor, for the merriment of Achilles.

In the "Tempest" we find, "the nerves are in their infancy again, and have no vigor in them," having reference merely to a state of debility; and in "Macbeth" we have, "Take any shape but that, and my firm nerves shall never tremble."

CHAPTER IV.

PHARMACOLOGIA.

Sleepy Drinks—Foster nurse of Nature—A liberal offer—A doctor's knowledge appreciated—What?—The perfumed dandy—Unbearable nonsense—What's in't?—Mandragora—Drowsy syrups—Superstition—Toxicology—The trusty pistol—Fashions of suicide—Difficulty of purchase—Poisoned by a monk—This tyrant fever—Swinstead abbey—Strange fantasies—North winds —A compound—Monks as physicians—Cardinal Beaufort—Liebreich anticipated—Republished—Was it chloral?—Comparison of conditions—Carefully noted—Meagre were his looks—What, ho!—Famine is in thy cheek—Death's pale flag—Thus with a kiss—A nest of Death—A slight discrepancy—Oxalic acid—Discovery repeats itself—The insane root—Drugging the posset—"Hashish"—The unction of a mountebank—Rabies canina—Curara—From what derived?—A failure apprehended—Trap with double triggers—Fencing match—An unlooked for termination—A jealous sister—Kills and pains not—Immortal longings—Easy ways to die—Zest to a tragedy—A specific—Alconcito—A royal student—Soliloquy—Most likely I did—Moreton preceded.

In arranging a chapter on pharmacology, it is the design to divide it into two portions:—the first to include all articles of the materia medica proper,—the other to be devoted to toxicology. The first is brief, for the simple reason that the material for its elaboration is limited; the material for the latter, being more voluminous, will extend the chapter to some length.

Narcotic remedies seem to have had an extended use in past ages, as we have them mentioned frequently in older writers, and pretty frequently in Shakespeare. Archidamus in the "Winter's Tale" says: "I don't know what to say.—We will give you sleepy drinks, that your senses, unintelligent of our insufficience, may though they cannot praise us, as little accuse us."

This "sleepy drink" probably referred to some form of alcoholic intoxicant, as the parties to the conversation belong to the revelers of a royal court.

The "sleeping potion" of Friar Laurence will be noticed more fully hereafter.

In regard to treating Lear for his disordered intellect, we find the following in A. iv. of that play:

Cordelia. "Alack! 'tis he: why, he was met even now, as mad as the vex'd sea: singing aloud; crown'd with rank fumiter and furrow weeds, with hoar-docks, hemlock, nettles, cuckoo-flowers, darnel, and all the idle weeds that grow. A century send forth; search every acre in the high-grown field, and bring him to our eye. *(Exit an officer.)* What can man's wisdom (do) in the restoring his bereaved sense? He that helps him, take all my outerward worth.

Doctor. There is medicines, madam: Our foster-nurse of nature is repose, the which he lacks; that to provoke in him are many simples operative, whose power will close the eye of anguish.

Cordelia. All bless'd secrets, all you unpublish'd virtues of the earth, spring with my tears! be aidant and remediate, in the good man's distress."

Then occurs a time when they are all absorbed in business, but Cordelia has not forgotten old Lear, who, it appears, she had left in the care of the doctor, for she makes inquiry, "how does the king? doctor.

Doctor. Madam, (he) sleeps still.

Cordelia. O, you kind gods, cure this great breach in his abused nature!

Doctor. So please your majesty that we may wake the king? he hath slept long.

Cordelia. Be govern'd by your knowledge, and proceed i' the sway of your own will. Is he array'd?

Doctor. Ay, madam; in the heaviness of his sleep, we put fresh garments on him.

Kent. Good madam, be by when we do awake him; I doubt not of his temperance.

Cordelia. Very well. *(Music.)*

Doctor. Please you, draw near.—Louder the music there.

Cordelia. He wakes, speak to him.

Doctor. Madam, do you, 'tis fittest.

Cordelia. How does my royal lord? How fares your majesty? Sir, do you know me?

Lear. You are a spirit, I know. Where did you die?

Cordelia. Still, still, far wide.

Doctor. He's scarce awake. Let him alone awhile.

Lear. Where have I been? Where am I? I am a very foolish, fond old man, four-score and upwards, not one hour more nor less, and to deal plainly, I fear I am not in my perfect mind."

Cordelia becomes pathetic, as we may very well imagine, and the kind physician requests her to "be comfortable, madam ; the great rage, you see, is cur'd in him ; and yet it is dangerous to make him even o'er the time he has lost. Desire him to go in ; trouble him no more till further settling."

Now, good my professional reader, what "simple" used the doctor wherewith he "closed the eye of anguish" in the foregoing case? Was it opium, chloral hydrate, bromide of potassium?— What? Most likely some vegetable narcotic, as such remedies as "hemlock" and other powerful agents of that class were much in vogue at that day. The doctor clearly presented the very best plan of treatment—enunciating *the* principle upon which the successful conduct of all such cases depends, namely, the "foster-nurse of nature—*repose.*" I doubt much, however, whether the gentle Cordelia did not forget the very fair promise in regard to the bestowal of her "outward worth," as my personal experience teaches me to regard with mistrust those who make loud pretensions of how handsomely we are to be paid—it usually culminating in the doctor failing of any fee at all, and with very little gratitude for his services. Regarding the pleasant effects of music on the weary mind and spirits, notice is taken of it in " The Tempest," thus :—"A solemn air, and the best comforter to an unsettled fancy, cure thy brains ;" and in the death-bed scene of Henry the Fourth, where he says— "let there be no noise made, my friends ; unless some dull and favorable hand will whisper music to my weary spirit." In Bucknill's " Mad Folk of Shakespeare " is to be found a long chapter on the beneficial effects of music in the treatment of the insane, in both ancient and modern times.

Hotspur's contempt for the perfumed dandy who asserted that "parmaceti for an inward bruise" was " the sovereign'st thing on earth," was commendable ; though it is exceedingly distasteful, we often are compelled to sit by in silence, and hear some vulgar ignoramus expatiate upon the value of this or that or the other procedure in medicine or surgery—ignoring our presence, and talking

with the face as of one with authority.   What doctor is there who
has not had to learn, over, many times, from the lips of some foolish
old woman, matters in his profession which, if not absurd or ridiculous, are at most puerile;—swallowing them with the gravity of one
who is listening to his sentence to the gallows?   What *unbearable*
nonsense do we tolerate and sometimes tacitly assent to for the
privilege of being physicians?   I set it down in print—in bold and
unmistakable language, that the doctor occupies the most unenvi-
able position of any member of modern society.

   "My noble mistress, here's a box; I had it from the queen:
what's in 't is precious; if you are sick at sea, or stomach-qualm'd
at land, a dram of this will drive away distemper."   " Cymbeline,"
A. iii., S. v.

   The " what's in 't " must have been bromide of potassium, good
wine, or else " effervescing nitrate of cereum," as these are said to
be the best remedial measures other than " position," if it is remembered aright.   Sea-sickness will likely always remain, in defiance of
the combat waged with it by therapeutics.

   The soliloquy of Juliet, as to how she should feel in the event of
her waking too soon and finding herself among the dead of "all
the Capulets," evokes this language:

   " Alack, alack! is it not like that I, so early waking,—what with
loathsome smells, and shrieks like mandrakes torn out of the earth,
that living mortals hearing them, run mad?"

   In " Antony and Cleopatra," we find, " give me to drink mandragora, that I might sleep out this great gap of time," in the language of Egypt's voluptuous queen.   The first only needs notice from
the fact of the superstition concerning it by the people of the middle
ages,—the latter only for that of its early employment as a
remedy,—especially for its soporific qualities, which were somewhat analagous to the poppy it is supposed.

   " Not poppy, nor mandragora, nor all the dreamy syrups of the
world, shall ever medicine thee to that sweet sleep, which thou
ow'dst yesterday," says the villain Iago, when he noted the tor-
tured Othello approaching him.

   Mandragora is not used as a medicine to any considerable extent
at the present day.   It is indigenous to European countries, and
not officinal in the United States.   In illustration of the super-
stitious notions connected with the may-apple, the duke of Suffolk,
in execrating the king for banishing him, uses this term,—" would

curses kill as doth the mandrake's groan "—an idea derived from a
mythological source, and founded on the notion that the may-apple
sprang from the remains of a dead criminal, and that when it was
drawn from the earth for the use of man, something must die. To
accomplish the extraction of the root with the least detriment to
animal existence, it was customary to loosen the soil about its roots,
tie a worthless dog to it and then run away, stopping the ears to
avoid hearing the shriek. The dog surely died.

"The dog surely died."

The "poultice" as a remedy for "aching bones" is suggested
by "Nurse" in "Romeo and Juliet."

We come now to the more voluminous, and we hope the more interesting, portion of this chapter—Part Second—or that which treats
more especially of the toxic materials used in the writings of
Shakespeare.

It may well be imagined that in a work abounding in tragedies,
and one in which women and sentiment played so conspicuous a
part, that poisons would occupy a conspicuous place in the catalogue of means whereby to put a quietus to a weary existence,—
and such is the fact. It is more common now, for those who reach
a point from which they view life as a failure, to resort to means
more in keeping with the spirit of the age; therefore they usually
resort to that ever handy and speedy agent, a trusty pistol; this
however is more strikingly true of suicide in *America*, whilst the
poisons are yet often resorted to in Europe, and among other
civilized nations. Under the heading "The Fashions of Suicide,"

Dr. Lankester, in his report of inquests for 1868–69 (noted in *Med. Press and Circular*), gives some interesting facts in regard to the subject. He says considerable change has taken place in the selection of poisons for suicidal purposes. That most frequently used during late years being *cyanide of potassium*; it is purchased without difficulty, and its action is most deadly. The next agent in most frequent use is *oxalic acid*, whilst the use of opium, hydrocyanic acid, etc., is on the decline, owing perhaps to the greater difficulty encountered in procuring them by purchase. The reason the other substances are more easily procured is that they are largely used in the arts, and are in the hands of numberless persons everywhere.

Although reference is made to poison in "The Tempest," A. iii., S. ii., and in one place again reference made to giving it so that it might "work a great time after," and spoken of also in "The Winter's Tale," A. i., S. i., and "rats'-bane" as a poison two or three times, there is nothing worthy of note said of it until in "King John," A. v., S. vi., where the following language occurs:

Herbert. (The king's chamberlain). "The king, I fear, is poisoned by a monk: I left him almost speechless, and brake out to acquaint you with this evil, that you might the better arm you to this sudden time, than if you had at leisure known of this.

Bastard. How did he take it? who did taste to him?

Herbert. A monk, I tell you; a resolved villain, whose bowels suddenly burst out: the king yet speaks, and, peradventure, may recover."

In this quotation Shakespeare does not appear to have kept close to the symptomatology, for the king had been sick a time before this poisoning should have happened. In Scene iii., whilst on the field of battle, the king was made to exclaim,—"Ah, me! this tyrant fever burns me up, and will not let me welcome this good news. Set on towards Swinstead; to my litter straight; weakness possesseth me, and I am faint." If the monk had been using treachery toward the king, then he certainly had been using "poison to work a great time after," because even prior to the facts last stated as to the condition of King John on the battle-field, the complaint is made by him,—"this fever that hath troubled me so long, lies heavy on me: O! my heart is sick."

The Bastard seemed fully persuaded of the truth of the report that the king was poisoned, as he hastily ordered the messenger,—"Away, before: conduct me to the king; I doubt, he will be dead ere I come." After reaching Swinstead Abbey the oft quoted soliloquy of Prince Henry occurred: "It is too late: the life of all his blood is touch'd corruptibly; and his pure brain (which some suppose the soul's frail dwelling-house), doth by the idle comment that it makes, foretell the ending of mortality."

Pembroke. "His highness yet doth speak; and holds belief that being brought into the open air it would allay the burning quality of that fell poison which assaileth him.

Prince Henry. Let him be brought into the orchard here.—Doth he still rage?

Pembroke. He is more patient than when you left him: even now he sung.

Prince Henry. O! vanity of sickness! fierce extremes in their continuance will not feel themselves. Death, having prey'd upon the outward parts, leaves them unvisited; and his siege is now against the mind, the which, he pricks and wounds with many legions of strange fantasies, which, in their throng and press to that last hold, confound themselves. 'Tis strange that death should sing."

The king is then brought to the open air, and thus rejoices: "Ah, marry, now my soul hath elbow-room, it would not out at windows, nor at doors. There is so hot a summer in my bosom, that all my bowels crumble up to dust: I am a scribbled form, drawn with a pen upon a parchment,—and against this fire I shrink up.

Prince Henry. How fares your majesty?

King John. Poison'd,—ill fare;—dead, forsook, cast-off; and none of you will bid the winter come, nor let (my kingdom's) rivers take their course through my burn'd bosom; nor entreat the north winds kiss my parched lips, and comfort me with cold. The poison is as a fiend, confin'd to tyrannize on unreprievable condemned blood."

The question for solution, when we analyze the foregoing extract, presents two points of interest: first, was the king poisoned at all? and, second, if he was poisoned, what substance had been used for that purpose?

In regard to the first of these propositions, it is pretty clearly apparent, to our mind, that he was not poisoned at all by the hand of a monk, or any one else—in fact was not poisoned at all in the light in which himself and attendants viewed the matter. This we shall attempt to establish clearly in a subsequent portion of this work.

As to the second proposition, there is more difficulty; he had not symptoms confined alone to the action of one virulent poison, but *some* common to several; therefore if he was poisoned, he had certainly been dosed with a compound. These too had been of both vegetable and mineral origin, if we may judge from the symptomatology. In the quotations, — "Doth he still rage?" and "the idle comment that it makes," with "many legions of strong fantasies," etc., all show a mind disordered, either from disease or poison. If from the latter, then it was from a narcotic or cerebrospinal poison, the class of which are usually of vegetable origin— acting *secondarily* if at all, upon the visceral structures; whilst those "fell poisons" which have "burning qualities" about them and produce "burn'd bosoms" and "parched lips," necessitating entreaties for flowing rivers of water and north winds, are usually of the corrosive mineral kinds — producing intense inflammatory action in the tissues with which they come in contact, but seldom acting upon the brain sufficiently to disturb the intellectual faculties. If in this case "poison" had contained "physic," it was an unfortunate circumstance; the monks often practiced the healing art, I believe, in those days—hence the king may have possessed an idiosyncrasy which was antagonistic to the prescription employed.

It is not very clear what is meant by the term used in connection with the monk who tasted to the king when it is said his bowels suddenly burst out. He was, no doubt, the subject of a hernial protusion and had the misfortune to have the intestine escape at the particular juncture named, and some movement or word of his betrayed the condition to those present at the king's attendance. They were anxious to find a pretext for his accusation and hence magnified even this accident to the poor monk's condemnation.

As to the singing of the king when thought to be dying, this is not very uncommon during the recovery from the influence of chloroform or in the intoxication of alcohol and some other poisons,· though in the very jaws of death from a congestive chill I have heard the sufferer sing and pray as if in a toxic or inebriated condition.

"Give me some drink; and bid the apothecary bring the strong poison I bought of him" are words from the lips of the dying Cardinal Beaufort, Bishop of Winchester.

As suggested before, the consideration of the soporific or "sleeping potion" of Friar Laurence is placed under the division of toxicology because of the characteristic effects of the remedy upon the animal economy—no remedy having such power, being free from toxicological properties when given in quantities, or to the susceptible or in peculiar conditions of the system ; it therefore takes *quantity* as well as *quality* to constitute a poison, — its poisonous properties only being judged by its effects.

It has been suggested by an ingenious writer, that the good Friar had certainly anticipated Liebreich in the discovery and use of the hydrate of chloral ; and a cursory view of the symptoms attending the action of the real and the mythical remedies upon the human system, might very easily cause any one to commit a like error ; but there is a great dissimilarity in their action, as we shall see. I will quote from an article of my own, written upon this subject, and published in the Leavenworth *Medical Herald*, some years ago: "I am of the opinion that if the correspondent of the ' *Michigan University Medical Journal*,' who seems to have made the important discovery of the identity of these drugs, had read the *whole* of the Friar's instructions, and not have mutilated them by making extracts, he could not have seen so striking an analogy in the action of the remedies. The full conversation ran thus:

Friar. 'Take now this phial, being then in bed, and this distilled liquor drink thou off ; when, presently, through all thy veins shall run a cold and drowsy humor ; *for no pulse shall keep his native progress, but surcease: no warmth, no breath shall testify that thou livest; the roses in thy lips and cheeks shall fade to paly ashes; * thy eyes' windows fall, like death when he shuts up the day of life ; *each part deprived of suple-government, shall stark and stiff and cold appear like death :* and in the borrow'd likeness of shrank death thou shall continue *two and forty hours*, and then awake as from a pleasant sleep.

Now, when the bridegroom in the morning comes to rouse thee from thy bed, there art thou dead: then, as the manner of our country is, in thy best robes uncover'd on the bier, *be borne* to burial in thy kindred's grave.' When discovered by her nurse and Lady Capulet, tremendous exertions were made to awaken her, but without avail; then comes Capulet himself, who thus exclaims: 'Ha! let me see her. Out, alas! she's cold! *Her blood is settled, and her joints are stiff;* life and those lips have long been separated.'

After a careful survey of the literature of the subject, I find the salient points of the action of the hydrate of chloral, on the bodily functions, to be the following:

Little or no impairment of the function of respiration; no abnormal condition of the pulse—the heart being the last of the vital organs to become affected by the agent. The face becomes flushed, and the eyes suffused and congested; unusual renal activity. *There is an especial relaxation of all the soft tissues of the body, with an exalted cutaneous sensibility. Sixteen hours the longest time recorded, during which a patient has been kept under its influence by a single dose,* and that in the case of a person suffering from stupor and melancholia,— hardly a fair test.

The hypnotic action of the drug, though very rapid, not morbidly profound like that of opium and some other narcotics;—*a hand on the door, a gentle word, or slight puncture being sufficient to arouse the sleeper to immediate and complete consciousness.* Now I am per- suaded that a careful collation of the two leading paragraphs of this article,—especially the italicised lines, will disclose the fact that hydrate of chloral produces few of the symptoms attributed by Shakespeare to his mythical drug; and that if Friar Laurence supplied the fair Juliet with a ' sweet oblivious antidote,' to rid her of an odious and troublesome suitor, it was *not* chloral hydrate.''

As stated before, the foregoing quotation was written a few months after the discovery of the '' hydrate,'' but the action of the agent was so carefully noted by those who had administered it up to that time that there have been no observations from its more extended use, which change the notions of the profession from the therapeutic facts as above related of it.

It must be admitted, however, that we have no remedy in our voluminous materia medica of which we are aware, that would come as near producing the *general* effects of the Friar's remedy as the hydrate of chloral; and it would really seem that to regard it in a general way, Liebreich has only reproduced a long lost article— known and used hundreds of years in the past—medicine as well as history repeating itself. If the powerful remedy used by Juliet was a mystery, we yet have another in the drug employed by Romeo in his tragic end.

" Well, Juliet, I will lie with thee to-night.   Let's see for means : O, mischief! thou art swift to enter in the thoughts of desperate men.   I do remember an apothecary, and hereabouts he dwells, which late I noted in tatter'd weeds, with overwhelming brows, culling of simples : meagre were his looks, sharp misery had worn him to the bones ; and in his needy shop a tortoise hung, an alligator stuff'd, and other skins of ill-shap'd fishes ; and about his shelves a beggarly account of empty boxes, green earthen pots, bladders, and musty seeds, were thinly scatter'd to make up a show. Noting his penury, to myself I said—and if a man did need a poison now, whose sale is present death in Mantua, here lives a caitiff wretch would sell it him.   O! this same thought did but forerun my need ; being holiday, the beggar's house is shut.—What, ho! apothecary !

Apothecary.   Who calls so loud?

Romeo.   Come hither, man.—I see that thou art poor ; hold, there is forty ducats : let me have a dram of poison ; such soon-speeding gear as will disperse itself through all the veins, that the life-weary taker may fall dead ; and the trunk may be discharged of breath as violently, as hasty powder fir'd doth hurry from the fatal cannon's womb.

Apothecary.   Such mortal drugs I have ; but Mantua's law is death to any he that utters them.

Romeo.   Art thou so base, and full of wretchedness, and fear'st to die? famine is in thy cheeks, need and oppression starveth in thine eye, contempt and beggary hang on thy back, the world is not thy friend, nor the world's law ; the world affords no law to make thee rich ; then be not poor, but break it, and take this.   (*Giving money.*)

Apothecary.   My poverty, but not my will, consents.

Romeo.   I pay thy poverty, not thy will.

Apothecary. Put this in any liquid thing you will, and drink it off; and if you had the strength of twenty men, it would despatch you straight." Supplied with the death-dealing agent furnished him in violation of the penal statutes of the government of Mantua, the grief-stricken representative of all the Montagues hastened from his exile to the 'tomb of all the Capulets,' where, upon discovering the still form of his bride, he thus soliloquized: "Death, that has suck'd the honey of thy breath, hath no power yet upon thy beauty: thou art not conquer'd; beauty's ensign yet is crimson in thy lips, and in thy cheeks, and death's pale flag is not advanced there. Ah! dear Juliet, why art thou yet so fair? I will believe that unsubstantial death is amorous; and that the lean abhorred monster keeps thee here in dark to be his paramour. For **fear** of that I still will stay with thee, and never from this place of dim night depart again: here, here will I remain with worms that are thy chambermaids; O! here will I sit up my everlasting

rest, and shake the yoke of inauspicious stars from this world-
wearied flesh. Eyes, look your last; arms, take your last embrace;
and lips, O! you, the doors of breath, seal with a righteous kiss a
dateless bargain to engrossing death.—Come, bitter conduct, come
unsavory guide! thou desperate pilot, now at once run on the dash-
ing rocks thy sea-sick weary bark. Here's to my love.—(*Drinks
his poison.*) O, true apothecary! thy drugs are quick.—Thus with a
kiss I die.''

(*Friar Laurence visits the tomb, and the lady wakes.*)

Juliet. ''O, comfortable Friar! where is my love? I do remember well where I should be, and there I am.—Where is my Romeo?

Friar.—"Lady, come from that nest of death."

Friar. Lady, come from that nest of death, contagion, and unnatural sleep. Come, come away; thy husband in thy bosom there
lies dead; come, I will dispose of thee among a sisterhood of holy
nuns. Stay not to question; come, go, good Juliet.—I dare no
longer stay.

Juliet. Go, get thee hence, for I will not away.—What's here? a cup, clos'd in my true love's hand? poison, I see, hath been his timeless end.—O churl! drink all, and leave no friendly drop to help me after?—I will kiss thy lips; haply, some poison doth yet hang on them, to make me die with a restorative. Thy lips are warm!''

Juliet then falls dead with Romeo's dagger buried deep in her heart. The old Friar explained the whole matter to the relatives of the two lovers in the following words:

" I will be brief, for my short date of breath is not so long as a tedious tale. Romeo there dead, was husband to that Juliet; and she there dead, that Romeo's faithful wife: I married them; and their stolen marriage-day was Tybalt's dooms-day, whose untimely death, banished the new-made bridegroom from this city,—for whom, and not Tybalt, Juliet pin'd. Then comes she to me, and with wild looks bade me devise some means, or in my cell there would she kill herself. Then gave I her, (so tutor'd by my art) a 'sleeping potion, which so took effect as I intended, for it wrought on her the form of death.

Prince. This letter doth make good the Friar's words, their course of love, the tidings of her death, and here he writes, that he did buy a poison of a 'poor apothecary.' ''

It will be noticed that the condition of Juliet at the time of Romeo's contemplation of her, and a description of her condition at the time of her first taking the remedy, are quite discrepant; in the first she is in the "likeness of shrank death," the " roses in her lips and cheeks are faded to paly ashes," whilst in the other it is said that " beauty's ensign yet is crimson in her lips and in her cheeks, and death's pale flag is not advanced there." The latter condition coincides more nearly with the conditions of one under the influence of chloral. It is a remarkable fact, that neither in language nor sentiment is there scarcely to be found a contradiction in all of Shakespeare's writings; the contradiction in the case of Juliet's condition being not of his making, as the five lines beginning, "Death that hath sucked the honey of thy breath," and containing the error or contradiction in idea is, in the copy from which I quote, the work of an " emendator;"—not to be found in older copies of the work, and notably absent from the quarto of

1597. This shows conclusively, that few men can correct errors for, or improve upon the works of Shakespeare.

In regard to the poison used by Romeo, it seems that oxalic acid comes nearer filling the physical and toxical conditions of the material than any other we possess at this day. "Put this in any liquid thing you will, and drink it off, and it will despatch you straight;" showing that it acted with celerity, and that it was necessary to dissolve or dilute it; nicotina or prussic acid might have been used in the event of the last suggestion, but the other is most plausible.

Oxalic acid is a colorless, crystallized solid, possessing a strong, sour taste; it dissolves in nine times its weight of cold, and in its own weight of boiling water; it dissolves in alcohol. It is a virulent poison in large doses, producing death with great rapidity and certainty in from ten to sixty minutes; it was not noticed as a poison until 1814, by Royston; since then by Percy, Thompson, and others; it is much used in the arts—particularly in calico printing, for discharging colors,—and therefore is quite a common agent in the hands of the suicide, even now. Cyanide of hydrogen, or prussic acid was first discovered by Scheele, in 1782, whilst nicotina was not known until quite recently; so that, if either of these articles were among the contraband in the stock of the poor apothecary of Mantua, we have only another instance of the fact that scientists are now discovering many things as new, which have been in use so long ago as to have fallen into disuse and have been forgotten.

Banquo, in a conversation with Macbeth soon after encountering the witches upon the heath of Fores, speculates in this way: "Were such things here, as we do speak about, or have we eaten on the insane root, that takes the reason prisoner?"

It is probable that the substance here referred to as the "insane root," was the modern cicuta or conium maculatum—the "hemlock" of the ancients, which was so popular as a weapon for the purpose of suicide and criminal poisoning; it is a most energetic poison, three drops of conia, the active principle of the plant, having killed a stout cat in a minute and a half; it acts upon the spinal cord, prostrating the nervous powers, paralyzing the voluntary muscular system, and destroys life by arresting the function of respiration. The brain does not seem to be influenced in any marked degree, even by a poisonous dose of the medicine; therefore the idea that it "takes the reason prisoner," is scarcely correct. In the fearful tragedy of "Macbeth," again, A. ii., S. ii., it is stated that Lady Macbeth "drugged the possets" of the king's attendants, "that death and nature did contend about them, whether they lived or died."

The half clear, half disturbed slumbers of these men, whilst Macbeth with bloody hands bent over their prostrated bodies, shows that they perhaps were laboring under the effects of some powerful toxical agent;—the "hashish," cannabis indica, or Indian hemp comes nearest meeting the characteristics in action upon the brain, of any of our modern substances; it is a powerful narcotic when given in sufficient quantity, but in a less dose it produces an intoxicated mind with delirious hallucinations—with, finally, drowsiness, stupor, etc., but has little effect upon the action of the heart. When taken into the stomach, it acts with much greater rapidity than opium, and most other vegetable toxicants; nor does it produce nausea as does opium occasionally.

There is in "Hamlet," A. iv., S. vii., recorded a conference between Laertes and the king, in regard to the assassination of Hamlet, as he seemed to stand directly in the path of their villainies. The former uses this language: "I will do 't; and for that purpose I'll anoint my sword. I bought an unction of a mountebank, so mortal that but dip a knife into it, where it draws blood no cataplasm so rare, collected from all simples that have virtue under the moon, can save the thing from death, that is but scratch'd withal. I'll touch my point with this contagion, that if I gall him slightly, it may be death."

We have the analogue of this "unction" in the virulent organic poisons,—those I mean of animal origin, and also a few cases in which they are probably of vegetable origin. In regard to those originating from the animal kingdom, it is a singular fact that they are not in any instance capable of being elaborated by the manipulations of the chemist, or by combinations brought about external to the living animal economy, but are, on the contrary, always, perhaps, generated by the animal organism in a state of vitality— most commonly during a state of *normal* vitality. As an illustration of the latter we have the poisons of the reptile and insect creations, one of which perhaps furnished the vindictive Laertes with his "contagion," whilst of the other, we may name the virulent products of rabies canina, glanders, etc., omitting entirely the products of animal decomposition, the specific poisons of small-pox, etc. All savage nations of the earth are in the habit of using these animal poisons for the purpose of tipping their arrows and spears,—but one vegetable poison being in use for this purpose within my knowledge, namely, the "curare" or "arrow poison" of British Guiana,—used by the natives for the purpose indicated by the name. This poison is as deadly as that of the rattlesnake, and, like it, exerts its most noticeable action upon the subcutaneous tissues; though the least abrasion of the mucous or cutaneous surfaces is sufficient to admit it into the body. It is claimed by most authorities that this wonderfully active production is derived from the bark of a ground-like plant, by aqueous extract; though there are others who claim that it is derived from the animal king-dom; and these are the most likely correct, from the simple fact that it has many analogues in that direction and none in the other.

The action of these three forms of poisons upon the animal economy is quite unlike in the main—those of vegetable origin acting for the most part upon and through the nervous system—producing little or no observable change in the structures of the body, while of mineral poisons, as before remarked, inflammatory and destructive metamorphosis is the common accompaniment of their action. Of the animal poisons, those generated in the living animal, as in rabies and the poison of serpents, etc., they multiply in the system when taken into the blood, and have thus always offered ample soil in which to propagate. As to the poisons gener-ated in the putrefactive process in animal products, and which generate the low fevers for example, these should no longer be re-garded as poisons proper, as they are now commonly recognized as belonging to and identical with parasitic, living, organisms—are real animals, as much so as are the lions and tigers found in the jungles of Central Africa.

Immediately succeeding the conversation in which Laertes boasts of having purchased the poison, he and the king continued,—

King. "Let's farther think of this; weigh, what convenience, both of time and means, may fit us to our shape.

If this should fail, and that our drift looked through our bad performance, 'twere better not assay'd: therefore, this project should have a back, or second, that might hold, if this should blast in proof. Soft!—let me see:—we'll make a solemn wager on your cunnings, I ha't: when in your motions you are hot and dry (as make your bouts more violent to that end), and that he calls for drink, I'll have prepar'd him a chalice for the nonce, whereon but sipping, if he by chance escape your venom'd stuck, our purpose may hold there." (This will be remembered as the plan for the termination of the fencing match, which had been arranged to take place between Laertes and Hamlet. They supposed that Hamlet knew nothing of the malice they bore him, but in that they were mistaken; he was better posted than his eccentricities would suffer them to acknowledge.)

"Set me the stoop of wine upon that table there. If Hamlet give the first or second hit, or quit in answer of the third exchange, the king shall drink to Hamlet's better breath.

Give me the cups; now the king drinks to Hamlet; come, begin;

Hamlet. Come on, sir.

Laertes. Come, my lord.

Hamlet. One.

Laertes. No.

Hamlet. Judgment.

Osric. (A courtier.) A hit, a very palpable hit.

King. Stay: give drink. Hamlet, the pearl is thine (the pearl was placed in the poisoned glass); here's to thy health.—Give him the cup.

Hamlet. I'll play this bout first; set it by awhile.

King. Our son shall win.

Queen. (Hamlet's mother.) He's fat, and scant of breath.— Here's a napkin; rub thy brows, my son: the queen carouses to thy fortune, Hamlet.

Hamlet. Good madam,—

King. Gertrúde *(the queen)*, don't drink.

Queen. I will, my lord: I pray you pardon me. *(Drinks.)*

King. It is the poisoned cup! it is too late. *(Aside.)*

Hamlet. I dare not drink yet madam; by and by.

Queen. Come, let me wipe thy face."

Laertes and Hamlet then play their third bout, when Hamlet is wounded, and by chance changes daggers with his antagonist and wounds him also; the queen falls—crying, the drink! the drink! I'm poisoned! *(Dies.)* Laertes then falls also, and as he does so he exclaims—"It is here Hamlet. Hamlet, thou art slain; no medicine in the world can do thee good: in thee there is not half

an hour of life: the treacherous instrument is in thy hand, unbated
and envenom'd. The foul practice hath turn'd itself on me; lo,
here I lie, never to rise again. Thy mother's poison'd; I can no
more. The king, the king's to blame.

Hamlet. The point envenom'd too! Then, venom, do thy work!
(*Stabs the king.*)

It is probable that the poison in the wine was the *conium maculatum*. It usually commences to operate in half an hour, when
taken in poisonous doses. It seems that the toxic agents of Shakespeare's imagination were of a potent quality whether those in the
drug shops of his cotemporaries were so or not, and certain it is, he
lacked no skill in using them with tragic effect.

In "King Lear," A. v., S. ii., we find another character disposed
of by poison; this is Regan, who was, through jealousy, poisoned
by her sister Goneril—she then committing suicide with a poniard.

The circumstances attending this tragedy are not drawn with the
minuteness and skill which characterize most other scenes of this
nature in Shakespeare's writings; therefore we have fewer grounds
for speculation. Othello spoke of poisons as an agent with which
to rid himself of the torments of jealousy, but he relinquished this
purpose in favor of the more trusty dagger. The defeat of Mark
Antony determined Cleopatra to take her departure to that bourne
from whence no pilgrim has ever returned, and she thus declares,
" Not the imperious show of the full-fortuned Cæsar ever shall be
broach'd with me; if knife, drugs, serpents, have edge, sting or
operation, I am safe." She finally decides upon the decisive act,
and thus addresses her attendant:—"Hast thou not the pretty worm
of Nilus there, that kills and pains not?

Attendant. Truly, I have him; but I would not be the party
that should desire you to touch him, for his biting is mortal: those
that do die of it, do seldom or never recover.

Cleopatra. Remember'st thou any that have died on 't?

Attendant. (*A clown.*) Very many, men and women too. I
heard of one of them no longer than yesterday: a very honest
woman, but something given to lie, as a woman should not do but
in the way of honesty how she died of the biting of it, what pain
she felt.—Truly, she makes a very good report of the worm; but
he that will believe all they say, shall never be saved by half what
they do. But this is most fallible, the worm 's an adder-worm.

Cleopatra. Get thee hence; farewell.

Attendant. I wish you all joy of the worm.

Cleopatra. Farewell.

Attendant. Look you, the worm will do his kind, remember.

Cleopatra. Ay, ay; farewell.

Attendant. Look you, the worm is not to be trusted but in the keeping of wise people; for, indeed, there is no goodness in the worm.

Cleopatra. Take thou no care, it shall be heeded.

Attendant. Very good. Give it nothing, I pray you, for it is not worth the feeding.

Cleopatra. Will it eat me?

Attendant. You must not think I am so simple, but I know the devil himself will not eat a woman: I know, that a woman is a dish for the gods, if the devil dress her not; but, truly these same whoreson devils do the gods great harm in their women, for in every ten that they make, the devils mar nine.

Cleopatra. Well, get thee gone; farewell.

Attendant. Yes, forsooth; I wish you joy of the worm. (*Ex. clown.*)

(*Enter female attendant.*)

Cleopatra. Give me my robe, put on my crown; I have immortal longings in me. Now, no more the juice of Egypt's grape shall moist this lip.—So, have you done? Come, then, and take the last warmth of my lips." (*They kiss, and the maid falls dead, when Cleopatra asks:*)—"Dost fall? have I the aspick in my lips? If thou and nature can so gently part, the stroke of death is as a lover's pinch, which hurts and is desir'd. Dost thou lie still? If thus thou vanishest, thou tell'st the world it's not worth leave-taking. (*To the adder.*) Come, thou mortal wretch, with thy sharp teeth, this knot intrinsicate of life at once untie: poor venomous fool, be angry, and despatch. (*To her maid.*) Dost thou not see my baby at my breast, that sucks the nurse asleep? (*She had applied the serpent to her breast.*) As sweet as balm, as soft as air, as gentle.—Nay, I will take thee too. (*Applies one to her arm.*) Why should I stay."—(*Falls down dead.*)

Cæsar, whose prisoner she was, then enters the room and enquires—" the manner of their deaths? I do not see them bleed. Poisoned, then. O noble weakness!—If they had swallow'd poison, 'twould appear by external swelling; but she looks like sleep. Here, on her breast, there is a vent of blood, and something blown the like is on her arm.

Attendant.   This is an aspick's trail.

Cæsar.   Most probable, that so she died, for her physician tells me, she hath pursu'd conclusions infinite of easy ways to die."

In the modern science of ophiology the *adder* is placed as a relative of the viper family, a species of serpent which usually inhabits dry, rocky and barren districts, and is not found in the vicinity of rivers and marshy grounds.   The poisonous animal to which reference is made under the name of the "worm of Nilus," most probably belonged to the *trigonocephalus piscivorus* of naturalists, which inhabits rivers and marshes in many southern latitudes, and the bite of which is speedily fatal.

The absence of *external* swelling would be no proof that poison had not been *swallow'd*, as Cæsar seems to have conjectured; but its absence might have been taken as some evidence that the parties had not died from the poison of a venomous reptile, as "external" swelling is an almost universal accompaniment of this virus when in contact with subcutaneous tissue.   There are no logical grounds for the idea of the maid's dying merely from the contact of her mistress' lips;—the matter gives zest to a tragedy, but will scarcely bear rigid scientific enquiry.   It is well known that the poison of most if not all herpetologic nature, is innoxious when in contact with unabraded cutaneous and mucous surfaces.   Cleopatra certainly learned originality, whether she succeeded in hitting upon an "easy way to die" or not; but that the poison of any of the snake tribe "kills and pains not" is hardly consonant with the experiences upon that point,—the most of them being extremely painful in their action; the bite of the tarantula, rattlesnake, etc., being attended with vomiting, cramps, suffocating spasms, coldness and great prostration of the nervous powers, and death.   Notwithstanding the fact that some of these poisons blast human life with the celerity of the lightning's stroke, yet it is probable that had an enlightened physician of the present day been present, he might have saved the life of Cleopatra, as, aside from the whiskey and ammonia treatment now so common and usually so successful, there has been recently discovered a specific for the evil; this is nothing else than the *gall* of the serpent so causing the wound,—one of the same species, or else the gall of some other species whose poison is more virulent than the one that did the biting.   The manner of using is to take ten parts of ninety-five per cent alcohol, or an equal quantity of the best whiskey, to one part of the gall, then dilute five drops of this mixture with half a tumbler (rather indefinite) of pure water, and give a teaspoonful every three or five minutes until all is taken. If the pain and swelling are not much benefited, repeat the process as before.

The author of this treatment is a medical gentleman who has long resided in India, and says that of fifty cases treated, he had to repeat the first quantity but twice, and every patient recovered.

The native Indians are said to use a tincture made from a plant called *alconcito*, or *solobasta*, for the bites of the most poisonous varieties, and with good success. They also *inoculate* with it as a prophylactic against the venom of all noxious animals. Our American aborigines are in the habit of using the *aristoloquia virginiana*, or *serpentaria*, for the same purpose, but with what success I don't know.

In Cymbeline, A. i., S. iii., we have the following:

Queen. "Now, master doctor, have you brought those drugs?

Physician. Pleaseth your highness, ay: here they are, madam: but I beseech your grace, without offence (my conscience bids me ask), wherefore you have commanded of me these most poisonous compounds, which are the movers of a most languishing death; but though slow, deadly.

Queen. I wonder, doctor, thou ask'st me such a question: have I not been thy pupil long? Has thou not learn'd me how to make perfumes? distill? preserve? yea, so that our great king himself doth woo me oft for my confections? Having thus far proceeded (unless thou think'st me devilish), is 't not meet that I did amplify my judgment in other conclusions? I will try the forces of these thy compounds on such creatures as we count not worth the hanging (but none human), to try the vigor of them, and apply allayments to their act, and by them gather their several virtues and effects.

Physician. Your highness shall from this practice but make hard your heart: besides, the seeing these effects will be both noisome and infectious."

It appears from this paragraph that Shakespeare held the notions of most laymen even of to-day in regard to vivisections and physiological experiments in general upon the lower animals. He puts his words in the mouth of a physician however,—a place from which would emanate very little of that teaching at this time—except, perhaps, it might so happen under exactly the same or analogous circumstances wherein the doctor was using only subterfuge—evading the unpleasant duty of directly offending a royal patron. The custom of such physiological experimentation of course then obtained, or had obtained, or Shakespeare would have had no data upon which to found an idea of it—unless it was another of his intuitions.

In another place, and when alone, the good Doctor Cornelius talks thus with himself: "I do not like her; she doth think she has strange lingering poisons: I do know her spirit, and will not trust one of her malice with a drug of such damn'd nature. Those she has will stupefy and dull the senses awhile; which first, perchance, she'll prove on cats, and dogs, then afterward up higher; but there is no danger in what show of death it makes more than the locking up the spirits a time to be more fresh reviving. She is fooled with a most false effect; and I the truer, so to be false with her." It is made evident that the queen had a homicidal mania; and in a passage in A. v., S. v., same play, it is said by Cornelius that the flight of Cymbeline's daughter was all that saved her from being "taken off by poison." The doctor then divulges the fact to the king, that he had very often been importuned by the queen to "temper" poisons for her, pretending that she only wanted to eradicate such vile things as cats and dogs, and things of no esteem; but he divining that her purpose was of danger to the life of something more important, did compound for her a certain stuff, which being taken, would cease the present powers of life; but, in short time, all offices of nature should again do their due functions.—"Have you taken of it?

Daughter. Most likely I did, for I was dead."

The action of this "stuff" of Shakespeare is most beautifully typical of chloroform; and had we the slightest evidence that a drug of that character had ever existed as such, save in the fertile brain of the greatest writer of the world, we well might doubt the priority of discovery of anæsthesia by both Morton and Wells. "*It will stupefy and dull the sense awhile, but there is no danger in what show of death it makes more than the locking up the spirits a time.*"

It seems that Shakespeare's wonderful mind not only comprehended matters of the past,—imbibed the ideas of his present, but with prophetic grasp anticipated the most important events which were to transpire ages after he ceased to be. In reference to the action of the drug of Cornelius on the human body, it will be remembered that when Imogen set out on her trip to Milford Haven, Pisanio presented her with a box, saying that it was from the queen, and extolling its virtues—a dram of it being sufficient to drive away distempers. She arrived at the cave of Belarius in an exhausted condition, where she says to herself, " I should be sick, but that my resolution helps me ; I am not very sick, since I can reason of it ;"—whilst again directly, after being left alone, she continues : " I am sick still ; heart sick.—Pisanio, I'll now taste of thy drug." The scene then occurs in which after the return from the hunt and the encounter with Cloten, they find Imogen in her stupor, and suppose her dead—her face being like the "pale primrose."

Belarius. "How found you him? (her.)

Arviragus. Stark, as you see." (*He had brought the body in in his arms.*) She then awaked as if from slumber, and anathematizes the good old Pisanio for giving her the box, in these words: " The drug he gave me, which, he said, was precious and cordial to me, have I not found it murderous to the senses?"

There is one assertion in the last quotation which would make the identity of the article used to be chloroform, and distinguish it from chloral, and that is, that the body was *stark*. It was *pale* also, another proof of chloroform.

CHAPTER V.

Prefatory—Wine for an ague—Objects of commiseration—A promise redeemed—Icy burning—A marshy residence—Magna charta—Allegorical—An idea of antiquity—"Would to bed"—"Falstaff, he is dead"—Congestive chill—Gad's-hill—Prince Henry and his "pals"—This man has become a god—Is Brutus sick?—Acerbity—The Appian Way—Foes to life—Malaria as a demoralizing agent—Cross gartering—The tourniquet as a remedy—Same as a cause of disease—Farewell to neuralgia—Brunonianism.

In summing up the material which Shakespeare furnishes us as a causation of disease we do not find much that is explicit or definite, and perhaps the matter could as well have been arranged under some other title as appropriately as that under which we have arranged it. There is one element connected with the matter which goes to make the chapter, however, that presents itself so prominently that it cannot well be placed under any other heading than the one given,—and that is malaria, If I chance, however, to introduce ideas in this connection which the reader may find irrelevant, I beg that he will remember the difficulty one must necessarily encounter in arranging the ideas of a non-medical person to make them strictly conform to scientific order. Hoping that my apology may be clearly comprehended and appreciated, I shall at once enter upon the subject matter proper to the text.

We find allusion to malaria first in "The Tempest, "A. ii., S. ii., thus:

Caliban. "All the infections that the sun sucks up from bogs, fens, flats, on Prosper fall, and make him by inch-meal a disease!" whilst in the latter portion of the same scene, there is faithfully portrayed an occurrence which may be witnessed any August day in the malarial districts of our own south and west. It is the place where the malingering Caliban was thought by the drunken butler,

Stephano, to have, " as I take it, an ague; he's in his fit now, and does not talk after the wisest. He shall taste of my bottle: if he have never drank wine afore, it will go near to remove his fit; if all the wine in my bottle will recover him, I will help his ague." This is but in accord with the popular notion of to-day, *i. e.*—that alcoholic stimulation or alcoholic *sedation* rather is a *sine qua non* in the treatment of some conditions dependent upon miasmatic poisoning;—not only that its good effects are manifested in some extreme conditions arising from that cause, but that " whisky " is a prophylactic for malaria.

The medical profession in this part of the country, I presume, is also fully persuaded of its value in these cases, as during a discussion upon typho-malarial fever, in the St. Joseph Medical Society, a few evenings since, it was claimed by members of large experience in managing such cases, that alcoholics are indispensable to the best treatment of the most dangerous of malarial poisoning cases—is *good* at all times and in all forms of Autumnal fevers which have marsh poisons as their cause. Not only is it *good* in malarial diseases of all grades and at all times, but that in *typhoid* fevers it is claimed by an eminent medical friend of my own to be *antidotal* to the etiological agent, and counteracts its influence just as, or in a similar manner as does it in the poison of the rattlesnake.

" My wind, cooling my broth, would blow me to an ague fit,"— " Merchant of Venice," A. i., S. i., is of no special import, but, " he will look as hollow as a ghost, as dim and meagre as an ague fit," in " King John," A. iii., S. iii., has grounds for reflection in it as conveying a good portrait of one laboring under ague. They are always objects of commiseration. In Richard the Second, A. ii., S. i., we see the words, " a lunatic lean-witted fool, presuming on an ague's privilege." These words were those of Richard himself in criticism of some plain words used by the former king, John of Gaunt, when he "breathed his last in wholesome counsel to his unstaid youth."

In this quotation we have it plainly asserted that John had an *ague* even at the hour of his dissolution,—the truth of which I fully acquiesce in after making a diagnosis from his symptoms and the previous history of the case. We stated in the chapter preceding this, whilst noting this case under the heading of toxicology, that although it was claimed by the persons about the king at the time of his last illness, and also by the king himself, that he had been *poisoned* by a monk, yet we did not coincide in that view regarding the king's malady; and that in a future portion of the book we would endeavor to present logical grounds for our opinion: in the following pages we propose to make good that promise.

The case of King John, bears a much closer analogy to a case wherein the hand of nature has been instrumental in saturating the system with poison, than does it to one in which a "villainous monk" had been the instrument. Miasmatic exhalations had no doubt wrought the evil in this case. "None of you will bid the winter come, to thrust his icy fingers *in my maw;* nor let my kingdom's *rivers take their course through my burn'd bosom;* nor entreat the *north* to make his *bleak winds kiss my parched lips, and comfort me with cold. There is so hot a summer in my bosom, that all my bowels crumble up to dust; against this fire, I shrink up.*" To this must be added the fact that he had been sick before, as will be remembered by his language on the battle-field, "Ah me! this tyrant *fever burns me up,*" and "*this fever that hath troubled me so long,* lies heavy on me; weakness possesseth me and I am faint."

In the most deadly forms of pernicious fever there is no symptom so horrible to the patient as this sense of burning heat; this is his agonizing torment when he is pulseless and his skin is icy cold—nay his breath is even cold, and his surface as blue and lifeless as the body of him who already tenants the grave,—the thermometer showing at the same time a great reduction in the normal temperature of the patient's body, whilst the oppressive internal congestions make him clamor for air, air;—bring him to the window, door,—into the yard, orchard, anywhere so that he may have air! and the exclamation often is, 'O! that I had a river of cold water running through me! I am burning up.' In all these malarial cases an unbearable *burning sensation* or pain in the stomach is one of the most distressing concomitants. Hence the exclamation, "Bid the winter come to thrust his icy fingers in my maw." *Quinine* is the only prompt and infallible agent for this symptom: opium, water, ice, etc., are *good,* but quinine is the cure. *He had been sick a time before his last severe illness,* and withal inhabited a marshy district, between the discharge of two considerable rivers—the Wash and the Humber, where the surface is so low that the ocean has in many places to be kept at bay by dikes, and where, to this day, thousands upon thousands of acres of the country are kept only for the support of the vast flocks of geese, both domestic and wild, which feed upon them. Moors and fen-lands characterise Lincolnshire to-day, after all the efforts with money and labor to reclaim it from the sea; and when we go back to the twelfth century, we ought surely to find it as malarial as the Pontine marsh of Italy, or the sloughs of our own Mississippi. In this district it is that lie buried the bones of Catharine Swinford, the wife of John of Gaunt; and in this district, at Newark on the Trent, died John, in the year 1216, at the age of forty-nine years. He signed the Great Charter the year before—1215.

The probable cause of the great dramatist's placing the death of John to the account of a monk, and that with poison, originates in the fact of there having been a great antagonism existing between John and the Roman church,—an antagonism which finally resulted in the complete and humble—nay *servile* submission of John. This perhaps is construed into a simile of real physical death—the poison represented by Shakespeare's own disdain for the Romish faith— that is if matters in religion ever gave him any concern at all.

Shakespeare, however, has managed the symptomatology of the case with such a masterly skill, that it might puzzle the most astute diagnostician of our time,—even his countryman, the great Watson himself, to say whether, from the symptoms, the king died with poison or malarial fever;—because they are sometimes very much alike.

The term "ague-fit of fear" is used by Richard the Second illustratively, whilst in the first part of Henry the Fourth, A. iii., S. i., Hotspur uses the term ague in the same sense—that is, to illustrate an idea; also in A. iv., S. i., of same play, he uses the words, "worse than the sun in March, this praise doth nourish agues;" thus pointing to the fact, that the notion yet prevalent among the mass of mankind that to bask in the sun at spring-time is to propagate agues, certainly can boast of antiquity as a basis, whether the idea itself be false or true. Sunlight alone never "nourished agues," whether in March or August, *directly;* the proximate principle in its causation,—malaria, however, doubtless is generated by the action of solar heat in conjunction with other agents, and, thus, if at all responsible, being so in a very roundabout way.

In King Henry the Fifth, we have a most artistic description of the influence of marsh poison in the case of the demise of Sir John Falstaff. He is first announced as "very sick, and would to bed," by the boy at the house of Mrs. Quickly, who requests Nym, one of Falstaff's followers, to " come in quickly to Sir John ; ah! poor heart, he is so shaked of a burning quotidian tertian, that it is most lamentable to behold ;" and further on, in concluding the career of this—one of the most marked characters that has ever figured in dramatic composition, Pistol urges the boy to " bristle his courage up, for Falstaff he is dead, and we must yearn therefore."

Bardolph. " Would I were with him, wheresome'er he is, either in heaven or in hell.

Mrs. Quickly. Nay, sure, he's not in hell: he's in Arthur's bosom. 'A made a fine end and went away, and it had been any Christian child ; 'a parted ev'n just between twelve and one, ev'n at the turning o' the tide : for after I saw him fumble with the sheets, and play with flowers, and smile upon his finger's end, I knew there was but one way ; for his nose was as sharp as a pen on a table of green freize. How now, Sir John? quoth I : what, man! be of good cheer. So 'a cried out—' God, God, God!' three or four times ; now I, to comfort him, bid him, 'a should not think of God ; I hoped, there was no need to trouble himself with such thoughts yet. So 'a bade me lay more clothes on his feet : I put my hand into the bed, and felt them, and they were as cold as any stone ; then I felt to his knees, and so upward, and all was as cold as any stone."

There are certainly many of the details which go to form the symptomatology of congestive chill omitted in this history ; but enough are present to show us that it is a fair picture of that malady—just as the practiced eye can tell the malady at the first glance, without asking previous history, in a case to which he may be called, in the miasmatic regions of our own and other countries. We regard miasm as the cause of the symptoms and death in the case above related as evidenced not only by the history and symptoms, but also by the habits, circumstances and age of the patient,— typhoid fever, with the which it would more likely be confounded, happening very seldom in a person of Falstaff's age, whilst it will also be remembered that the haunts of Prince Henry and his notorious " pals" were in the county of Kent, about Rochester and Gad's-hill,—the surface of the country being low and covered in many places with swamps and forests. Of the million and forty-one thousand acres composing this county, nine hundred thousand are meadows and arable land,—even the Kentish and Surrey portion of the city of London lying in many places several feet below the highest tides. I think it is somewhere said that in former years this portion of London was often subject to malarial fevers of a severe type, though it is against the rule for this to be so in cities generally.

"Ague" stayed the Duke of Buckingham "a prisoner in his chamber" on an important occasion; and Patroclus allows (in Troilus and Cressida) that "those wounds heal ill which men do give themselves"—an assertion acknowledged by the whole medical world, and which has, perhaps, a better foundation for its truth than has the next—which says that "danger, like an ague, subtly taints." Coriolanus likens fear to an ague also, whilst we find an animated discussion of Cæsar's merits between Cassius and Brutus in this language:

Cassius. "And this man is now become a god; and Cassius is a wretched creature, and must bend his body, if Cæsar carelessly but nod to him.

He had a fever when he was in Spain, and when the fit was on him, I did mark how he did shake: 'tis true, this god did shake: his coward lips did from their color fly; and that same eye, whose bend doth awe the world, did lose his lustre. I did hear him groan; ay, and that tongue of his, that bade the Romans mark him, and write his speeches in their books, alas! it cried, 'Give me some drink, Titinius,' as a sick girl. Ye gods, it doth amaze me, a man of such a feeble temper doth get the start of the majestic world, and bear the palm alone." Now when the matter is considered in all its relations, we have in this extract another case arising from marsh poison—palpable, plain, unmistakable. We find a case something on the same order in that of Brutus himself, when his wife Portia uses this language: "Is Brutus sick, and is it physical, to walk unbrac'd, and suck up the humors of the dank morning? What! is Brutus sick, and will he steal out of his wholesome bed to dare the vile contagion of the night, and tempt the rheum and unpurged air to add unto his sickness?" and when met in the senate chamber on the day of the assassination, Cæsar jocularly assures Brutus that he is not so much his enemy as "that same ague which hath made him lean," and he then invites Brutus and the others to drink some wine, with the view perhaps to neutralize the acerbity which he knew to be present in their bosoms.

The neighborhood of Rome, where this scene transpired, is notoriously the most malarial district in Europe. The poison of the Pontine marsh, before referred to, is so pestilential in its concentration, that an unacclimated person passing the great "Appian Way" from Rome to Naples at night time, and in the hot season of the year, may imbibe enough to dangerously compromise his existence.

Macbeth, in his extremity, while shut up in his castle at Dunsinane, thought to resort to the very common expedient of exterminating his enemies by drawing them into pestilential districts, there to be prey'd upon silently by "pale distemperatures and foes to life," as 'twas said by many would be the fate of the Union soldiers on our southern coasts during our civil war. In the stead of the yellow fever, which was relied upon to do its share in perpetuating the reign of "King Cotton," Macbeth placed his reliance on the same unreliable alliance, and depended upon "ague" to "eat them up,"—A. iv., S. v.

Lear prays thus to be avenged upon his undutiful daughter, Goneril: "You nimble lightnings, dart your blinding flames into her scornful eyes; infect her beauty, you fen-suck'd fogs, drawn by the powerful sun, to fall and blast her pride."

I do not know of an agent more potent to ravish beauty of its charms, than a residence in a malarial locality. Marsh poison blights—"subtly taints" the whole vital economy, and renders those reared mid its foul pollutions dull and the victims to hebetude, mentally, physically and *morally*. The latter assertion may seem queer to those who know nothing of malarial districts and their people; but I know from experience that what I assert is *true;*— they are as a general proposition lacking in the *moral* principles, so much so that physicians are commonly loth to attend the best of them, as he expects to realize little or nothing for his services; and I have never seen a sprightly physical or mental organization reared from infancy to adult age in such an atmosphere.

"This does make some obstruction in the blood, this cross-gartering"—so says Malvolio in "Twelfth Night,"—A. iii., S. iv. The custom among the women of civilized countries, of ligating or constricting the legs in keeping their hose in place, is no doubt productive of serious evils. It has been suggested as an expedient worthy of trial in cases of retarded or suppressed menstruation— and also in puerperal eclampsia, to resort to ligation of the thighs (arms also, in the latter), in the first to throw the force of the sys temic circulation upon the pelvic organs more directly, and in the latter to cut off *transiently* a supply of blood to the brain, but not to lose it to the system at large, as would be done in direct abstraction. Now, if there is any just ground for such a theory as the above, it follows as a necessity that there would be conditions in which this practice would be inadmissible, and where its adoption would be hurtful. These cases might be enumerated somewhat in the following order: menorrhagia, cases prone to abortion, placenta previa, all cases of hemorrhagic diathesis, in rectitis, hemorrhoids, cystitis, metritis, nephritis, cellulitis, etc., etc., as connected with the pelvis, whilst varix, phlebitis, etc., might result to the extremities themselves. These are not all, but convulsive conditions themselves may be engendered from this cause as effectually as from a loaded rectum and gravid womb, provided the condition is forcibly persisted in; and, again, the blood so impeded in a free circulation through its normal channels becomes itself a toxic material.

These considerations should be held sufficient for placing the system of "gartering" among our women in the same category with tight-lacing, low-neck dresses and high-heeled shoes. Let them all go down to oblivion together, and the days of hysteria, "palpitations" and neuralgias will in a great measure take their departure.

In "Twelfth Night" also, we find the term "Brownist" used in a sense of derision. A foot-note in the edition from which we quote says that the Brownists were a sect (whether in medicine, or what, is not stated), afterwards called the "Independents," who were much ridiculed by the writers of the time. This perhaps had reference to the followers of John Brown, an Englishman (not, however, the lately departed "friend" of Queen Victoria), who held to the opinion that the proximate cause of all fevers was nothing more than a general depression of the vital powers of the whole body, and that treatment based upon that supposition was the only rational method. These ideas were vehemently assailed by Broussais and his followers, who declared that fevers were all symptomatic—that they had their origin in a preceding local lesion, and that therefore the treatment must be shaped to suit the altered pathology.

The term "devouring pestilence hangs in the air" is found in Richard the Second, but is of no significance in its application to Shakespeare's medical knowledge.

CHAPTER VI.

DERMATOLOGY.

The beginning—Serpigo—A voluminous curse—Was it small-pox?—The cursed hebenon — Acarus scabiei — The disease in Paris—Falstaff as a " wen "—Kibes—Probably vaccinated—A string of rhymes—Good fruit only from a good tree—Transmissibility of defects—Gynæcological phenomena—The " convulsive zone "—Spreading it on " thick "—Rouge and pearl powders—'Tis beauty truly blent—Commendable caution—Danger in the dark—A fastidious scoundrel—Supposition strengthened—We catch of you, Doll—Baths in syphilis—Ricord and Bumstead—A beautiful picture—Durability of a tanner—A curious but not creditable truth—A needed reform—Venesection in the right iliac fossa.

For the sake of convenience, and to avoid a multiplication of short but separate classifications, all diseases affecting the superfices of the body noticeably, will be considered under the above caption. This will necessarily bring into close proximity affections of a very diverse pathology—some which might be very properly classed under other heads perhaps had we more material of the same kind—but many of the subjects touched upon are in themselves very brief, and though demanding their share of attention, yet are too short for any purpose save condensation or incorporation into an article general in its character; for this reason, and also because syphilis almost always involves the cutaneous structures to a greater or less extent, it will likewise be noticed in connection with dermatologic medicine.

" Serpigo " is an affection of the skin of the " tetter " family,—sometimes seemingly related more closely to the " herpetic " group; it is mentioned in "Measure for Measure " and also in "Troilus and Cressida," where Therestes uses it in his maledictions upon the managers of the siege of Troy; and the same character, whose tongue was caustic as a red-hot scalpel, in his wrangle with Patroclus, talks thus:

164

Therestes. "Why, thy masculine whore. Now, the rotten diseases of the south, the guts-griping, ruptures, catarrh, loads o' gravel i' the back, lethargies, cold palsies, raw eyes, dirt-rotten livers, wheezing lungs, bladders full of imposthume, sciaticas, lime-kilns i' the palm, incurable bone-ache, and the riveled fee-simple of the tetter, take and take again such preposterous discolourers.

Patroclus. Why, thou damnable box of envy, thou, what meanest thou to curse thus?"

This quotation, although containing a little of everything, could not be separately stated, and we therefore give it for what it is worth. The ghost of Hamlet's father in his story of how he was most foully murdered by his brother and his own queen, speaks of a "loathsome crust:"

Ghost. "But, soft; methinks, I scent the morning air: brief let me be.—Sleeping within my orchard, my custom alway in the afternoon, upon my secure hour thy uncle stole, with juice of cursed hebenon in a phial, and in the porches of mine ears, did pour the leprous distillment; whose effects holds such an enmity with the blood of man that swift as quicksilver, it courses through the natural gates and alleys of the body; and with a sudden vigor it doth posset, and curd, like sour droppings into milk, the thin and wholesome blood: so did it mine: and a most instant tetter bark'd about, most lazar-like, with vile and loathsome crust all my smooth body."

There are few morbific agents which will strictly answer in every particular the characteristics of the contents of the phial, in this case. It must have been some powerful animal toxic, similar to, or identical with the virus of small-pox; the only plea which could be deducted against this hypothesis, from the quotation itself, being the "sudden vigor" with which it acted. This, however, is an indefinite assertion, and "sudden" might be a week or ten days in one case, whilst it might be only a few moments or hours in another.

It is possible that the word "hebenon" may have had a meaning similar to our "narcotism" or "narcotic," and that it was used this time in relation to the supposed effects upon the system,—the term likely having its origin in the word "hebes"—dull, obtuse, heavy, sluggish. *Hebenon* is not found in any lexicon to which I have access. The "itch mite" intrudes itself upon our notice in

"Romeo and Juliet."—"Her wagoner, a small gray-coated gnat, not half so big as a round, little worm pick'd from the finger of a milk-maid." The arachnoid insect, known among naturalists as the acarus scabiei or common itch insect, is here certainly referred to. It was formerly supposed that this parasite found its way into the human skin from many of the animal species, as the dog, and others of our domestic animals. Several persons in Paris were said to have contracted the disease whilst attending upon a diseased camel. We see in the extract that milk-maids were thought to suffer from it, which would give us to think it communicable from the cow, if we agree with the text. There is an insect somewhat akin to the one under notice, which infests cheese, but it never affects the human or animal system. The true acarus scabiei is now universally believed to be propagated through raw or brown cane sugar; hence the term "finger of a grocer's maid" would in truth have been more appropriate in the case in question than was that of milk-maid. The vaccine disease, afterwards so thoroughly studied by Jenner, may have fallen under the notice of Shakespeare, and it may be that to this he refers in the quotation. This would get the itch and cow-pox only a little mixed. "Hal," afterwards Henry the Fifth, likens Falstaff to a "wen."

Prince Henry. (To Poins.) "I do allow this wen to be as familiar with me as my dog;" and again in "Merry Wives of Windsor:"

Falstaff. "Well, sir, I am almost out at heels.

Pistol. Why then let kibes ensue."

We recognize no such a malady as "kibes" in our modern nosology; but in former times it was in use, and meant to "chap" or crack open from cold, as in chilblains. The term is said to be of Persian origin,—the affection being, as intimated by Pistol, most common about the heels.

"You rub the sore, when you should bring the plaster—and, most chirurgeously."—"The Tempest."

"To strange sores, strangely they strain the cure."—"Much Ado About Nothing." Was the elastic bandage here presaged?

Thersites tells us what he knew about boils, as does also Coriolanus in his anathemas upon his ungrateful countrymen. Timon of Athens speaks of "ulcerous sores," whilst Charmian, in "Antony and Cleopatra," excuses herself from a game of billiards on the score of a sore arm. (Wonder if she hadn't been vaccinated.)

The following extract is from " A Midsummer Night's Dream:"

> " So shall all the couples three,
> Ever true in loving be ;
> And the blots of Nature's hand
> Shall not in their issue stand:
> Never mole, hare-lip, nor scar,
> Nor mark prodigious, such as are
> Despised in nativity,
> Upon their children be."

And in "Cymbeline:" " On her left breast a mark cinque-spotted, like the crimson drops i' the bottom of a cowslip," and " upon his neck a mole, a sanguine star: it was a mark of wonder."

In speculating upon the first of these extracts, it may be remarked that the " fates " probably understood few of the " tricks that are *not* vane " in the hands of nature,—if they had, it is hardly probable that so rash a promise as that their children should possess neither " mole, blot nor scar," would have been made,— as it is an unalterable fact that to have sound fruit we must have perfect parentage; [parents who are either morally, mentally or physically imperfect may transmit their characteristics to their progeny, and it seems to be an established fact as regards *acquired* imperfections as well as those that are inherent in individuals : thus crop your dog's tail, and his offspring may appear minus the caudal appendage,—if not in the first or second—may be in the third generation—atavism. This will happen the more surely if both the male and female parents be so treated. Blumenbach remembered a man whose little finger of the *right hand* was left crooked after an injury ; several of his sons at birth had the identical deformity in *their right hand.* Two brothers at Brussels were micropthalmic in the left eye ; their father had lost the left eye fifteen years before his marriage. A lady at Dover, England, was frightened by a ferret whilst *enciente;* every child born after that had eyes like the animal, and they all became blind, or nearly so, at the age of puberty. Brown-Sequard noted a case where a man became epileptic after a fall in which the dorsal vertebræ were shattered; he married and his son became epileptic, though there had not before been epilepsy in the family previous to the father's injury. I myself know a circumstance where the mother, and daughters in three generations following,—that is to say, from child to great grandmother, each had a small encysted tumor of the scalp *exactly* in the same situation, and all of the same nature. But the most beautiful and satisfactory results of this power of transmission are seen in the inferior animals, where many of the traits may be directly propagated from one living and mature being to another mature being,—of the same species or not, and afterwards these characteristics may be transmitted to the progeny. This is illustrated by the stripes on the shoulders and legs of the horse colt when the mother has previously borne mules ; and is sometimes also seen in the human family when the children of a second husband resemble in physical, mental or moral traits the mother's former husband. Through the relation of *parentage* the husband and wife may also impress upon each other their peculiarities—as in becoming to resemble each other in personal appearance, tastes, habits, mental traits, etc. *Association*, in young married people, together with the identity of conditions of physical and mental growth, may contribute to this end, but for its most complete attainment they must have "mingled bloods" in the great office of propagation. But as I started out to say before, these strange powers of transmission are best seen in the lower orders of animal creation,—as for instance in the guinea-pig.

Experiments upon nervous phenomena by Dr. Brown-Sequard show that in the guinea-pig exposure of the spinal cord, or severe injury to a large nerve trunk, will be followed by convulsions by irritating what he calls the " epileptic zone,"—a small spot of skin near the ear. In animals before mentioned as having received a nervous injury, convulsions may be produced at the pleasure of the experimenter by touching this special point of the cutaneous surface. When recovery of the injured nerve takes place, the hair always falls from the " convulsive zone ;"—but what I more particularly wished to notice is the fact that the young of these epileptic animals, brought forth after recovery, have the same epileptic seizures, and recovery is preceded by falling off of the hair in precisely the same place ! And further,—he remarked that the animals under experiment often eat off the toes of a paralyzed limb, and that in the young of the toeless father or mother the progeny would also appear with the same member missing ! This is a curious and interesting subject, and merits the close attention of the physiologist and gynæcologist.

It appears that æsthetics received a proper share of attention in

past ages, as well as in this present "fast" age of the world.
"Timon of Athens" in his misanthropic rage talks thus:

"Whore still: *paint till a horse may mire upon your face*," and
in "Cymbeline" he speaks of "some jay of Italy, who smothers
her with painting, hath betrayed him," thus giving us information
to the effect that the "rouge" and "pearl powders" found their
votaries in old times as they do to-day, mainly among the *demi
monde*. That *sensible* people then looked upon the custom of
"painting" as they now do, we may infer from a passage in
"Twelfth Night:"

Olivia. "Have you any commission from your lord to negotiate
with my face? We will draw the curtain and show you the picture.
Look, you, sir; such a one I am at this present: is't not well done?
Viola. *(In the garb of a youth.)* Excellently done, if God did
all.
Olivia. 'Tis ingrain, sir; 'twill indure wind and weather.
Viola. 'Tis beauty truly blent, whose red and white nature's
own sweet cunning hand laid on. Lady, you are the cruelest she
alive, if you will lead those graces to the grave, and leave the
world no copy."

The term "let her paint an inch thick," is also used, which tells
us that the habit of "spreading it on heavy" was perhaps not a
strange proceeding to the "ancient fair," whilst the same is hinted
at by "Clown" in "Measure for Measure."
The second portion of this chapter, as previously intimated, will
be devoted to the consideration of syphilography.
In "Measure for Measure" Lucio, the fantastic, in conversation
with two gentlemen:

1st Gentleman. "Do I speak feelingly?
Lucio. I think thou dost; and, indeed, with most powerful feeling of speech: I will, out of mine own confession, learn to begin
thy health; but, whilst I live, forget to drink after thee.
1st Gentleman. I think I have done myself wrong, have I not?
2d Gentleman. Yes, thou hast, whether thou art tainted or free.
Lucio. Behold, behold, where Madam Mitigation comes!
1st Gentleman. I have purchased as many diseases under her
roof, as comes to——
2d Gentleman. To what, I pray?

Lucio. Judge.

2d Gentleman. To three thousand dollars a-year.

1st Gentleman. Ay, and more.

Lucio. A French crown more.

2d Gentleman. Thou art always figuring diseases in me; but thou art full of error: I am sound.

Lucio. Nay, not as one would say healthy; but so sound as things that are hollow: thy bones are hollow; impiety hath made a feast of thee."

In the first paragraph of the foregoing it will be perceived that direct reference is made to the throat lesion of secondary syphilis, the lesion of articulation, and the danger incident to drinking after (from the same vessel) a person so contaminated is almost directly stated. Lucio proved his own wisdom in that matter, if he knew nothing else of value; and his determination to always forget to drink after the gentleman is worthy to be imitated by every thinking person. Indeed *I* have long practiced the habit of avoiding all places of public resort for the purpose of taking a drink of water, because syphilitic and other loathsome affections often cling to the lips and fingers of those resorting to them; particularly is the syphilitic poison wide-spread among the transient portion of mankind; and one does not know what moment he might innocently place this the most loathsome contagion to his lips, by the use of a public dipper, or by the hand-towel in the wash-room of an hotel.

The ravages made by pock upon the osseous system seems to have been clearly comprehended by Shakespeare, from the language used at the conclusion of the extract; and though the disease had then been of comparatively recent introduction into Europe (it is claimed from America), yet it had been pretty thoroughly studied we may suppose from this apparent familiarity with it by the unprofessional.

This same pedantic fellow, Lucio, in a conversation with the Duke thus demeans himself. *(Duke in disguise.)*

Lucio. "I was once before him (the duke) for getting a wench with child.

Duke. Did you such a thing?

Lucio. Yes, marry did I; but I was fain to forswear it: they would else have married me to the rotten medlar." ('Twould have been too good for him.)

Falstaff's quandary as to whether he was afflicted with gout or syphilis has been touched upon in the chapter on neurology; in the remarks there made, it is stated that notwithstanding the fact of the pain which gave rise to the thought, being situated in the great toe in place of the "shin," yet knowing the lascivious habits of "Sir John," and the exceedingly diverse phases which syphilitic lesions assume, we were inclined to believe "a gout o' this pox" true in this case of the "knight." We are strengthened in the position there taken, by the following conversation:

Falstaff. "How now, Mistress Doll?

Hostess. Sick of a calm: yea, good sooth.

Falstaff. So is all her sex; an they be once in a calm, they are sick.

Doll. You mauddy rascal, is that all the comfort you give me?

Falstaff. You make fat rascals, Mistress Doll.

Doll. I make them? Gluttony and diseases make them: I make them not.

Falstaff. If the cook helps to make the glutton, you help to make the diseases, Doll: we catch of you, Doll, we catch of you; grant that, my virtue, grant that."

As to the treatment of syphilis it is apparent that local treatment in the form of baths must have been common in Shakespeare's time if we look to the following in "Timon of Athens:"

Timon. "Art thou Timandra?

Timandra. Yes.

Timon. Be a whore still! they love thee not that use thee: give them diseases, leaving with thee their lust. Make use of thy salt hours; season the slaves for tubs and baths; bring down rose-cheeked youth to the tub fast, and the diet."

Perhaps it is the worse for *our* patients that we do not adopt a rigid course of bathing and personal purification in syphilis; especially might it benefit those in whom the cutaneous system is deeply involved; cleanliness is a most God-like virtue, and as a prophylactic measure—nay often a *curative* means, its worth is beyond estimate.

Ricord, Videlle nor Bumstead could hardly paint a better pen-picture of the ravages of syphilis than did this same cynical old Timon on another occasion when in conversation with one whom he accuses of harlotry.

Timon. "Consumption sow in hollow bones of men; strike their sharp shins, and mar men's spurring. Crack the lawyer's voice, that he may never more false title plead, nor sound his quillets shrilly; down with the nose, down with it flat; take the bridge away from him, make curl'd pate ruffians bald; and let the unscarr'd braggarts of the war derive some pain from you."

There cannot be found in the writings of the ablest medical authority of this age, a more terse and truthful picture of syphilis than is seen in these words of the sour old Timon. His description is indeed a marvel of accuracy. Witness the allusion to the throat, nasal and other osseous lesions—the fauces, vomer, tibia, etc., being special points of involvement in the tertiary state of the malady.

Hamlet. "How long will a man lie i' the earth ere he rot?
Clown. 'Faith, if he be not rotten before he die (as we have many pocky cases now-a-days, that will scarce hold the lying in), he will last you some eight year, or nine year: a tanner will last you nine year."

Thus it is seen that the "owner of a foul disease" (Hamlet, iv., i.) is punished even in the solitudes of the grave, by returning to dust much more rapidly than do virtuous men.

Lysimachus, in "Pericles," enquires of the bawd: "How now, wholesome iniquity! have you that a man may deal withal, and defy the surgeon?"

And the same gentleman in his interview with the virtuous Marina whose ill-luck had placed her in this den where "no heretics were burn'd but wenches' suitors" (Lear, iii., ii.), she assured him that "since I came (here), diseases have been sold dearer than physic,"—a truth which holds good even now whilst I write. It is known to every doctor that the degraded scoundrel who gives his last five dollars for the privilege of getting the malady will spend thirty in trying to evade the payment of the twenty he owes his surgeon for curing him.

When the medical profession makes it four times as costly for this class of patients to get rid of the malady as it is to catch it, there will be less need of "contagious disease acts" and "bawdy-house inspectors," and all that,—and the service will then only be awarded pay according to its worth. There is no class of practice in which the fees are so loosely and foolishly conducted as this;

and it is to be hoped that medical organizations everywhere will sometime make it incumbent upon members always to " bleed" this class of patients—not in the " bend of the arm " but in the purse. The idea that syphilis may be propagated through the blood of a person so affected, and that by microscopic observation we may detect in it certain syphilitic characteristics, finds some old footing in an assertion made by Andreas Cæsalpinus to the effect that when the Spaniards abandoned the town of Somma, near Mount Vesuvius, they mixed blood from the patients in the hospital of St. Lazarus with all the wine in the place, and thereby infected with syphilis all who drank it. This happened early after its alleged American origin. The bacterial theory might account for this.

CHAPTER VII.

ORGANOLOGY.

The stomach—Power of mind over function—Voluntary inanition—Its Pathology—What a physiologist!—Dietetic ideas of a hostess—An apt comparison—The irritability of hunger—A plain road—An error explained—The woodman and his belt—Seat of the affections—Gin-drinker's liver—Cause for effect—Smiling at grief—Lewdness and poverty—Illustrated—Sentiment reversed—The badge of cowardice—The truth in popular ideas—Then live, Macduff—Sleep in spite of thunder—Pulmonary gangrene—Benedick, the married man—Thaw'd out—A pertinent conclusion—A blind philosopher—How are you 'fraid!—Latent senses—The green flap—Some new infection—An enquiry—An amusing incident—"Hal's" vocabulary—Renal functions—Sympathetic fibrillæ—Carry his water to the wise woman—What says the doctor to my water?—A sensible doctor, for a wonder—Changes in the kidney—Nose painting—A sure sign—Taste not—A cheap article—"When I was about thy years, Hal"—The lean and hungry Cassius—He smiles in such a sort—Drawing the fire out—A parody—An exploded barbarity—Mr. Stribling, the druggist—The blood is the life—Blasting a good resolve—Man improves with his condition—A plea for the lancet—Palpitation—Good air as an agent—Much effuse of blood, etc.

Though not of the most rigidly appropriate character, it is proposed to include under the title "organology" all subjects pertaining to the different organs and structures of the body that have not before been noticed, and whilst we are aware that the arrangement may not escape criticism, we can only ask that he who may find fault with it may find the inclination, at some future time, to accomplish the very same task *better*.

The first organ to claim our notice is that fundamentally important one—the stomach.

It has been said in a former page, that unquiet meals make ill digestions,—the truth of which has forced itself upon the notice of most persons, no doubt. It seems that the function of alimentation is more closely allied to the proper working condition of the brain and nervous system than most other functions of the body. Strong emotional conditions of the mind may not only *suspend* the normal functions of this viscus,—*impair* them for a time, but may in rare instances totally *destroy* them, Within the last week, a man arrested and confined in our county jail, on a clear charge of murder, refused food from the time of his arrest, until his death took place from inanition,—in perfect health, otherwise, seemingly. In these cases there is actually no demand for food, from the simple fact that the nerves,—the gastric distribution of the parvagum, lose, through the powerful mental shock, their proper function,—and no hunger is felt. In cases of *voluntary* abstinence, like that of Tanner and others, the freedom from mental perturbation is the main factor in their power of indurance, though after a time, this same "abstinence" may and does "engender maladies" as its sequence, as we have it asserted in "Love's Labor Lost."

In "Richard the Second," John of Gaunt is made to say— "things sweet to taste prove in digestion sour," which would lead us to believe that the chemistry of the assimilative process was understood by Shakespeare as well as most of our modern physicians,—whilst we may exclaim, what a physiologist he might have become! This remark may, however, be applied to other appetites besides that of the stomach; and doubtless John only used it as a metaphor.

It appears that in the day of Mrs. Quickly it was not thought meet that one tax their digestive powers too far,—and Mrs. Quickly, who was an innkeeper, seems to have been one to entertain thoughts of so wholesome a kind. We hear her arguments upon this subject

"Hal came down on Sir John's pate with a bottle."

upon an occasion when "Hal" came down on "Sir John's" pate
with a bottle for likening the king to a singing-man of Windsor.

Mrs. Quickly. "Thou didst swear to me then, as I was washing
thy wounds, to marry me, to make me "my lady" thy wife. Canst
thou deny it? Did not good-wife Keech, the butcher's wife, come
in then, and call me gossip Quickly? coming in to borrow a mess
of vinegar? telling us she had a good dish of prawns, whereby
thou didst desire to eat some, whereby I told thee they were ill for
a green wound." The term "green wound" is also used in "Henry
the Fifth," an idea erroneous enough certainly, but part and parcel
of the notions of that day it appears.

Henry the Fourth likens the stomach to fortune that gives single-
handed;—"she either gives a stomach and no food—such are the
poor (in purse); or else a feast and no appetite,—such are the rich
that have abundance and enjoy it not: but the illustration of

Menenius, who compares with the digestive system the governor of
a province, is very good.

Menenius. "There was a time when all the body's members
rebell'd against the belly; thus accus'd it:

That only like a gulf did it remain i' the midst of the body, idle
and inactive, still cupboarding the viands, never bearing like labour
with the rest; where the other instruments did see and hear, devise,
instruct, walk, feel, and mutually participate, did minister unto the
appetite, and affection common to the whole body.

The belly answered.—

Citizen. Well, sir, what answer made the belly?

Menenius. I will tell you, if you will bestow a small (of what
you have a little) patience awhile, you'll hear the belly's answer.

Citizen. Y' are long about it.

Menenius. Note me this, good friend; your most grave belly
was deliberate, not rash like his accusers, and answered: 'True is
it, my incorporate friends,' quoth he, 'that I receive the general
food at first, which you do live upon; and fit it is, because I am
the storehouse, and the shop of the whole body: but if you do
remember, I send it through the rivers of your blood, even to the
heart, the brain, the strongest nerves, and small inferior veins;
they all receive from me that natural competency whereby they
live;' " and the irritable humor of a hungry man, is given by this
same Menenius, in good style, in a conversation with Sicinius, one
of the "tribunes of the people:"

Menenius. "He was not taken well (meaning that he was not
approach'd at the proper time); he had not dined: the veins unfill'd,
our blood is cold, and then we pout upon the morning, are unapt
to give or to forgive; but when we have stuffed these pipes, and
these conveyances of blood with wine and feeding, we have suppler
souls than in our priest-like fasts: therefore, I'll watch him till he
be dieted to my request, and then I'll set upon him.

Brutus. You know the very road into his kindness, and cannot
lose your way."

It is quoted by Darwin, as the saying of a certain physician, that
this irritability of temper so conspicuously noticeable in a hungry
man, is often converted by him, unconsciously, into actual *anger*—
in or by which state he is *stimulated* into a more bearable condition,
both mentally and physically.

This same authority tells us a truth but *partially* when he says that "good digestion waits on appetite, and health on both," because it is well known that there is often an abundance of appetite with no digestion at all;—yet we admit the truth of the latter portion of the paragraph, as healthy appetite attended by good digestion are the almost certain concomitants of good health.

It seems that the great author was in error as to the *modus operandi* of a dinner in producing a placid mind; it cannot be the "filling of the vein"—neither the "stuffing of the pipes and conveyances," as a result of drinking and feasting, which bring about this praiseworthy result, for in that event it would only be manifested some hours perhaps after meals, whereas it usually supervenes very speedily after a sumptuous dinner. I suspect that it is this gastric division of the "eighth pair" that here again raises the quarrel, and that the savory viands very soon apply their pacifying antidote to the millions of its fibrillæ which ramify upon the inner or mucous coating of the stomach; these same victuals perhaps also acting mechanically in some degree in producing the same effect,—and thus for once transforms a cross and oft-times unreasonable nondescript into a benign and pleasant husband and gentleman.

Speaking of the mechanical action of food upon the stomach—it will be recollected by the reader that this "pressure" upon the nerves and tissues of the organ need not always be made from the interior of its cavity; but that pressure from *without* will in some degree produce the same effect.

Remember the woodman who prepared himself to be absent at his camp a fortnight, and who in the place of food supplied himself with a broad leathern belt supplied with buckles and twelve holes; he took up his belt one "hole" each day, and at the end of two weeks was as sprightly as the "buck" of his native woods.

The liver was, by the ancients, supposed to be the seat of the affections, and in this fact we have an explanation of B*i*ron's (not B*y*ron's) talking of—"this is the liver vein," after having read some lines of erotic poetry; the line is found in "Love's Labor Lost."

Gratiano, in "The Merchant of Venice," puts matters in a sensible shape, thus: "With mirth and laughter let old wrinkles come, and let my liver rather heat with wine, than my heart cool with mortifying groans. Why should a man whose blood is warm within, sit like his grand-sire cut in alabaster? sleep when he wakes, and creep into the jaundice by being peevish?''

Here we have an honorable and ancient precedent for "hobnail liver," and he who chooses to follow the example can do so without the fear of being charged with a design to innovate upon the old and well established customs.

The woodman who prepared himself with a leathern belt.

In regard to a man's "creeping into jaundice through peevishness"—the effect is mistaken for the cause; old "Shake" got his cart before the horse that once. He had doubtless "let his liver heat with wine" on that occasion. This same idea as to the effects of excessive alcoholic stimulation upon the liver is seen also in "Antony and Cleopatra," A. i., S. ii.; and the confounding of cause and effect named above is corrected in a line in "Troilus and Cressida," when he says "what grief hath set the jaundice on your cheeks?"

The idea—erroneous as it is, and though antiquated as the ever-

lasting hills,—which makes the liver the seat of love and pusillanimity, finds many places to crop out in the writings of Shakespeare; of the former, Rosalind gives a negative attest when she
wishes to "wash the liver of Orlando as clean as a sound sheep's
heart, that there shall not be one spot of love left in 't," whilst in
"Twelfth Night" "The Duke" and Viola speculate on the connexion between the liver and the tender passion in this style:

Duke. "Alas! their love may be called appetite, no motion of
the liver, but the palate, that suffers surfeit, cloyment, and revolt;
but mine is hungry as the sea, and can digest as much;" when
Viola, detailing the depths of her own affections,—she "pin'd in
thought, and with a green and yellow melancholy, she sat like
Patience on a monument, smiling at grief." In this we see the
notion of a close relationship between melancholia and a deranged
hepatic function. "This wins him, liver and all," says Fabian,
whilst listening to the reading of the letter by his dupe Malvolio.
"Put fire in your heart and brimstone in your liver," was another
of the shrewd suggestions of the same fellow.

In an allusion to the supposition that lewdness and poverty go
hand in hand, Prince Henry speaks of "hot livers" and "cold
purses," and Falstaff, in his wrangle with the Chief Justice, assures
him that "you, that are old, consider not the capacities of us that
are young: you measure the heat of our livers with the bitterness
of your gall."

Pistol, one of the riotous companions of Sir John, gives us an
idea as to the causation of hepatitis, in the instance when he informs
"Knight Falstaff" of the news pertaining to his "Doll," and
"Hellen of his noble thoughts,"—the which thought would "in-
flame his noble liver." It would be extremely difficult to say
what, in a constitution like that of Falstaff, might serve to produce
an inflamed liver; if cowardice, love or wine should be considered
etiologic of liver complaint, we should expect such an unmitigated
old lout as he to be a continued series of afflictions.

Leontes in his jealous obliquity remarked that if his "wife's liver
were infected as her life, she would not live the running of one
glass." In this quotation we again find sentiment reversed:—
"Were my wife's life affected as her liver, she would not live the
running of one glass," would do very well, and would be in har-
mony with the general tenor of the sentiment on this subject, for
it will be remembered that he claimed his wife to be in love with
Polixenes.

Falstaff comes in again as an authority upon the liver question as affecting the principles of heroism. He says: "The second property of your excellent sherries is, the warming of the blood, which, before cold and settled, left the liver white and pale, which is the badge of pusillanimity and cowardice."

The "boy" spoken of before in connection with the demise of Sir John Falstaff, speaks of the courage of Bardolph in this light vein: "He is white liver'd and red faced, by the means whereof 'a faces it out, but fights not," whilst Sir Toby Belch declares of one of the characters in "Twelfth Night," that the blood in his liver would not clog the foot of a flea. The same notion as to the color of the liver under similar circumstances is found in "Richard the Third," whilst the term "lily liver'd" in connection with a lack of personal courage, is used in both "Macbeth" and "King Lear." The notion that anger is productive of an increased physiological condition of the liver, finds expression in "Henry the Eighth," and also in "Troilus and Cressida," A. i., S. iii.

It is said that most all notions which find credence among the public at large, no difference how improbable they may seem to those who are better informed, yet have some truth in them; this, no doubt, is the fact in regard to the wide-spread belief that the hepatic function is such that it leaves the liver white in all cowards; though here, as in a former instance or two, ¦the confounding of effect and cause is apparent. The influence which excited states of the mind exert upon the various organs and their functions is well known to persons conversant with the science of physiology,— and that the liver should bear a prominent share in these derangements of function we need not be at a loss to suppose when noting the important place it holds in the vital economy. That the mental emotion denominated *fear* makes pale also the heart we have evidence in "Macbeth," who uses the memorable words—"Then, live, Macduff: what need I fear of thee? But yet I'll make assurance doubly sure, and take a bond of fate: thou shalt not live; that I may tell pale-hearted fear it lies, and sleep in spite of thunder." It is not only fear that exercises a depleting influence over the liver in Shakespeare's estimation, but he says, in "Troilus and Cressida," that "reason and respect make livers pale, and lustihood deject." "Spotted livers" are noted there also, but seem to have no special significance.

The lungs are spoken of in "The Tempest," where lord Adrian

allows " the air breathes upon us here most sweetly," to which Sebastian replies—" As if it had lungs, and rotten ones," whilst Antonio concludes the fancy by suggesting, " or as 'twere perfumed by a fen,"—having reference to the very offensive eminations which escape from low and marshy grounds during hot weather.

We find here a connection of the two conditions of the lungs which go to constitute a case of that exceedingly rare malady— pulmonary gangrene. Whether Shakespeare was reasoning from analagous conditions as observed in other decomposing animal material, or had been the accidental observer of a case of real putrefaction of the lung tissue (progressive, of course), we of course have no means of knowing; but sure it is, he came very near the facts for a person who was merely guessing.

Benedick, "the married man," does not seem to have been so fastidious upon the health conditions of the woman he designed to make his wife, as would be one of our youths in 1884; for whilst Beatrice asserted that she only consented to wed *him* through pity, he avers he only took *her* because he had been told she was in a consumption! This would go near to be the truth perhaps, if Beatrice was old and wealthy, and lived in the United States at this era (I mean not the consumption, but the motive). But Beatrice had no tuberculosis—only a " whoreson cold, sir; a cough, sir," which soon left her when her frigid nature was thaw'd out by the workings of her nuptial pleasures.

The extract relative to the demise of Henry the Fourth, noticed in this work in the chapter on neurology, and reading thus :

" More would I, but my lungs are wasted so, that strength of speech is utterly denied me," appears to have been merely predicated upon a generally exhausted condition of the vital powers rather than to have depended upon an actual local pulmonary lesion. This conclusion is reached from the fact that no antecedent symptoms connected with the case are sufficient to warrant a different one.

Old Pandarus, who figures quite conspicuously in the courting affairs of Troilus and Cressida, "had it bad" if we are to place much credence in the old fellow's accuracy of judgment after having our faith so badly shaken in him upon remembering his failures on the woman question. He says: "A whoreson phthisic, a whoreson rascally phthisic so troubles me, and the foolish fortune of this girl; and what one thing, and what another, that I shall leave you one o' these day ;

I'll sweat and seek about for eases,
    And at that time (death?) will bequeath you my diseases."

It seems probable that if this person had a whoreson phthisic at all, that it was likely of a syphilitic origin, as in the two last lines quoted he gives us some hint in that direction; and the language of Troilus, whose confidence he had shamefully abused in the matter of his representations respecting the virtues of Miss Cressida, goes far toward substantiating the conclusion:

Troilus. "Hence, brothel-lackey! ignominy and shame pursue thy life, and live aye with thy name.

Pandarus. A goodly medicine for mine aching bones! O world! world! world! thus is the poor agent despised." The mere assertion, however, that he would bequeath his disease does not make it positive that he had not a whoreson phthisic, for the reason simply that it is now proven beyond a doubt that tuberculosis is directly transmissible from one person who is suffering from it to another who is in good health. The germs,—bacteria—may be carried into the system of a sound person through several avenues, or by more than one means, viz.: by inoculating, either with the blood, or directly with tubercular matter; or by inhaling the detritus from the expiration of a tubercular patient; and also, perhaps, by absorption—cutaneous and mucous, as in occupying the same couch with a tubercular patient.

The matter pertaining to the pathology of the respiratory system having been noticed, we come next to its physiology. In this direction we have such phrases as "so shall my lungs coin words till they decay," "thou but offend'st thy lungs to speak so loud," and "the heaving of my lungs to ridiculous smiling," etc., etc., are some of them.

An extract from "A Midsummer Night's Dream," which is interesting to the physiologist, is found in the following:

" Dark night, that from the eye his function takes,
    The ear more quick of apprehension makes;
    Wherein it doth impair the seeing sense,
    It pays the hearing double recompense."

Under ordinary circumstances the above is not true—as for example in the case of a physician who is necessarily out much of nights; but I do believe a person learns to, or acquires the power to see better by being trained in the school of night perambulations; the *transient* suspension of any one of the special senses will not be compensated for by any one of the others assuming its duties in part or in whole, but it is certainly true that the total obliteration of one or more of them, and a long schooling of those which remain perfect, render them much more acutely sensitive to their wonted stimulus, and may thus often in some degree fill the principle of compensation.

I had Shakespeare's idea, as above expressed, very fairly illustrated some years ago in my own family. There was sojourning in the village where we then resided, a gentleman of fine intelligence who was congenitally blind. My wife chanced to be calling at the house of a lady where he was stopping, and he heard her name called, and also had some conversation with her; from that time forward he could always recognize her in name and in person by the voice alone; I was much from home about this time, and my wife was considerably exercised as to the probability of the "blind man's" wanting to stay a time at our house, as he had been complimenting most of the neighbors with his company for a few days each. One day she had been down the street on an errrand, and whilst on her return she discovered on the other side of the street, but considerably in advance of her, the "blind man," Mr. Flemming, making his way in the same direction; she instantly said in a low tone to a companion who was with her — "Yonder goes the blind man ; I don't want him to go to our house, for I am afraid of him."—"How are you afraid !" suddenly rang out sharp and clear from the poor man's lips. She was much surprised, as she supposed that at that distance no ordinary ear was able to distinguish the sound of an ordinary conversation, little less the exact words. Here this power of compensation had doubtless been educated to the point of the nicest acuteness as a *necessity* to the welfare of the individual, as otherwise he no doubt would have encountered many dangers in his perambulations about the country entirely alone.

Apropos of this subject, a strange story comes to us from Europe, in the work of Mr. W. H. Levy, entitled "Blindness and the Blind," in which he tells of himself that although he is totally blind yet he has the power to distinguish one object from another— to tell perfectly well when near to an object, etc., almost as well as though he was possessed of vision ; he can distinguish a house from a shop, or a board fence from a stone wall,—tell how high an object near him may be,—distinguish a stump from a horse, etc., with much precision. This power he terms "facial perception," or the power of seeing with the face, as he loses the faculty when the face is covered, and cannot perform the function with any other portion of the surface, though it be uncovered. Writers call this power the "latent sense," but at best it is not very clearly understood. "Sand-blind," "high gravel blind," are terms used in the "Merchant of Venice," and seem to be of the same significance as our term "stone blind."

"I do see the cruel pangs of death, bright in thine eye," is found in "King John," whilst Thersites, in "Troilus and Cressida," tells us what he knows about ophthalmia and its therapeutics when he likens Patroclus to a "green sarcinet flap for a sore eye;" and the man Benvolio, in "Romeo and Juliet," gives us his in the oft-quoted couplet:—

> "Take now some new infection to thine eye,
> And the rank poison of the old will die."

I have often wondered why the "green flap" is universally worn in these cases; I can think of no optical law which makes it either desirable or necessary. In the couplet is embodied the whole principle of the *treatment* of ophthalmic affections, namely: the production of a *new* or of another condition in the structures of the eye.

"Come on my right hand," for this ear is deaf," says Cæsar to Antony. This infirmity is one of grave annoyance, as the writer can attest from a past experience; and, like Cæsar (in one particular at least), he always wants his companion on his right hand; indeed it is unpleasant for one to ride or walk to his left, though it be in silence, so confirmed is the habit. An incident occurred in this connection a year or so ago, when on a horseback ride into the country with a strange gentleman. He, upon starting, got to my left hand,—as I supposed by chance; it was no great while until an opportunity offered, which I made the most of, by riding in a careless manner on his left; this process was repeated several times during the trip, until at last it was evident that on his part as on my own, the change was not by accident but by design; and upon enquiry it was found that the worthy gentleman was in the same unpleasant predicament as Cæsar and myself,—he always wanted his Antony on his right hand, as his left ear was deaf.

Epistaxis is noticed in "The Merchant of Venice," and pleuritis or pleurodinia, "side stitches that shall pen the breath up," in "The Tempest," while "the dropsy drown this fool," and "that swollen parcel of dropsies," are terms in the vocabularies of Calaban and Prince "Hal." If we take the latter as veritable fact, it gives us another argument in the chain of evidence that old "Sir John" was miasmatic, as it is a well known fact that abdominal dropsies are a very frequent concomitant of malarial poisonings, and the term was applied by the prince to his old friend—"Jack Falstaff, gentleman."

The renal function is noticed first in the "Merchant of Venice," in this way: "Some are mad if they behold a cat; and others, when the bagpipe sings i' the nose, cannot contain their urine for affection." In this quotation we see again the power of emotional conditions of the mind over the organic functions; in cases of the character just alluded to we find the analogue of the peristaltic action of the intestinal mucous membrane through the excitation of the sympathetic fibrillæ which supplies it, in cases of fear; or in the lachrymal apparatus through the patheticus.

The tormentors of poor Malvolio, in "Twelfth Night," concocted a plan by which they attempted to make him believe they were in earnest as to his lunacy; they proposed to "carry his water to the wise woman"—a proceeding very popular in a certain class of our profession only a few years ago. The "urine doctors" do not flourish to the same extent in this country as in days gone by. Falstaff does not escape in this matter either; "what says the doctor to my water?

Page. He said, sir, the water itself was a good water; but for the party that owned it, he might have more diseases than he knew of." A sensible and conscientious doctor, for a wonder.

In "Macbeth" it is given out as a fact that "drink" is a great provoker of three things, viz.: "Nose-painting, sleep and urine." Lager beer for the latter always.

As in the case of the liver, so with the kidneys,—the alcoholic stimulants exercise a very marked influence over their functions; what may at first constitute only an augmented functional activity through the stimulating effects upon the renal organs, will, in the end, if long continued, lead to structural change in the kidney in the form of granular degeneration, or atrophy, or some other abnormal condition which is a sure precursor of toxæmia, dropsical effusions, and other perversions of the healthy life which ultimate in death; even the sleep itself which "drink" promotes is one morbid in its action; whilst the nose-painting which seems only a matter for sport, to those who observe superficially, is a sure sign to others that the alcohol has commenced its destructive processes in the system in earnest. It is claimed of late that some skilled artizan has discovered a process by which the illuminated proboscis may be bleached, and rendered as good as new. The only remedy, however, known to physicians is to "leave sack."

Falstaff even had to bear the odium of being fat attached to his other sins.

Prince Henry. "Here comes lean Jack, here comes bare bones. How long is't ago, Jack, since thou sawest thy own knee?

Falstaff. My own knee? when I was about thy years, Hal, I was not an eagle's talon in the waist; I could have crept into any alderman's thumb-ring: a plague of sighing and grief! it blows a man up like a bladder." Then after a wrangle, in which much laughable matter occurs between them, they conclude in this way:

Falstaff. "The king himself is to be feared as the lion. Dost thou think I'll fear thee as I fear thy father? Nay, an I do, I pray God, my girdle break!

Prince Henry. O, if it should, how would thy guts fall about thy knees! But, sirrah, there's no room for faith, truth, nor honesty, in that bosom of thine; it is filled up with guts and midriff."

The dissimilarity in the mental organization is on a par with that of the physical when we compare another of Shakespeare's characters with his inimitable Falstaff. Reference is made to Cassius, whose physique and mental make up are thus placed in contrast with that of Sir John.

Cæsar. "Let me have men about me that are fat; sleek-headed men, and such as sleep o'nights. Yond' Cassius has a lean and hungry look; he thinks too much: such men are dangerous. Would he were fatter; but I fear him not; yet if my name were liable to fear, I don't know the man that I should avoid as soon as that spare Cassius. He reads much; he loves no plays, he hears no music, seldom smiles, and when he does, he smiles in such a sort as if he mock'd himself, and scorn'd his spirit that could be moved to smile at anything." Falstaff would have been a man after Cæsar's own heart.

It is very clearly perceived and forcibly illustrated in the fore-going selection that Shakespeare had observed the fact that ali-mentive and intellectual capacity are not likely to be twins—or, in other words, to reside in the same person. Stomach work and brain work are not generally compatible, from physiological reasons as given in a former chapter.

"And make each petty artery in his body, as hardy as the Numean lion's nerve."—*Hamlet*. " My veins are chill, and have no more of life, than may suffice to give my tongue that heat to ask your help." A case of extreme debility in the person of Pericles. Veins and their contents are noticed in "A Winter's Tale," and "As fire cools fire within the scorched veins of one new burn'd " in " King John ; " whilst another passage in the same reads " or if that surly spirit, melancholy, had bak'd thy blood, and made it heavy, thick, which else runs trickling up and down the veins."

In the first of these quotations from "John," it is evident that it had a deep hold upon the popular mind ; as we see ninety-nine out of a hundred common people, even now, hold to and act upon the notion that exposing a fresh burn to the fire afterward will " draw the fire out." The process of roasting the victim of a coal oil explosion slowly before a red-hot stove as a healing process has no good grounds in the philosophy of therapeutics ; we might well *cõmmit* a parody and exclaim O Science, O Medicine, what barbari-ties are enacted in thy name!

In " King John " we also find a line which reads thus : " That whiles warm life plays in that infant's veins "—only an idea in veri-fication of the old scripture—" the blood is the life thereof."

Falstaff, after marching up and throwing down the body of the dead Percy, claiming that he had slain him, whilst pleasantly con-templating his chances of growing renowned over his feat, talks thus to himself :

" He that rewards me, God reward him ; if I do grow great, I'll grow less ; for I'll purge and leave sack, and live cleanly, as a nobleman should."

Poor Sir John, the grounds upon which he built his good resolves proved as fallacious as the mirage of the desert ; but the *resolve* alone teaches us to remember the fact that man always rises with his condition ; place a boor on a seat of rosewood and he will think twice before cutting it, or place him in a room with Brussels carpets, and he will scarcely eject his saliva.

As to curtailing his obesity by purging, it was of doubtful propriety, but the resolve to leave off sack and live cleanly were the very essence of philosophy. The fat in his system represented the hydro-carbon that should have been consumed in the respiratory process; but the system being always supplied with an abundance of that material in the sack, the respiratory fires were kept burning with that fuel, and the fat was laid by for a rainy day, or for a period of hybernation as it were. So of the cleanliness: remove the dirt from the surface, and oxydation of the superfluous tissues will be hastened.

The subject of fever is a little too general to come appropriately under the present head; but as there seems no more convenient place for the little that is named of the subject, I shall introduce it here nevertheless. I quote two or three lines from "Love's Labor Lost:"

Dumaine. "I would forget her, but a fever she reigns in my blood, and will remember'd be.

Biron. (Aside.) A fever in your blood? why, then, incision would let her out in saucers," (evidently refering to the custom of venesection),—whilst we find in "King John" some lines reading thus: "This fever that hath troubled me so long, lies heavy on me," and "ah me! this tyrant fever burns me up;" "entreat the north to make his bleak winds kiss my parched lips, and comfort me with cold." These words were quoted before in the chapter on etiology, and their causation and pathological significance placed to the action of malaria, instead of "poison tasted to him by a monk." We also find the idea, as expressed in the words of Biron, embodied in a conversation between the Archbishop of York and the Earl of Westmoreland, in "Henry the Fourth;" and, though only used in an allegorical sense, yet it conveys a good notion of the practice of the times.

Archbishop. "We are all diseas'd; and with our surfeiting, and wanton hours, have brought ourselves into a burning fever, and we must bleed for it; of which disease, our late king, Richard, being infected, died."

The condition of the circulation in fever is noted in "Troilus and Cressida," as appears in the following:

Pandarus. (Speaking of Cressida.) "She's making her ready. She'll come straight: you must be witty now. She does so blush, and fetches her wind so short, as if she was frayed with a sprite: I'll fetch her. It is the prettiest villain: she fetches her breath so short as a new-tak'n sparrow. *(Ex. Pandarus.)*

Troilus. Even such a passion doth embrace my bosom: my heart beats thicker than a feverous pulse, and all my powers do their bestowing lose."

The foregoing is a very fair pen-picture of the excitement incident to venereal anticipation in the modest young man. This from old Timon, is after his usual style: "Go, suck the subtle blood of the grape, till the high fever seethe your blood to froth, and so 'scape hanging: trust not the physician; his antidotes are poison, and he slays more than you rob," whilst may be mentioned again the charge against Cæsar: "He had a fever when he was in Spain, and, when the fit was on him, I did mark how he did shake." "Hectic," is used in "Hamlet." In "Love's Labor Lost" we have a precedent for "open air" exercises held now as so essential for health. "So it is, besieged with sable-coloured melancholy, I did commend the black-oppressing hour to the most wholesome physic of the health giving air; and, as I am a gentleman, betook myself to walk. The time when? About the sixth hour; when beasts most graze, birds best peck, and men sit down to that nourishment called supper. So much for the time when. Now for the ground which; which, I mean, I walk'd upon; it is ycleped the park. Then for the place where; where, I mean, I did encounter that obscene and most preposterous event, that draweth from my snow-white pen the ebon-coloured ink, which here thou viewest, beholdest, surveyest or seest." So much for the exhilaration of an evening's walk.

In "The Winter's Tale," Leontes says: "The blessed gods purge all infection from our air, whilst you do climate here," whilst we see in "King John" the faith in good air: "His highness yet doth speak; and holds belief, that being brought into the open air, it would allay the burning quality of that fell poison," etc.

The horrors of pestilential vapors are thus presented:

"A many of your bodies shall, no doubt, find native graves, upon the which, I trust, shall witness live in brass of this day's work; and those that leave their valiant bones in France, dying like men, though buried in yon dunghills, they shall be fam'd; for there the sun shall greet them, and draw their horrors up to heaven, leaving their earthly parts to choke your clime, the smell whereof shall breed a pestilence in France," whilst the hurtful influence of air to an early wound is thus stated: "The air hath got into my deadly wounds, and much effuse of blood doth make me faint."— "Henry the Sixth," A. ii., S. vi.

The deleterious effects of the local action of even *pure* air upon open wounds is clearly recognized even now. Filter it—removing all germs and mechanical irritants, and yet the oxygen or some other constituent admitted with it will cause the wound to progress in a manner different from one hermetically closed.

CHAPTER VIII.

Grows stronger for the breaking—Mistaken principle—Patching the over-coat—Bad practice—Syncope—Mistakes in prognosis—Spare the blood—Shakespeare a poor surgeon—A scar covered veteran—The money changer—The surgeon's fee—Professional failing—Doctors and the clergy—A man with a soul—The surgeon's tools—Surgeon's fort—Honors to whom honor, etc.—Trichina spiralis—Who is responsible?—Doctors and their doings—Little change—Cowardly knave—Jester for an hospital—The least merit—A precedent for doctor "she"—"Malignant fistulæ"—Potent remedy—Popular ignorance—The reformed hod-carrier—Professional honor—Another comparison—A lame impostor and his lame detection—Doctor's untimely end—The English Nero—Dr. Butts, the scoundrel—A want of faith—Woful mistake—Danger of expectancy—In Macbeth—An absurd credulity—God Almighty as a visiting physician—How does your patient, doctor?—Needs a divine—No mean psychologist—Indiscreet—A self-constituted doctor.

There will be united in the present chapter all the matter pertaining to the specialty of Surgery,—the surgeon, therapeutics, and the physician ; at the same time taking care to keep the specific material of each as distinct from the other as possible.

It is asserted in the second part of "Henry the Fourth" that a "broken limb united, grows stronger for the breaking;" and in the same "thou hast drawn my shoulder out of joint."

Now the first of these propositions is perhaps predicated upon the assumption that because the deposition of bony material at the site of fracture is usually more voluminous than the original normal bone, the *strength* of the new structure will be greater also. This conclusion is opposed to the principles of repair not only in histogenetic operations, but also in the ordinary physical and mechanical appliances. This principle, in its application to living tissues, used to be fairly illustrated by the late Prof. Linton, of St. Louis, in this way : "The neoplasms are all formed of materials of a less perfect vitality than the normal original tissue of the part where they may chance to be located;—that in cicatricial tissue in particular is this so marked, that he could illustrate the difference in no better way than to liken it to patching your over-coat with a bit of your cotton shirt." This principle holds good with the osseous as well as all other tissues, and demonstrates conclusively that we have caught Shakespeare in one error at least. When once we have a broken femur, we may, under the most favorable circumstances, never hope to have it "just as good as new;" or, "just as good as *old*" rather.

In "As You Like It" we find the following: "And here, upon his arm, the lioness had torn some flesh away, which all this while had bled; and now he fainted, and cried in fainting upon Rosalind. Brief, I recover'd him, bound up his wound," etc. Shakespeare here observed the caution to not make a patient dangerous as to hemorrhage from a lacerated wound; though he lets him bleed enough to make him fall into a syncope; the damage, however, was not lasting, as we are assured that Orlando was again soon " strong of heart." In "Henry the Fourth" occurs another passage in regard to a swoon into which the king had fallen.

Somerset. " Rear up his body; wring him by the nose." This teaching as to changing a person to an upright or semi-upright position in a common syncope is averse to the very law and resource of nature,—the falling into a horizontal position being the very means adopted by unassisted nature to restore such cases. As to the " wringing by the nose" to revivify a fainting patient, that method was never any part of nature's plan, but is doubtless the offspring of some miserable botch. The loss of blood is also recognized as a source of syncope in the case of Clifford where he tells us that " much effuse of blood doth make me faint." We have another failure in Shakespeare to sufficiently weigh surgical principles, in the fact that he did not discriminate between lesions of a serious nature and those which are comparatively unimportant:— thus, he makes the loss of an eye and part of the cheek as very early fatal in the case of Salisbury in " Henry the Fourth;" he makes the case as speedily fatal as would be a wound of a vital organ—as the lung, liver, kidney, etc., whilst another error is in the words—" the blood I drop, is rather physical than dangerous to me"—found in Coriolanus. It is axiomatic in all surgical practice that the less blood we have from a traumatism or following the use of the surgeon's knife, the better for the patient. The same rule holds true in obstetric practice, as it is a truism that the most dangerous cases of metritis and other complications arising to post parturient patients in my hands have followed usually in cases preceded by profuse hemorrhage.

The grave apprehensions entertained for the safety of a patient with fractured ribs, as seen in "As You Like It," would also add weight to the conclusion that tho' Shakespeare was good at most all things else, he was sadly deficient as a writer upon surgical science. There is a notice of a character having had his "shoulder blade" "torn out" in "Winter's Tale," and in "King Lear" we find "flax and whites of eggs" recommended as a hemostatic. The wound in "Portia's thigh" has nothing significant in it, whilst only a military surgeon would be interested in the scar-covered veteran Marcius who had one wound i' the shoulder, one i' the left arm, seven hurts i' the body, one i' the neck and two i' the thigh, etc., making in all twenty-seven. "The Winter's Tale" also has "I fear my shoulder blade is out," as a conclusion to "Shakespeare as a Surgeon."

The term "surgeon" is used quite frequently. In "Midsummer-Night's Dream" is a witticism that "with the help of a surgeon he (one of the number of fops) might yet recover, and yet prove an ass"—an assertion that is too true of many, many of the surgeon's clients.

In the case of Shylock, the Jewish money-changer, the court enjoined the necessity of having "some surgeon" at hand when he cut his "pound of flesh," "to stop his wounds, lest he do bleed to death." Shylock failed to cut, therefore the surgeon's skill was not brought into service; wonder if he got his fee? I suspect he did not, as it is the amount of *physical* labor, and the *quantity* of medicine administered in a given case, which entitles the practitioner to *pay* in the estimation of a majority of mankind. We find a very good illustration of the character of the cases which surgeons are often called to treat in the case of a riot between Sir Toby Belch, Sir Andrew Ague-check, and Sebastian in "Twelfth Night," and also a stab at the morals of some of our "Surgeon Dicks" who get "tight," and get their "eyes set at eight i' the morning." Unfortunately for themselves and for their patrons, it was the custom, not long in the past, for many of the best minds in the surgical and medical professions to drink immoderately; but I am of the opinion from an extended observation, that the "whisky habit" has grown much less common among medical men during the last twenty years.

The morals of medical men as a class, seems to me not inferior to that of an equal number of persons chosen from any class in society—not even omitting the clergy. It has been said: "Show me three physicians, and I will show you two sceptics," as an illustration of the religious status of the profession. This happens, no doubt, from the fact that physicians are usually men who do not swallow blindly the teachings of others; they think and reason for themselves, and the consequence is that they find much that is put forth by the theoretical propagators of Christianity as too futile for a moment's serious consideration; they are men who look up from nature to nature's God, and worship accordingly. If you want a man with a *soul* go to the ranks of the true physician, and you will be sure to find him.

"Surgeon's box" is mentioned in "Troilus and Cressida," and "fetch a surgeon" in "Romeo and Juliet" in the case of Mercutio.

Romeo. "Courage, man, the hurt cannot be much.

Mercutio. No, 'tis not so deep as a well, nor so wide as a church door, but 'tis enough; 'twill serve: ask for me to-morrow, and you will find me a grave man."

Now in reference to the "surgeon's box," we suppose that the case in which surgeons keep their "tools"—(to use the unmistakable language of a young medical gentleman of our acquaintance) is meant; whilst "go get him surgeon," is the language of Duncan in behalf of a wounded soldier.

"Let me have a surgeon, I am cut to the brain," was the request of old King Lear in one of his fantasies; and Iago, that impersonation of the sum of all villainies, proffered to "fetch a surgeon" for Rodrigo, who had been set upon by his own hired assassins.

It is apparent that the practice of surgery was even at that early day looked upon with much more respect than the practice of medicine; thus it is to-day, and thus it will ever be.

There is one very obvious cause for this, and one which all may and do more or less observe—and that is the surgeon's work is always tangible to the naked eye of the populace, no comprehensive thinking or philosophizing being brought into requisition for the recognition of the surgeon's power; whilst the intricacies which the doctor proper has to meet and overcome are far beyond the scrutiny of the ordinary observer.   Whilst, really, the surgeon is only an ordinary mechanic in many instances, and the physician a deep and genuine philosopher, the one carries the palm amongst a thoughtless community, whilst the other is set down as an old fogy. It seems, too, that the profession is half inclined to honor the surgeon more than the physician, and it may be that it is from the fact that the peculiarities of the science and art of surgery proper are not cursed with the multitudes of parasites to which the practice of medicine is exposed—the practice of medicine, owing to the advantages which may be taken of it, having to bear the odium of a million professional (?) leeches sucking at its integrity.   The great profession legitimate medicine, reminds me of a strong man who partakes of an underdone pork steak, and in process of time becomes afflicted, heart, brain and all, with trichina spiralis.   Quackery is everywhere; it pervades the high places as well as the low, flourishes in the palace of the rich as well as in the hovel of the poor, and is so fastened upon and rooted into the profession and society that there is no feasible way in which to get rid of the evil.   The profession itself is in some degree responsible for this; but in the mean it is due to the willful ignorance of the populace.   Our American people will be humbugged, and the pretenders in medicine make them pay dearly for their willing pliability.

As Part II. of Chapter VIII., we design adding what we have upon the subject of "Doctors and their doings;" and, though constituting the bulk of the chapter, we hope it may not prove less interesting on that ground.   Of materials we have an assortment: we have the "regular" and the "mountebank,"—doctor "she" and the "tooth-slinger," each in his sphere; little observable change in the quantity or quality of the "goods" in three hundred years.

The renowned "French physician"—Doctor Caius, whose misunderstanding with Sir Hugh Evans is so well described in the "Merry Wives of Windsor," is a true representative of the advertising fraternity of this day; and when Sir Hugh avowed that his antagonist had "no more knowledge of Hibbocrates and Galen,—and he is a knave besides;—a cowardly knave," he no doubt hit upon the exact truth.

We find a strange bargain as to service in an hospital in "Love's Labor Lost," in the matter of the courtship between Rosaline and Biron:

Rosaline. "If you my favor mean to get, a twelvemonth shall you spend, and never rest, but seek the weary beds of people sick.

Biron. Studies, my lady? Mistress, look on me: behold the window of my heart, mine eye, what humble suit attends the answer there; impose some service on me for thy love.

Rosaline. Oft have I heard of you, my lord Biron, before I saw you, and the world proclaims you replete with mocks, comparisons, and wounding flouts, which you on all estates will exercise, that lie within the mercy of your wit: to weed this wormwood from your fruitful brain, and, therewithal, to win me, if you please, without the which I am not to be won, you shall this twelvemonth term, from day to day, visit the speechless sick, and still converse with groaning wretches; and your task shall be, with all the fierce endeavor of your wit, to force the pained impotent to smile.

Biron. To move wild laughter in the throat of death? it cannot be; it is impossible: mirth cannot move a soul in agony.

Rosaline. Why, that's the way to choke a gibing spirit, whose influence is begot of that loose grace, which shallow laughing hearers give to fools. A jest's prosperity lies in the ears of him that hears it, never in the tongue of him that makes it: then if sickly ears, deaf'd with the clamours of their own dire groans, will hear your idle scorns, continue there, and I will have you, and that fault withal; but, if they will not, throw away that spirit, and I shall find you empty of that fault, right joyfully of your reformation.

"I'll jest a twelvemonth in an hospital."

Biron. A twelvemonth? well, befall what will befall, I'll jest a twelvemonth in an hospital."

It appears to me that there is less merit—less applicability, less pretext for the above quoted matter, and that the occasion was less appropriate for the exercise of such a train of thought, than is to be found in connection with almost any single passage or reflection in the entire writings of Shakespeare. The only merit I am able to discover in it is the *originality* of the idea of employing a " jester " to an hospital; the idea being new, whether its application would be of value or not. It is not every day that we stumble on original thought even of doubtful merit, and we will prize this accordingly.

The champions of female physicians may find a precedent for their doctrines in " All's Well That Ends Well," in the case of Lady Helena, who ministered to the king successfully.

The old lord, Lafeu, in a conversation with the Countess of Rousillon, in answer to the enquiries as to the health of the king, remarked—" He hath abandoned his physicians, madam; under whose practice he hath persecuted time with hope, and finds no other advantage in the process, but only the losing of hope by time.

Countess. "This young gentlewoman *(meaning Helena, her ward)* had a father,—O, that had! how sad a passage 'tis,—whose skill, almost as great as his honesty, had it stretch'd so far, would have made nature immortal, and death should have played for lack of work. Would, for the king's sake, he were living! I think it would be the death of the king's disease. He was famous, sir, in his profession.

Lafeu. He was excellent, indeed, madam: the king very lately spake of him, admiringly and mourningly; he was skilled enough to have lived still, if knowledge could be set up against mortality.

Bertram. What is it my good lord, the king, languisheth of?

Lafeu. A fistula, my lord."

King. (Another Scene.) "How long is it, count, since the physician at your father's died? He was much fam'd.

Bertram. Some six months since, my lord.

King. If he were living, I would try him yet:—lend me an arm;—the rest have worn me out with several applications: nature and sickness debate at their leisure."

Then follows a lengthy conversation on other matters, and then the king's malady is again brought up:

Lafeu. "I have seen a medicine that is able to breathe life into a stone, quicken a rock, and make you dance canary with spritely fire and motion; whose simple touch is powerful to upraise King Pepin, nay, to give great Charlemain a pen in's hand, to write to her a love line.

King. What her is this?

Lafeu. Why, doctor she. My lord, there's one arriv'd, if you will see her:—now, by my faith and honor, if seriously I may convey my thoughts in this my light deliverance, I have spoke with one, that in her sex, her years, profession, wisdom, and constancy, hath amaz'd me more than I dare blame my weakness. Will you see her (for that is her demand), and know her business? That done, laugh well at me.

King. Now, good Lafeu, bring in the admiration, that we with thee may spend our wonder too, or take off thine by wond'ring how thou took'st it."

Lafeu then brings in Helena, and remarks—" This is his majesty; say your mind to him: a traitor you do look like; but such traitors

his majesty seldom fears. I am Cressida's uncle, that dare leave
two together. Fare you well.

King. Now, fair one, does your business follow us?

Helena. Ay, my good lord.   Gerard de Narbon was my father;
in what he did profess well found.

King. I knew him.

Helena. The rather will I spare my praises towards him; knowing him is enough.   On 's bed of death many receipts he gave me;
chiefly one which, as the dearest issue of his practice, and of his
old experience the only darling, he bade me store up as a triple
eye, safer than mine own two, more dear.   I have so: and hearing
your high majesty is touch'd with that malignant cause, wherein the
honor of my dear father's gift stands chief in power, I came to tender it, and my appliance, with all bound humbleness.

"Helena and the King."

King. We thank you, maiden, but may not be so credulous of cure: when our most learned doctors leave us, and the congregated college have concluded that labouring art can never ransom nature from her inaidable estate, I say, we must not so stain our judgment, or corrupt our hope, to prostitute our past-cure malady to empirics; or to dissever

> Our great self and our credit, to esteem
> A senseless help, when help past sense we deem.

Helena. My duty then shall pay me for my pains: I will no more enforce my office on you; humbly entreating from your royal thoughts a modest one, to bear me back again.

King. I cannot give thee less to be called grateful.

> Thou thought'st to help me, and such thanks I give
> As one near death to those that wish him live;
> But what at full I know, thou knowest no part,
> I know all my peril, thou no art.

Helena.

> What I can do can do no hurt to try,
> Since you set up your rest 'gainst remedy.
> He that of greatest works is finisher
> Oft does them by the weakest minister.

King.

> I must not hear thee; fare thee well, kind maid.
> Thy pains not used, must by thy self be paid:
> Proffers, not took, reap thanks for their reward.

Helena.

> Dear sir, to my endeavors give consent;
> Of heaven, not me, make an experiment.
> I am not an impostor, that proclaim
> Myself against the level of mine aim;
> But know I think, and think I know most sure,
> My art is not past power, nor you past cure.

King. Art thou so confident? Within what space hop'st thou my cure?

Helena. The greatest grace lending grace,

> Ere twice the horses of the sun shall bring
> Their fiery torcher his diurnal ring;
> Ere twice in murk and occidental damp
> Moist Hesperus hath quench'd his sleepy lamp;

> Ere four and twenty times the pilot's glass
> Hath told the thievish minutes how they pass,
> What is infirm from your sound parts shall fly,
> Health shall live free, and sickness freely die.

King. Upon thy certainty and confidence, what dar'st thou venture?

Helena. Tax of impudence, a strumpet's boldness, a divulged shame, traduced by odious ballads; my maiden's name

> Seared otherwise; the worst of worst extended,
> With vilest torture let my life be ended.

King.

> Methinks, in thee some blessed spirit doth speak,
> His powerful sound in this, an organ weak;
> Sweet practiser, thy physic I will try,
> That ministers thine own death, if I die."

We see in the above quotation but a reflection of the ideas of the ignorant masses from that day to the present; the matter is only the notions of to-day presented in their most feeble aspect. Ninety-nine hundredths of the people of this March, 1884, would quit the "most learned doctors, and congregated college," and run wild after some " Indian doctor," the which is only another name for some reformed hod-carrier. Even " kings and potentates," and others whose common sense ought to be a guarantee of better actions, trust the lives of their *children*—sometimes themselves, to the medical care of some creature having less skill than a boot-black.

Our lady friends who are ambitious to become specialists in the department of " malignant fistulae " may in the foregoing case find an ancient and honorable precedent.

Apropos of the cure of fistulas, it was the fortune—good or bad— of this city, a few years ago, to be visited by an old and impudent negro, who called himself Dr. Sunrise. He made a specialty of treating " fistulæ." He " *pulled them out!* " and never failed of a cure. He took quarters in a hovel in the purlieus of the city, before the door of which might be seen any day the carriages of the wealthy,

"Dr. Sunrise" in St. Joseph.

while the common people thronged the streets, all seeking to be healed. He would not receive his pay in a check on a city bank—*he had no time to spare in running to the bank for his fee!* It must be paid, cash in hand, or no treatment did he mete out! $3,000, it was said, rewarded his three weeks' scattering of handbills and flippant arrogance. The profession of this era is certainly cursed to the very full with this kind of stuff, but medical men may console themselves (when reading the foregoing) by remembering that this is not the only age and generation that has been cursed with the incubus.

In "Richard the Second" we find an appeal to God to put it into a physician's mind to help his patient to his grave immediately.

It is somewhat singular that among the multitude of villainies we constantly see or read of, it is one of the rarest to hear of a physician abusing the confidence of his patients. A physician's purposely murdering his patient is one of the rarest of crimes. There have been two cases in the United States within my recollection where this crime has been charged upon physicians, but fortunately for the honor of the profession, and the ends of justice it is to be hoped, both parties were acquitted of the charge; I allude to the case of Dr. Schoeppe in Pennsylvania, and that of Dr. Madlicott in Kansas; the one for the murder of Miss Stenick through motives of avarice, the other of Mr. Ruth for the purpose of inheriting his widow. These were the charges.

The most debased wretch who has the hardihood to enter the medical profession, seems to regard fully the duty of holding sacred the trusts of his patrons as tenaciously as he does his own private secrets. I have hardly known this trust betrayed in more than a single instance. I have known but a single case where the morals of the family of any one have been directly polluted by the family doctor.'

Can we say as much of any other calling? How stands even the immaculate clergy upon this point? This merit alone in the physician should entitle him to the confidence and esteem of all the world, and make him revered as a patron of virtue, if for nothing else. It is not the man, but the calling, however, that makes him what he is in this regard.

"Physician" is mentioned in "Henry the Fourth," "Richard the Third," and in "Henry the Sixth." In the latter we find detailed the doings of an impostor, which is worth transcribing:

(Enter one, crying a miracle! a miracle!)

Glocester. "What means this noise? Fellow, what miracle dost thou proclaim?

One. A miracle! a miracle!

Suffolk. Come to the king: tell him what miracle.

One. Forsooth, a blind man at St. Alban's shrine, within this half hour hath recover'd his sight; a man that ne'er saw in his life before.

King Henry. Now, God be prais'd, that to believing souls gives light in darkness, comfort in despair.

(Enter Simpcox and his kinsfolk.)

Cardinal. Here come the townsmen in procession, to present your highness with the man.

King. Great is his comfort in this earthly vale, though by his sight his sin be multiplied.

Glocester. Bring him near; his highness' pleasure is to talk with him.

King. Good fellow, tell us here the circumstance; has thou been long blind, and now restor'd?

Simpcox. Born blind, an't please your grace.

Wife. Ay, indeed was he.

Suffolk. What woman is this?

Wife. His wife, an't like your worship.

Glocester. Hadst thou been his mother thou could'st have better told.

King. Where wert thou born?

Simpcox. At Berwick in the North, an't like your grace.

King. Poor soul! God's goodness hath been great to thee.

Queen. Tell me, good fellow, camest thou here by chance?

Cardinal. What! art thou lame?

Simpcox. Ay, God Almighty help me!

Suffolk. How cam'st thou so?

Simpcox. A fall off a tree.

Wife. A plum-tree, master.

Glocester. How long hast thou been blind?

Simpcox. O, born so, master.

Glocester. What! and wouldst climb a tree?

Simpcox. But that in all my life, when I was a youth.

Wife. Too true; and bought his climbing very dear.

Glocester. 'Mass, thou lovest plums well, that would venture so.

Simpcox. Alas, good master, my wife desir'd some damsons, and made me climb with danger of my life.

Glocester. A subtle knave; but yet it shall not serve;—let me see thine eyes:—wink now;—now open them.—In my opinion yet thou seest not well.

Simpcox. Yes, master, clear as day; I thank God.

Glocester. Say'st thou me so? What colour is this cloak of?

Simpcox. Red, master; red as blood.

Glocester. Why, that's well said. What colour is my gown of?

Simpcox. Black, forsooth; coal black as jet.

King. Why, then, thou know'st what colour jet is of?

Suffolk. And yet, I think, jet did he never see.

Glocester. But cloaks and gowns before this day, a many.

Wife. Never before this day, in all his life.

Glocester. Tell me, sirrah, what's my name?

Simpcox. Alas, master, I know not.

Glocester. What's thine own name?

Simpcox. Saunder Simpcox, an't please you, master.

Glocester. Then, Saunder, sit thou there, thou lyingest knave in Christendom. If thou hadst been born blind, thou might'st as well have known all our names as thus to name the several colours we do wear. Sight may distinguish of colours; but suddenly to nominate them all, it is impossible. My lords, would ye not think his cunning to be great, that could restore this cripple to his legs?

Simpcox. O, master, that you could! "

Glocester then sends for a whip and stool, gives Mr. Simpcox a good thrashing,—he leaps from the stool and runs away, the people following and shouting—a miracle! a miracle!

There was little show of erudition or even good sound sense in the effort to expose the malingering of this fellow Simpcox; no person, however expert, can distinguish, in many cases, by a mere examination of the physical appearance of the eye, whether or not its optical powers are perfect; and the plea that the inability of Simpcox to individualize the parties present by their several names was sufficient to brand him as an impostor is simply ridiculous. If he had been afflicted with congenital cataract, and had that day been operated upon successfully, why then he would not have been able to say of colours which was red or which black; he might have acquired the power very soon from a process of education, but not in a few hours. The readiness with which he recognized colours rendered it certain that he either had not been blind at all, or else had been operated upon at sometime prior to that present day. He had not been blind from birth if he could *immediately* distinguish colors—that is certain.

Doctor Shaw, a notorious political intriguer, is named in "Richard the Third," but not in connection with medical matters; and Doctor Peace had held a place of trust and honor in the government, until displaced through the jealousies of Cardinal Wolsey. It is said that through grief at this misfortune, he ran mad and died.

In "Henry the Eighth" we find mention of one Doctor Butts, the king's physician;—a man who seems to have been as heartless and unprincipled as his bloody master. It happened that this self-important doctor did not like Cranmer, the Archbishop of Canterbury, and when this august functionary was humbled to the dust by the cold-blooded English Nero,—Henry the Eighth,—this same Butts, contrary to the instincts of the true physician, triumphed in his degradation, and took delight in making the fallen prelate feel it to the utmost. He acted a contemptible part.

Menenius, in "Coriolanus," says:

"It gives me an estate of seven years' health; in which time I will make a lip at the physician: the most sovereign prescription in Galen is but empiric physic, and to this preservative, no better than a horse-drench," thus giving little credit to the powers of medicine.

The notion prevails among a large portion of mankind, that the doctor has really little power over disease, and from this belief springs the patronage which in most instances falls into the hands of the class of empirics known under various names, and outside of the pale of regular medicine—the idea being prevalent among the common people that they will do no harm if they do no good. If such reasoners would carry their arguments a little further, they would surely see that they had better employ no person at all, as one that is neither competent for good nor for evil is simply a nonentity, save in the matter of fees. But they who take up the idea that even the common disease of rheumatism is not dangerous, and will get along quite as well when not treated at all, are wofully mistaken. The plan was tried in the Massachusetts General Hospital, during the past summer, of leaving cases of rheumatism without active treatment, and the progress of the cases noted. Ten ordinary cases, eight with first attacks, and two with a second attack—all young or middle-aged adults. *Two died*, three of seven examined got heart disease, and the average duration of the disease was about six weeks! This was an appalling record for nature as a doctor, and shows us, as definitely as so few cases can, the dangers of trifling with life.

The idea of Macbeth,—"throw physic to the dogs, I'll none of it," is doctrine of the same worthless sort. Whilst I know full well the many abuses cloaked under the guise of the healing art,—and certain as I am of the murderous work it performs in the hands of the ignorant, yet it is a God-like calling, in its purity; and separated from the evils which beset it in the shape of unworthy pretenders, and there is nothing in the way of human ministrations productive of more good to the human race.

In "Macbeth" we find the doctor occupying a conspicuous place, notwithstanding his low estimate of physic. We find the old notion in regard to the power of a touch of the royal hand in curing scrofula:

Malcolm. "Well; more anon.—Comes the king forth, I pray you?

Doctor. Ay, sir; there are a crew of wretched souls, that stay his cure: their malady convinces the great assay of heart; but at his touch, such sanctity hath heaven given his hand, they presently amend.

Malcolm. I thank you, doctor.

Macduff. What's the disease he means?

Malcolm. 'Tis called the evil: a most miraculous work in this good king, which often since my here remain in England, I have seen him do. How he solicits heaven, himself best knows; but strangely-visited people, all swollen and ulcerous, pitiful to the eye, the mere despair of surgery, he cures; hanging a golden stamp about their necks, put on with holy prayers; and, 'tis spoken, to the succeeding royalty he leaves the benediction. With this strange virtue he hath a heavenly gift of prophecy, and sundry blessings hang about his throne, that speak him full of grace.'' The absurdity of the idea that a ''swollen and ulcerons'' person affected with king's evil can be cured by '' charms and incantations'' has not entirely passed from the minds of living generations. I was reading in a medical periodical no longer ago than yesterday where a medical gentleman gravely proposed the setting apart of a certain ward in an hospital into which patients of exactly the same class as those in the other wards should be admitted, and who, in addition to the identical treatment given to the others, should receive special and persistent prayers for their recovery, and that the success of the plan be carefully noted. It seems to me that this plan would imply the ridiculous idea that the patients in the wards of our hospitals as now conducted are removed entirely from the recognition of a benignant Providence, and that the salvation of their inmates is left entirely to the care of the nurses and physicians. It is certainly said that ''the prayers of the righteous availeth much,'' but I am persuaded that they are not of sufficient power in these latter days to amputate a thigh, or supersede the anti-periodic powers of quinine. If the plan proposed by the good doctor should prove a success, I presume the practice of the healing art would go back into the hands of the monks and barbers. The same doctor who had such faith in the king's virtues as a ''healer'' was called to see Lady Macbeth for her sleep-walking, and with commendable con-scientiousness announced the disease as ''beyond his practice,''— '' yet,'' says he, '' I have known those who walked in their sleep, who have died holily in their beds.'' During the course of the treatment it was asked by

Macbeth. '' How does your patient, doctor?

Doctor. Not so sick, my lord, as she is troubled with thick-coming fancies that keep her from her rest.

Macbeth. Cure her of that. Canst thou not minister to a mind diseas'd, pluck from the memory a rooted sorrow, raze out the written troubles of the brain, and with some sweet oblivious antidote cleanse the stuff'd bosom of that perilous grief, which weighs upon the heart?

Doctor. Therein the patient must minister unto himself.''

It is apparent that Macbeth had entertained the hope that the powers of the physician might avail something in the restoration of his wife's mental faculties, which had been so perturbed since the murder of Duncan; and that it was only after the doctor declared his inability to do her good that he passionately exclaimed—"throw physic to the dogs, I'll none of it"—a loss of confidence which seems to have had some grounds for it, as in his extremities he had hoped much, and received no help.

It is probable that the case of Lady Macbeth would have been benefitted in the hands of many of our modern psychological experts; and there is little doubt but that if the power of persistent prayer is necessary for the restoration of the sick, Lady Mac. would have been a fit subject upon which to have made experiment; she was sick morally as well as mentally, and if a white neck-cloth and lugubrious physiognomy ever do good in the restoration of suffering humanity it is in maladies like hers.

We find a metaphoric expression in Hamlet to this effect: "Your wisdom should show itself more richer, to signify this to his doctor; for, for me to put him to his further purgation, would perhaps plunge him into more choler." In "Lear" we find a doctor mixed up in the matters considerably, and in association with the treatment of old Lear's mental alienation proves himself to be no mean psychologist; his treatment of the case, as fully detailed in the chapter on pharmacologia, testifies to his ability in his professional acquirements, and to the matter as it is there stated we may refer the reader again.

True to his mission of justice and mercy, we find the physician, Cornelius, in "Cymbeline," thwarting the evil designs of the heartless queen. "She doth think she has strange lingering poisons: I do know her spirit, and will not trust one of her malice with a drug of such damned nature," whilst he comes in for a charge of a lack of discretion by Cymbeline, for simply announcing that the queen was dead:

Cornelius. "Hail, great king! To sour your happiness, I must report the queen is dead.

Cymbeline. Whom worse than a physician would this report become? But I consider, by medicine life may be prolong'd, yet death will seize the doctor too."

We find one of that numerous and detestable class—self-constituted doctors, making himself prominent in attending the shipwrecked persons in "Pericles:" "Get fire and meat for these poor men; it has been a turbulent and stormy night. *(To a servant.)* Your master will be dead ere you return: there's nothing can be minister'd to nature, that can recover him. Give this to the 'pothecary, and tell me how it works. 'Tis known, I ever have studied physic, through which secret art, by turning over authorities, I have (together with my practice) made familiar to me and to my aid, the blest infusions that dwell in vegetables, in metals, stones; and can speak of the disturbances that nature works, and of her cures. Make fire within: fetch hither all the boxes in my closet. Death may usurp on nature many hours, and yet the fire of life kindle again the over-pressed spirits. I heard of an Egyptian that had nine hours lain dead, who was by good appliance recovered."

How like the boastful lies of this class—the mountebanks of this day! And the benighted public swallow the stories as gospel truths. Verily humanity is composed of the selfsame ingredients among all people and in all ages.

The recent law passed by the legislature of Missouri and other states, lodging in the hands of Boards of Health the power to grant this class of men *exclusive* privileges, in the practice of their nefarious traffic—traffic in human life—is a shame to the age, and is the extreme realization of the idea called the BLACK ARTS *in Medicine*. *One Hundred Dollars* to the "State Board" and *any man* may have issued to him a certificate authorizing him to practice medicine in the great and enlightened States of Missouri, Illinois, West Virginia, and some others perhaps; and the would-be reformers in the profession—those who are loud mouthed and boisterous in their clamor for a "higher standard of medical education," are the willing agents of these mountebanks in endangering the lives of helpless and unsuspecting women and children. The *people* should see to it that such laws are removed from the statute books of the state. This recent medical legislation in the various states is in the interest of designing cliques, and the hands of those with whom the power for the execution of the laws has been placed have never been raised a single time against quackery,—but, on the contrary, have smote none but legitimate practitioners.

[l The licence law mentioned above is, to the practice of medicine, what the "high licence law" is to the dram shops—places a monopoly of the itinerant medicine business in the hands of him who has money, but summarily stops the "wheels of progress" of the impecunious and less fortunate quack. I am not aware of any case

"I have my licence from the State Board of Health, and here is your medicine."

yet where any one has taken out the hundred dollar licence, but if any do not avail themselves of the opportunity to revel in the benefits of a rich monopoly, it is certainly no fault of the law.

CHAPTER IX.

MISCELLANEOUS.

A vile caricature—The Hunchback—Now is the winter of my discontent—Listening to the whispers of Vanity—I ll be at charge for a looking-glass—Troublous dreams—Sleep that knits up the raveled sleeve—Our life is two-old—Sleep hath its own world—From Byron – Neuralgia—No guaranty of truth—Riot—Position in sea-sickness — Old quarantine regulations — The plague—From the cradle to the grave—Characteristics of senility—Take a man of honor, Kate—He brings his physic after his patient's death—An awkward predicament—Tests for death—Life a failure—Ay! but to die? Grim Death!

Under the above title will be included various subjects which could not be well arranged under a different heading, and which did not embrace material sufficient in volume to entitle it to a place in the work as a whole chapter. The principal subjects noticed here will be Cyphosis (hunchback), Sleep, Senility, Necrology, etc., together with other minor matters of little importance, with which the volume will close.

In commenting upon the physical deformities of Richard the Third in a preceding chapter, it was mentioned that a quotation at more length depicting also his mental and moral traits in connection with other physical defects (those not mentioned there), might be found in the present place. This work, claiming to be an embodiment of Shakespeare's medical knowledge, would, it is thought, be incomplete without his complete description of that hideous caricature of humanity; and, although it may seem that a large portion of the matter is irrelevant to actual medicine, yet it is hardly possible to comprehend the medical point found in it unless we take them in their full connection.

Richard the Third, King of England, occupied the throne from 1483 to 1485, and the foul crimes enacted during his brief lease of authority made his history a blot upon the human character. He was killed at the battle of Bosworth Fields, where his army of twelve thousand men was completely defeated by one of half the number under the command of the Earl of Richmond, who then became King Henry the Seventh.

Nowhere in Shakespeare's whole productions is his power of delineating human character more manifest than in his pen-picture of this individual; it is perfect, both as to his physical, moral, and mental developments. The description shows Richard to have been a fit representative of his class, both as to physical and mental characteristics; it being a noticeable fact that in their mental organization they (hunchbacks) almost invariably possess a piquancy and subtility unequaled by most persons of a better physique, and whilst their mental traits do not give them just claims to profundity, yet they are commonly shrewd in the management of the business affairs of life, and their witticisms are often hurled with blighting effect at any they may not chance to like; and their *moral* distortions are commonly of so pronounced a type as to have originated among the Germans an old adage, that "he upon whom God has set a mark, watch him, for he has surely come to bite the world."

Richard thus descants upon his own deformity: "Love forswore me in my mother's womb; and, for I should not deal in her soft laws, she did corrupt frail nature with some bribe to shrink my arm up like a withered shrub; to make an envious mountain on my back, where sits deformity to mock my body; to shape my legs of an unequal size; to disproportion me in every part, like to a chaos, or an unlick'd bear-whelp, that carried no impressions like the dam." Then after he had murdered the king, Henry the Sixth, with his own hand, on his blooody march to power, he thus cogitates: " Now is the winter of my discontent made glorious summer by the sun of York; and all the clouds that lowered upon our house, in the deep bosom of the ocean buried. Now are our brows bound with victorious wreathes; our bruised arms hung up for monuments; our stern alarums chang'd to merry meeting, our dreadful marches to delightful measures. Grim visaged war hath smoothed his wrinkl'd front; and now, instead of mounting barbed steeds, to fright the souls of fearful adversaries, he capers nimbly, in a lady's chamber, to the lascivious pleasing of a lute. But I that am not shaped for sportive tricks, nor made to court an amorous looking-glass; I, that am rudely stamp'd, and want love's majesty, to strut before a wanton ambling nymph; I, that am curtail'd of these fair proportions, cheated of features by dissembling nature, deformed, unfinish'd, sent before my time into this breathing world, scarce half made up, and that so lamely and unfashionable, that dogs do bark at me as I halt by them; why I, in this weak, piping time of peace, have no delight to pass away the time unless to see my shadow in the sun, and descant on mine own deformity; since heaven hath shaped my body, so let hell make crook'd my mind to answer it; and therefore, since I cannot prove a lover to entertain these fair well spoken days, I am determined to prove a villain, and hate the idle pleasures of these days."

Notwithstanding these vows, the foul toad found a time when he could listen to the whisperings of vanity and be influenced thereby; he even got so that he thought well of his own good looks; hear him after he had been paying court to Annie, the widow of the murdered Edward:

"And will she yet abase her eyes on me that cropp'd the golden prime of this sweet prince, and made her widow to a woful bed? On me that halt and am misshapen thus? My dukedom to a beggarly dinner, I do mistake my person all this while; upon my life she finds, although I cannot, myself to be a marvelous proper man. I'll be at charge for a looking-glass, and entertain a score or more of tailors, to study fashions to adorn my body; since I am crept into favor with myself, I will maintain it with some little cost."

The most complete bibliography of malformations resulting from incomplete (intra uterine) development of parts does not claim that the fœtal extremities—the arm or leg—are *abridged* in development. They may *fail of development* utterly and the child be born either armless or legless, but not with an arm " shrank up like a withered shrub," nor " legs of an unequal size," as was the case with Richard, according to his own account. Constrictions, as of the looping around an extremity by the umbilical cord, *might* have retarded their growth, but the fault is placed to the credit, seemingly, of the same agencies which placed the " envious mountain on his back." The action of a constricting funis could not be properly accused of this. As was shown in a former chapter, when speaking of teratologic condition of the fœtus, that the departures from the normal almost always consist of *lack* of development and not in an *excess* of development; hence the conclusion may be fairly entertained that the mountain which sat mockingly upon the back of Richard was not of intra uterine growth, but perhaps occurred during his early childhood. He also testifies to the fact that he was lame, as the dogs barked at him as he " halted " by. This was much more likely to have been of post natal origin than to have been part of a congenital deformity. It is not uncommon to see the lower extremities become of unequal length in spinal affections which occur subsequent to birth, as in rickets for example.

Growths of such a character as the one situated upon his back if of intra uterine origin are known usually to consist of an extra fœtus more or less perfect, constituting a tumor covered by integument. It is not impossible but that the tumor we write of was of this nature, though his mother, not being free from a suspicion of some constitutional sexual vice, would be less likely to make an effort in the way of over-production than she would to transmit a constitutional taint which should in childhood manifest itself in curvature of the spine. This latter seems to have been the real deformity in the case under consideration, although Shakespeare puts forward the testimony of more than one witness to the fact that it was congenital.

It will be remembered that he had murdered the husband of Annie with his own hand at Tewkesbury, and he meets her on the way to the grave with her husband's body and proposes marriage to her, which she, to his utter amazement, accepts. Queen Margaret thus gives us his portrait: " Thou elvish marked, abortive rooting hog! thou that was sealed in thy nativity the strain of nature and the scorn of hell! Thou slander of thy mother's womb! thou loathed issue of thy father's loins!"

Constance speaks thus of one she could not love. She was speaking to her fair boy, Arthur:

" If thou, that bidd'st me be content, wert grim, ugly. and slanderous to thy mother's womb,—full of unpleasing blots, unsightly stains, lame, foolish, crooked, swart, prodigious, patch'd with foul moles, and eye-offending marks, I would not care, I then would be content; for then I should not love thee; but thou art fair, and at thy birth, dear boy, nature and fortune joined to make thee great."

The physiological process called sleep is spoken of in " Macbeth," " Julius Cæsar," and " Henry the Sixth." In the latter the " troublous dreams this night doth make me sad " says the " hunchback." on one occasion during the time he was scheming for the crown ; whilst the first (Macbeth) says " the innocent sleep ;—sleep, that knits up the ravell'd sleave of care, the death of each day's life, sore labour's bath, balm of hurt minds, great nature's second course, chief nourisher in life's feast." The innocent sleep thinks Cæsar when he says: "let me have men about me that are fat; sleek-headed men, and such as sleep o' nights; yond' Cassius hath a lean and hungry look;—he thinks too much."

"Our life is two-fold: sleep hath its own world, a boundary between the things misnam'd death and existence; sleep hath its own world, and a wide realm of wild reality. And dreams in their development have breath and tears and tortures, and the touch of joy; they leave a weight upon our waking thoughts, they take weight from off our waking toils, they do divide our being; they become a portion of ourselves as of our time, and look like heralds of eternity; they pass like spirits of the past,—they speak like sybils of the future; they have power, — the tyranny of pleasure and of pain; they make us what we were not—what they will, and shake us with the vision that's gone by, the dread of vanish'd shadows—Are they so? Is not the past all shadow? What are they? Creations of the mind?—The mind can make substance, and people planets of its own with beings brighter than have been, and give a breath to forms which can outlive all flesh."

I introduce the above quotation from Byron, that readers may find diversity of sentiment, and in this instance have the chance to see side by side the ideas of two of the most profound minds that ever looked into the human heart.

"Before the curing of a strong disease, even in the instant of repair and health, the fit is strongest."—*King John.*

"The same diseases heal by the same means."—*The Merchant of Venice.*

The first of these assertions is certainly correct, as the disease must reach its acme before the decline commences; in that instant repair must gain the ascendancy over waste, though the instant of absolute health is not yet reached the moment repair is begun. There is neither anything shrewd nor illogical in the second assertion.

"Indeed, we feared his sickness was past cure," in "King John," had reference not to physical infirmity, but to the political danger of Prince Arthur. "John" also contains the proposition to "heal the inveterate canker of one wound, by making many"—an idea only used illustratively, but one which finds application very often in practical medicine and surgery. A quotation from "Richard the Second" to the effect that "they breathe truth that breathe their words in pain" is recognized as a basis of action in admitting certain testimony in our courts of justice. If a person make a statement whilst under the impression that he cannot long survive, we, as a rule, give great regard to its probable truthfulness; but whether such credence could be placed in the veracity of one who was simply laboring under an attack of neuralgia without any apprehension of danger to life, we are not so well satisfied. Under these considerations of the fact a party would have to be laboring under pain, to his or her mind evidently speedily mortal, before much special significance could be given to their utterances.

In "Henry the Fourth" there is a laughable incident where Falstaff takes up the quarrel of Mrs. Tearsheet, and thereby precipitated a riot with Pistol, who, with his sword, made thrusts at Falstaff's belly and stabbed him in the groin, Sir John at the same time hurting Pistol in the shoulder; the reader must turn to the original, and get the matter in its full connection, to enjoy a good laugh.

A very early, and also a very tardy case of dentition is noticed in "Richard the Third," and "it is time to give them physic, their diseases are grown so catching" is seen in "Henry the Eighth." "Then recovered him again with aqua vitæ, or some other hot infusion" is found in the "Winter's Tale;" the term "aqua vitæ" being used in one other place in Shakespeare, also. "Hot infusions" are the popular domestic resort even to this hour, and when after scalding, steaming and roasting a patient his friends or parents cannot "recover" him, the physician perhaps is invited to undertake the then no easy task.

"Sea-sick" is also noticed in the "Winter's Tale," but no ideas as to its true pathology or best treatment are advanced. Observations as to *position* being the cause, and the change of that position into a (philosophically) more proper one as a prophylactic, and also a curative measure, appear to be the most logical ideas ever entertained and promulgated upon this distressing condition, Dr. Beard to the contrary notwithstanding. It is to be hoped that experience may prove the value of the suggestions. The phrase "with a mind that doth renew swifter than blood decays" is found in "Troilus and Cressida," and probably has reference to the mere coagulation of the blood; as blood does not really undergo the change of putre-faction sooner than many other organic compounds.

Upon the subject of sanitary science, we find the following in "Romeo and Juliet" in regard to quarantine:

"Going to find a bare-foot brother out, one of our order, to asso-ciate me, here in this city visiting the sick, and finding him, the searchers of the tower, suspecting that we both were in a house where the infectious pestilence did reign, seal'd up the doors, and would not let us forth." This was the story of Friar John after his return from Mantua, whither he had been on the mission to Romeo to acquaint him with the condition of Juliet as she lay bound by the Friar Lawrence's "sleeping potion" in the "tomb of the Capulets."

It seems that quarantine regulations were more rigidly enforced at that early day than at present; and it is likely that the "infectious pestilence" referred to was either small-pox or plague, as barring doors would have little effect in warding off the subtle germs that propagate cholera. The "plague" is named by "Timon;" though it is probable that this scourge had not lately visited the British islands, as this is the only instance in which Shakespeare speaks of it in his entire writings; had he, however, lived half a century later, at the time when London was almost depopulated from this dreadful malady, he would doubtless have given the world a graphic descrip-tion of its horrors; it was his strong point to seize upon every salient feature of an age, and present it in a light, and with a force of thought, never attained by any other individual. It will be remem-bered that the plague visited London in 1665, and the great fire in 1666, just fifty years after the death of Shakespeare.

The oft-quoted "all the world's a stage" is a truism; "they have their exits and their entrances, and one man in his time plays many parts,—his acts being seven ages. At first the infant, mewling and puking in his mother's arms; then, the whining school-boy, with his satchel, and shining morning face, creeping like snail unwillingly to school. And then the lover, sighing like furnace, with woful ballad made to his mistress' eye-brows. Then a soldier, full of strange oaths, and bearded like the pard, jealous in honor, sudden and quick in quarrel, seeking the bubble reputation even in the cannon's mouth. And then the justice in fair round belly, with good capon lin'd, with eye severe and beard of formal cut, full of wise saws and modern instances; and so he plays his part.

The sixth age shifts into the lean and slipper'd pantaloon, with spectacles on nose and pouch at side ; his youthful hose, well sav'd, a world too wide for his shrunken shanks, and his big manly voice, turning again towards the childish treble, pipes and whistles in his sound.

Last scene of all, that ends this strange eventful history, is second childishness, and mere oblivion ; sans teeth, sans eyes, sans taste, sans everything "—the listless old man sits in his quiet corner, his hands resting on the top of his cane, waiting patiently for the final summons.

The Chief Justice and Falstaff get the matter in this shape :

Falstaff. "You that are old, consider not the capacities of us that are young.

Chief Justice. Do you set down your name in the scroll of youth, that are written down old with all the characters of age? Have you not a moist eye, a dry hand, a yellow cheek, a white beard, a decreasing leg, and increasing belly? Is not your voice broken, your wind short, your chin double, your wit single, and every part about you blasted with antiquity, and will you yet call yourself young? Fie, fie, fie, Sir John.

Falstaff. My lord, I was born about three of the clock in the afternoon, with a white head, and something of a round belly ; for my voice—I have lost it with hollaing and singing of anthems. To approve my youth farther, I will not : the truth is, I am only old in judgment and understanding ; and he that will caper with me for a thousand marks, let him lend me the money and have at him.''

" Hal " gets off a pretty good thing in the same direction during his courtship with his Kate : " While thou livest, dear Kate, take a fellow of plain and uncoin'd constancy, for he perforce must do thee right, because he hath not the gift to woo in other places ; for these fellows of infinite tongue that can rhyme themselves into ladies' favors, they do always reason themselves out again. A good leg will fail, a straight back will stoop, a black beard will turn white, a curled pate will grow bald, a fine face will wither, a full eye will wax hollow—but a good heart, Kate—" while Hamlet finishes it in this wise : " This satirical rogue here, says that old men have grey beards ; that their faces are wrinkled ; their eyes purging thick amber and plum-tree gum ; and that they have a plentiful lack of wit, together with most weak hams.'' Though after all these pictures of decay, it is claimed by the cynical philosophy of the blind Gloster, in "King Lear," that but for the hatred we have for the world —engendered by its strange mutations, life would never yield to the inroads of time, and our existence on earth would become perpetual. It no doubt occurs to every one who has had experience in the vicissitudes of earthly existence, at some time in their career, to ask themselves the question—"To be or not to be? or whether 'tis nobler in the mind, to suffer the stings and arrows of outrageous fortune; or to take arms against a sea of troubles, and by opposing end them?" Or, like Constance, in "King John," who in the "extremity of her griefs" says of the "grim monster"—"No, I defy all coun. sel, all redress, but that which ends all counsel, true redress, death, death. O, amiable, lovely death! thou odoriferous stench! sound rottenness! arise from forth the couch of lasting night, thou hate and terror to prosperity, and I will kiss thy detestable bones."

In "Henry the Eighth" we find a simile in regard to his marriage, in these words: "He brings his physic after his patient's death"— an occurrence by the way not unfrequent in the career of many doctors of medicine.

Experience teaches us that this fact is often more embarrassing than the matter would seem to warrant; but really, one who has practiced medicine in the rural districts and has many times called to see his patient and finds him twenty-four hours dead, can fully appreciate my meaning. The writer of these lines not long in the past practiced in the country, and when approaching the house of a patient whom he had left in a critical condition at the last visit, it was customary to scan closely the premises, and if he found a number of horses tied along the fence—many of them with side saddles on, he at once felt crestfallen, and without further information concluded that "he brings his physic after the patient's death."

The language of Capulet, once before noted in these pages—"Out, alas! she's cold! her blood is settled and her joints are stiff; life and these lips have long been separated; death lies on her like an untimely frost," is a fair picture of the ending of mortality; though if one swallowed all the ideas and speculations he reads of, he might reach the conclusion that after all, it is a difficult matter to say positively when a person is dead. For the more satisfactory demonstration of its certainty, numerous tests are given, one of the most recent being to ligate the finger of the party suspected, and if it swells beyond or on the distal side of the constriction, then the circulation goes on and of course the person lives. Another is to apply the flame of a candle to the point of the finger, and if the burn is followed by vesication the person lives,—if it remain parched and brown then he is dead ; whilst again if the fingers of the suspected party be held between the eye of the observer and a strong light, as the sun at noonday, if they are transparent then life remains, if opaque or dark, then death has done his work ; whilst yet another test is to drop a solution of atropine in the eye, and if it dilates, all right,—if not, then we may begin to suspect something wrong.   I suspect however that the test of old Lear—that of placing a looking-glass before the lips of the party suspected, and if the " shine is moistened" by the condensed expired vapors, then he lives—otherwise he is *caput mortuum*.   The wafting of a feather by the breath is also suggested as a test in "King Lear."

Of easy ways to die I know of no one who has given the subject more special attention than the voluptuous Cleopatra, who studied the matter well with a view to its practical application in her own person.   The assertion that one recovered after having nine hours lain dead, is only a marvelous story from the lips of a quack— the analogue of cases with which we meet every day.

Apropos of the dying and the dead, we find a case in medical jurisprudence in "Henry the Sixth "—a case which if " not positively proven " is very well argued upon a basis of hypothecation.   The case referred to is the death of the duke of Gloster, who it was claimed had been murdered at the instance of the queen and her paramour, the earl of Suffolk.

Warwick. "I do believe violent hands were laid upon the life of this thrice-famed duke.

Suffolk. A dreadful oath, sworn with a solemn tongue !   What instance gives Lord Warwick for his view?

Warwick. See how the blood has settled in his face.   Oft have I seen a timely parted ghost, of ashy semblance, meagre, pale, and bloodless, being all descended to the laboring heart ; who in the conflict that it holds with death attracts the same for aidance 'gainst the enemy ; which with the heart there cools, and ne'er returneth to blush and beautify the cheek again.   But see, his face is black, and full of blood ; his eye-balls farther out than when he liv'd, staring full ghastly like a strangled man : his hair upraised, his nostrils stretch'd with straining.   His hands abroad display'd like one that grasp'd and tugg'd for life, and was by strength subdued.   Look, on the

sheets, his hair you see, is sticking; his well proportioned beard
made rough, rugged, like to the summer's corn by tempest lodged.
It cannot be but he was murdered here; the least of all these signs
were probable.''

The annals of forensic medicine do not furnish a more consistent
and graphic picture of death by hanging or by strangulation than is
here presented. The endeavor, however, to point out negative signs
as evidence of the duke's murder is rather lame and inconclusive.
Shakespeare falls into such an error but seldom indeed.

It was said a few paragraphs back, that no doubt was entertained,
that most persons who had encountered for a time the vicissitudes of
life, had often concluded that after all, life is an unsatisfactory state
of existence, that life is a failure, and that there are few things here
below worth living for; but then ''to die, and go we know not
where; to lie in cold obstruction and to rot; this sensible warm motion to become a kneaded clod; and the delighted spirit to bathe in
fiery floods, or to reside in thrilling regions of thick-ribbed ice: to
be imprison'd in the viewless winds, and blown with restless violence
round about the pendent world; or to be worse than worst of these—
'tis too horrible! The weariest loathed worldly life, that age, ache,
penury and imprisonment can lay on nature, is a paradise to what
we fear of death.''

In regard to the terror manifested by Shakespeare at the bare idea
of the uncertainties of a future existence, it appears a little puerile
to myself. To the philosophic mind the thought of a future oblivion
in which we *may be* should possess no more of dread than the oblivion
in which we *were*. Indeed, as I *was* one hundred years ago is, to
my mind, the condition in which *I will be* one hundred years hence.
To my thinking the analogue is complete. If I am hereafter imprisoned in the viewless winds or lie in cold obstruction, what is it
more than I have been? We have this life certainly which we may
present as an analogical conclusion for another; but on the other
hand *we know*, from observation, of *two* states of non-existence for
these forms of ours—the remove from the beginning, and from the
ending of the present one—and so ''I take my leave.''

THE END.

INDEX.

PAGE

Abortion........24, 25, 58, 61, 64
A boon to nineteen 127
Acumen, Professional......... 58
Age, Nubile............. 24
Alcohol and venery...... 36
All the world's a stage 218
Anæsthesia............154
Anger............ 120
Anorexia 22
Antidote 84
Appetite, Craving............ 21
    "   Sexual............107
Arrow-poison 148
Asperity 35
Atavism 167
A very old head 130
Avon, Bard of...... 28

Balance, Nutritive....... 21
Banquo............. 80
Barker, Dr., of Dumfries 33
Baths in syphilis............ 171
Bearing-cloth 38
Beau Nash 89
Biron 197
Blasted 219
Blood, Smell of 80
Blue-eyed hag 18
Blumenbach 167
Boards of Health 210
Bowlsby, Alice............ 18
Brownist............163
Brown-Sequard 167
Bryant, W. C. 96
Bucknill, Dr. 71, 78, 85, 101
Bullen, Anne 47
Byron, Lord 216

PAGE

Cæsarian section 64
Campbell, Lord............ 28
Cataclysm, Final............ 95
Carry his water 186
Cataract......... 206
Cave of Belarius... 155
Cephalalgia 128
Chastria, Mrs. 120
Chemistry of digestion 175
Child, A thankless 65
Chlorosis 37
Chosen, by what?... 43
Coma and speech 124
Come back 48
Come on my right 185
Conclusions............117
Consanguinity 27
Conspiracy 74
Convulsions, Puerperal 68
Cornelia 53
Country swain 19
Cramer, Jennie 19
Cramp in drowning...... 125
Cut-throat 46
Cyphoses 44, 212

Dankish vaults 74
Death of Falstaff............160
DeBoismont 82, 87, 91
Deformities, Double 45
Degeneracy, Mental 55
Delineation, Farcical 73
Dentition, a guide......... .. 57
Dialectical society 36
Digestion and sleep 94
Diseases dearer than physic 172
Disturbances, Mental......... ... 73

	PAGE
Down grade of life	35
Do you nothing hear?	86
Drama and education	42
Dreams, always involuntary	83
Drinks, Sleepy	132
Duhaget, Dom.	82
Dyspareunia	70, 119
Early marriages	54, 55
Earth and its girdle	23
Eclampsia	68
Elimination	22
Emendator, Error of	145
English common law	32
Envy	120
Epilepsy	121
Epistaxis	185
Etiology	156
Existence, A future	222
Expert, Medical	33
Expression and bromides	123
Facial perception	185
Fact, the only evidence	33
Falling sickness	121, 123
Families, Aristocratic	28
" Rural	60
Farmed out	57
Female physicians	198
Fencing match	149
Fever, Typhoid	22, 92
Few can correct errors	146
Fibroids, Uterine	60
Fleming, the phrenologist	184
Fools not mad folks	97
Foscari, Cell of	74
Garrulous nurse	56, 62
Garters, an evil	162
Gentleman, Lusty	32, 33
Germ-life	47
Give her an hundred marks	49
Give me some drink	161
Gland, The mammary	56
Gout	131
Green sickness	37, 62
Groans, Night of	47
Grocer's maid	166
Gynæcology	17

	PAGE
Halitus, Pulmonary	102
Hallucinations	90, 91, 147
Handkerchief	42
Hatred, Immoderate	30
Harangue	121
Headache	129, 130
Head, Compression of	128
Hebenon	165
He reads much	187
Hernia	113
He upon whom God sets a mark	213
Histo-genetic operations	192
Hobnail liver	179
Hope	41
Horse, with side-saddle	220
Hospital, Guy's	37
How stand the clergy?	204
Hunchback, The	42
Hypnotics	141
Idea, A paramount	100
Idiosyncrasy	139
Ignorance of the populace	196
Illegitimacy	31, 32, 34, 55
Imagination, Scientific	92
Immortality	93
Inanition	57
Incident, Ludicrous	39
Indian, American	30
" doctor	202
Inebriate "Homes"	75
Infanticide	64
Infantile vitality	68
Influences, Septic	22
Insane hospitals	74
Irritability of hunger	177
Jealousy	101, 103, 104, 105
Jones, John, of Albany	127
Jorisenne, Dr.	40
Knowledge, Intuitive	72
Knowing him is enough	200
Lactiferous period	56
Lady, English	30
Language, Irrelevant	98

	PAGE
Lankaster, Dr.	137
Lebreicht	140
Le Sage	88
Lex scripta	29
Letter, A veritable	116
Licence, Sexual	107
Liquidating a bill	84
London, Tower of	42
Love powders	115
" marks	109
Lugubrious physiognomy	209
Lunacy, courts of enquiry	76
Lust	112
Lying-in chamber	50
Macbeth, Lady	79
Madness and emotion	101
Mad-folk of Shakespeare	134
Maid, A fun-loving	77
Malaria and mortality	162
Male accoucheurs, none	54
Malformations	26
Malignancy and milk	60
Mammary glands 56, 58,	61
Mandragora	135
Mantua, Apothecary of	142
Man's procreative capacity	107
Marriage in 1884	182
" Early, and morals	55
Marshall, Minnie	116
Massachusetts gen. hospital	207
Mastication, Organs of	58
Medical Soc'y of St. Joseph	157
Medicine, Forensic	29
Medlicott, Dr.	203
Menses	28
Mental phenomena, Aberrant	71
Metamorphosis	21
Milk 30, 56, 57, 60, 62, 63,	82
Midwives, Commission of	39
Mind, the offspring of matter	91
Molière	78
Money-bags	31
Monkey as an expert	76
Monogamistic relations	108
Montagues, The	142
Mormon society	108
Morbi materies	22
Motion	91, 93
Murder, Picture of	221
Music as a remedy	133
Narcotics	132
Night, Dismal	42
Nipple, The 55, 56,	63
Non medical men	21, 24
Not from Shakespeare	112
Not pregnant, When	40
Normal pregnancies, Ten	59
Notions, Antiquated	19
Nubility and fourteen	24
Nursing, Attachments of	63
" her own child sacred	58
Odontalgia	128
Offspring, Limitation of	54
Olivares, Duke of	88
On death	222
Opium	84
Organology	174
Orleans, Maid of	39
Ovariotomy, Normal	24
Ovulation	60
Ovid	115
Pabulum of thought	96
Painting, Face	196
Paramour, A black	51
Pen, The	22
Pen of a master	50
Perfumes of Arabia	80
Phonograph	23
Physiology of sleep	215
Pierre Châtel	82
Poisoned by a monk	137
Pontine marsh	159
Prather, Miss	126
Prayer vs. quinine	208
Pregnancy, Diagnoses of	40
" Signs of	40
Pretty worm of Nilus	150
Printing press, The	23
Private retreats	75
Privilege, Child-bed	30
Procreative life of women	59
Prunes, Stew'd	22
" Longing for	20

PAGE

Psychology 70, 72
Puck 23
Pulse as a guide 85
Pure air deleterious 191
Pythagoras................... 78

Quack, A 67
Quack, The impecunious 221
Quick at second month 22

Race, Yankee...... 55
Rape, but no conception 118
Reade, Charles 76
Red-hot stove, curative ... 188
Reproduction, when complete 61
Resuscitation, Writer's mode 69
"Retreats," Private 75
Revolver, The trusty 111
Rosenweig, Dr. 18
Royston 146

Sack 38
Sagacity of Shakespeare 21
Scheele 146
Schoeppe, Dr. 203
Scientific use of the imagina-
tion 92
Sea-sickness, Position in. 135, 217
Section, Cæsarian 64
Sexual relations, Equality in. 106
Shaftesbury, Lord 107
Shakespeare, a contradiction 31
Shylock, the Jew............ 194
Sims, Dr. J. Marion 40
Singing man of Windsor 176
Skeleton..................... 90
Sleeplessness 73
Sleep, Physiology of 93
Smile, sir 34, 102
Snake bite 152
Social science 36
Solohasta 153
Somnambulism 81, 82
Soul, The 93
Specifics, Love 114
Spectres, etc. 87
Spencer, Herbert 36
Squaw, Labor of 30

PAGE

Sterile condition 110
Storm, Relentless 90
Study of Shakespeare 71
Suicide, Fashions of 136
Sunrise, Dr. 203
Surgery 192
Swinstead Abbey 138
Syphilis, Baths in 164

Tanner, resists decay 172
Tanner, the faster 175
Tearsheet, Mrs. Doll ... 38, 130
Telephone 23
Temptation, A terrible 76
Teratology 44, 214
Tewkesbury and Gov. Butler 75
Then live, Macduff 181
The public dipper 170
The Wash and the Humber .. 158
Thorn, A jealous 105
Tissue, Plastic 44
Trust not the physician..... 190
Truth and popular idea...... 180
Tubercular bacteria 183
Tubercle and syphilis....... 129
Twins, Siamese 45

Utah 108
Uterus a mobile organ 27

Vaccine disease 166
Varden, Dolly 109
Villain, what hast thou? ... 52
Vision, Obliquity of 103
Vivisection 153
Von Helmont 115
Vulgarian 134

Waggish old man 122
Wedlock no evidence......... 34
Whistle, The seaman's 66
Wilkes, Dr. 37
Wine and blood............. 173
Witticisms 45
Woman, a dish for the gods .. 151
Woodman, The 178
Young flirt, The 110
Zone, Epileptic............. 168